FIELDS of DREAMS

FIELDS *of* DREAMS

A GUIDE TO VISITING AND ENJOYING ALL 30 MAJOR LEAGUE BALLPARKS
Revised and Updated

JAY AHUJA

CITADEL PRESS
Kensington Publishing Corp.
www.kensingtonbooks.com

CITADEL PRESS books are published by

Kensington Publishing Corp.
850 Third Avenue
New York, NY 10022

All Kensington titles, imprints, and distributed lines are available at special quantity discounts for bulk purchases for sales promotions, premiums, fund raising, educational, or institutional use. Special book excerpts or customized printings can also be created to fit specific needs. For details, write or phone the office of the Kensington special sales manager: Kensington Publishing Corp., 850 Third Avenue, New York, NY 10022, attn: Special Sales Department, phone 1-800-221-2647.

Citadel Press logo Reg. U.S. Patent and Trademark Office
Citadel Press is a trademark of Kensington Publishing Corp.

First printing April 2001

10 9 8 7 6 5 4 3 2 1

Printed in the United States of America

Library of Congress Cataloging-in-Publication Data

Ahuja, Jay.
     Fields of dreams : a guide to visiting and enjoying all 30 major league ballparks / Jay Ahuja.
          p.   cm.
     "A Citadel Press book."
     ISBN 0–8065–2193–7 (pbk.)
     1. Baseball fields—United States—Guidebooks.   2. Baseball fields—Canada—Guidebooks.   3. Stadiums—United States—Guidebooks.   4. Stadiums—Canada—Guidebooks.   I. Title.
     GV879.5.A48   1998
     796.357′06′873—dc21
                                                                                          97–45700
                                                                                                CIP

DEDICATION

To John and Steve, who were a big part of nearly all of my journeys. To Paul, Elizabeth, "Dr. Hook," Matt, Dubber, Jackie, Diane, Kathy, Patti, Jim, Dave, Phil, Tracy, Rob, Mike, Jacki, Rick, Dan and everyone else who joined up with us along the way, provided a place to crash, or helped in so many other ways.

I'd also like to thank Carrie, Barbara, Donna, Pat, Missy, and Charles for helping turn my many scattered thoughts into a book.

To my parents, who instilled in me an unquenchable desire to travel, discover, and enjoy.

To Karen, who was behind me when I first came up with the idea of writing *Fields*, stood beside me as I traveled to many of the cities herein, kicked me in the rear when I needed to get busy writing, and married me when it was done.

CONTENTS

Dedication   v
Preface   ix
Introduction   xii

THE EAST

Atlanta   Turner Field   3
Baltimore   Orioles Park at Camden Yards   10
Boston   Fenway Park   18
Cleveland   Jacobs Field   26
Miami   Pro Player Stadium   33
Montreal   Olympic Stadium   41
New York   Shea and Yankee Stadiums   47
Philadelphia   Veterans Stadium   60
Pittsburgh   PNC Park   67
Tampa Bay   Tropicana Field   74
Toronto   SkyDome   82

THE MIDWEST

Arlington   The Ballpark   91
Chicago   Comiskey Park and Wrigley Field   102
Cincinnati   Riverfront Stadium   115
Denver   Coors Field   121
Detroit   Comerica Park   129
Houston   Enron Field   137
Kansas City   Kauffman Stadium   145
Milwaukee   Miller Park   152

Minneapolis   Hubert H. Humphrey Metrodome   160
Saint Louis   Busch Stadium   169

THE WEST

Anaheim   Anaheim Stadium   177
Los Angeles   Dodger Stadium   185
Oakland   Alameda County Stadium   194
Phoenix   Bank One Ballpark   200
San Diego   Jack Murphy Stadium   206
San Francisco   Pacific Bell Park   214
Seattle   Safeco Field   225

Appendix A: On Your Own Versus Taking a Tour   232
Appendix B: Spring Training   236
Bibliography   239

PREFACE

I travel not to go anywhere, but to go.

ROBERT LOUIS STEVENSON

What started ten years ago as just another vacation has since become a passion. It began one spring, when I came across a major league baseball schedule printed in a local Charlotte, North Carolina, paper. I hadn't been to a major league game since I left New York, six years earlier. At the time, the nearest pro baseball team was the Orioles AA farm team, the Charlotte O's. They had some great young talent but were playing in a temporary park since their old one had burned to the ground. Somehow that didn't quite cut it.

It was too late in the year to plan a spring training trip, so I looked into the idea of spending a week seeing as many regular season games as possible. I mentioned the idea of a "baseball-intensive road trip" to a few people at the office, and before I knew it, I was planning a trip up the East Coast with two sportswriters, John Glennon and Steve Wiseman. After spending a little time with the schedule, we decided on a route—Philadelphia, New York, Boston, New York, Baltimore, and back to Charlotte. Six games, four big-league cities, five ballparks, and more than twenty-three hundred miles in nine days. The beauty of our plan was that it allowed enough time to see the cities themselves, as well as the ball games and ballparks.

Prior to that first trip, the only major league ballparks I had been to were Shea and Yankee stadiums. While they are both fine parks, it wasn't until I had seen a few others—some better, some worse—that I realized that, unlike any other team sport, the game of baseball is a product of its surroundings. Each ballpark, with its varied outfield dimensions, uneven fences, wide or narrow foul territories, distinct elevation, and wind patterns, affects each and every game. As Leonard Koppett so adeptly put it in *The New Thinking Fan's Guide to Baseball,* "The idea is to win *this* game, on *this* field, under *these* conditions, at *this* time. The conditions are supposed to be the same for both teams, but only here and now, not at all times everywhere."

I also realized that in addition to affecting play on the field, the individual quirks of ballparks give them an ambience that affects the fans. Fenway Park's Green Monster and manual scoreboard in left field, Kansas City's fountains and waterfalls beyond the outfield fence, Camden Yards' warehouse wall in right field, and Wrigley Field's ivy-covered walls and rooftop seats across the street make them worth visiting, even if a game isn't being played. In Camden Yards' inaugural year 14,200 people did just that, paying $5 for a guided tour of the park on nongame days. During the 1994 strike, a friend who was disappointed that he wouldn't get to see the Red Sox while in Boston stopped by Fenway Park. He was surprised to learn from a security guard that people had been stopping by "all day, every day" since the strike began.

Avid golf fans often refer to Augusta National, where the Masters is played each year, as "Heaven on Earth." A baseball fan might very well say the same about his or her favorite ballpark. There is something special about walking through the tunnel toward your seat, a hot dog and a cold pop in your hand, and getting your first glimpse of that sea of green grass. The smells, sounds, and sights of a ballpark somehow have a way of returning you to days gone by—perhaps back to when you saw your first ball game as a kid, hoping to catch a ball or see your favorite player knock one out of the park.

I've taken several nonfans to see their first big-league ball game. After seeing it in person, they generally wondered aloud why they hadn't been to a game before. Almost without exception, they had seen a few games on TV and thought the sport was too methodical. In person, they discovered that a baseball game is an altogether different experience. They were awed by the sight of the playing field, basked in the smells and sounds, and even exchanged high fives with complete strangers when the home team scored.

I've never been much of an autograph hound, but America's ballparks offer ample opportunity to get your favorite player's John Hancock. Many teams will allow you to gather near the dugout before and during batting practice to ask players for autographs. Another place folks seek autographs is outside the players' parking lot at the stadium. Player lots are generally located on the complete opposite side of the stadium from the main entrance gate. Lastly, visiting team hotels offers the chance to "bump into" a player. Of course, you have to recognize a player in civilian clothes in order to get his signature. Bear in mind that players are often overwhelmed by autograph requests and may not always get to sign your card, ball, or program simply because they have other things to take care of. Generally speaking, players are glad to do it if you ask politely and are not interrupting them.

Visiting America's major league ballparks, as well as spring training in both Florida and Arizona, has certainly been fun. What I'm most thankful for is that my baseball trips have allowed me to catch up with old friends who have moved to various parts of the country. These trips have also enabled me to see cities and sights I might never have otherwise seen, including the Grand Canyon, Niagara Falls, the Gateway Arch, the Vietnam War Memorial, the Sixth Floor JFK Memorial, the Golden Gate and Brooklyn bridges, Central Park, the Sears Tower, and the Smithsonian Museums.

I've partied at Rush and Division Streets in Chicago, Greenwich Village in New York, Pioneer Square in Seattle, Buckhead in Atlanta, Covington Landing across the river from Cincinnati, Deep Ellum in Dallas, Hennepin Avenue in Minneapolis, Lacledes Landing in St. Louis, Fells Point in Baltimore, Larimer Square in Denver, the Flats in Cleveland, as well as Prince Arthur and Crescent Streets in Montreal, and even Revolucion Boulevard in Tijuana, Mexico.

America's major league cities also offer a wealth of cultural highlights. Some of those I've enjoyed most are the Metropolitan Museum of Art, the Museum of Natural History, the Museum of Modern Art, and the Guggenheim (all in New York); the Art Institute of Chicago, the Museum of Science and Industry, and the Field Museum of Natural History in Chicago; the Nelson-Atkins Museum in Kansas City; the Sixth Floor Museum in Dallas; the Andy Warhol Museum in Pittsburgh; Alcatraz Island in San Francisco; the Museum of Natural History and the Museum of Art in Denver.

By now, you've probably figured out that the purpose of this book is not only to discuss the game of baseball and its ballparks, but also to provide a guide to America's major league cities, share some of my own experiences, and highlight some of the attractions that might appeal to a baseball fan. I've been to some cities and ballparks as many as six or seven times, while others I've visited only once. As a result, I probably do a better job with some cities than I do in others. I'll let you be the judge. If I've missed anything important, I hope you'll let me know.

Suffice it to say that there is an awful lot to do and see out there between Seattle and Miami. And what better excuse than a few major league ball games to make you go and check it out. It worked for me. I hope you'll find something in the pages that follow to make you want to do the same.

INTRODUCTION

The game begins in the spring, when everything else begins again, and it blossoms in the summer, filling the afternoons and evenings, and then as soon as the chill rains come, it stops and leaves you to face the fall alone.

A. BARTLETT GIAMATTI

Half the fun of a baseball trip is in the planning and anticipation. Each winter when the major league baseball (MLB) schedule is released, I pull out a pen, a pad of paper, and my atlas to see what I can come up with. The official schedule is available in February from the office of Major League Baseball at 350 Park Avenue, New York, NY 10022. If you really want to get a jump on things, unofficial schedules can generally be found in mid-January in national baseball tabloids such as *Baseball Weekly* or *Baseball America*. On the Internet, check out www.majorleaguebaseball.com for schedule information.

My first step in planning a trip is to decide on a time frame: How many days do I want to spend and at what time of the season? If I'm thinking about starting a trip with opening day, I'll avoid places like Cleveland, Detroit, Milwaukee, and Denver—simply because my idea of a great day at the ballpark doesn't include snow or temperatures in the thirties. If I'm considering games in Atlanta, Florida, or Texas, I'll probably look at early spring or late fall, to avoid the sweltering heat associated with those places in the dead of summer.

Another possibility at the beginning of the season is exhibition games, as good tickets to these are easier to come by than tickets to opening day games. In 1993, just before the start of the season, I was surprised to see that the Red Sox were playing the Braves in Atlanta, only four hours from my home. Four years later I saw a rematch of the '96 World Series when the Braves hosted the Yankees for a pair of games at brand-new Turner Field. While an exhibition game may not count, it does involve two major league teams playing in a major league stadium. How bad could that be?

I generally plan to spend around nine days—Saturday through the following Sunday—using only five of my precious vacation days. The advantage of a trip of this length is that it's possible to see several cities and games at a nice leisurely pace. The actual number of games depends on you and the MLB schedule. You may also want to plan your trip around a holiday, thereby extending the trip by a day or saving a vacation day. Holiday flights, rental vehicles, and hotel rooms may cost more, however, and tickets are more likely to sell out. So if you decide to go this route, be sure to make all your reservations well in advance.

I try to see between five and eight games in a nine- to ten-day period. I might see more games if possible, but not at the expense of seeing what a city has to offer other than baseball. Besides, there is only so much ballpark food you can take!

In the summer of '93, a few guys from Princeton University saw all twenty-eight major league ballparks in twenty-eight days. At that rate, they probably spent as much time rushing to and from airports as they did at the games. Nevertheless, seeing that many parks in such a short period of time is an impressive accomplishment, given the complexity of the MLB schedule.

The first time I went to the Midwest on a baseball trip, I saw eight games in seven ballparks and six cities. But try as I might, I couldn't manage to see Milwaukee play at home because the Brewers were on a nineteen-day road trip at the time. Alas, you see what you can and save some things for another time.

The more cities and ballparks you try to see, the trickier the scheduling becomes. Oftentimes, in cities that have two teams, like New York, Chicago, or the San Francisco/Oakland and Los Angeles/Anaheim areas, you'll have to catch one team's final game of a home stand and the other's home opener in order to see both teams on the same trip. Sometimes you'll have to spend a day in town without seeing a ball game. There are other times when your only option will be to see one team, leave for a day or two, and come back. You could, for instance, go to Shea to see the Mets, then leave town to see Boston or Philadelphia, and come back to watch the Yankees. Still, in other cases, you can see two games in two different ballparks on the same day. A day game at Wrigley and an evening fray at Comiskey are probably the most common example of this.

Once you've decided how many days you can spend on your trip, it's time to choose where to go. One way to do a baseball trip is to follow a particular team on a road trip. This is a fairly easy way to plan a trip. All you have to do is look at your favorite team's road schedule and pick a time to go along. One disadvantage of this method is that you aren't likely to see more than two or three ballparks and teams in a nine- to ten-day span.

Another point worth mentioning is that a trip can become a real bummer if you catch your favorite team in the midst of a losing streak. Since I've been taking these trips, the Red Sox are 1 for 8 with me in the stands. At one point, they were 0 for 7 until I finally saw them beat the Yankees at Fenway Park. The all-time low was when Roger Clemens got food poisoning in Baltimore and was scratched as the starter. My friends and I decided to go see the sights of Washington, D.C., instead. The Red Sox probably won that game.

The way I prefer to plan a trip is to pick out five or six ballparks that are close enough to each other that I can see as many games as possible, with a minimum amount of time spent traveling from city to city. Most people I've talked to who have done a baseball road trip have centered their trip around either New York or Chicago for that very reason. The Los Angeles/Anaheim and San Francisco/Oakland areas offer a tremendous number of nearby sights and attractions, but, other than minor league parks, baseball-related options within a short drive from those cities are somewhat limited.

When it comes to deciding where to go, it's really a matter of individual preference. Which teams and individual players do you want to see, what parks and cities are of the most interest, and where are you starting from? Chicago has Wrigley Field and the new Comiskey Park, as well as relative proximity to Milwaukee, Detroit, and Cleveland. Saint Louis, Minneapolis, Toronto, and Dyersville, Iowa (home of the Field of Dreams) are a little farther away, but still well within reach by car.

New York offers two parks, Yankee and Shea stadiums, with Boston, Philadelphia, Baltimore, Montreal, and the Hall of Fame in Cooperstown, New York, not too far away. The West Coast has seven major league teams, although Seattle and Phoenix are a long way from the other five.

Cities such as Chicago, San Francisco, Los Angeles, and New York offer a wealth of things to do besides baseball. Nightlife in any of the four cities compares favorably with the best in the country. You'll also find a number of outstanding museums, historic landmarks, tourist attractions, parks, and shopping.

Once you've settled on "when and where," the next step is to sit down with the schedule and plot your trip. You may find that the trip you'd like to make is not practical because teams are on the road or off on the day you hoped to be in a particular city. But don't forget to look at the trip in reverse order, starting with the final destination. It may just work out that way.

On our California trip, my buddies and I found that if we started in San Francisco and worked our way south, we weren't able to see all five California teams play. But during the same time frame, if we started in San Diego and drove north, we had no problem seeing them all. We also discovered, with the help of a travel agent, that it was cheaper at that time to fly into San Diego and out of San Francisco than it was to do the opposite. An added benefit was that it was only a little more expensive (including the rental car one-way drop-off fee) to do it that way than it was to fly in and out of the same city. Considering the amount of driving time saved, it was a no-brainer on our part.

As you tinker with the details and a trip begins to fall into place, you'll probably get to see most, if not all, of the teams, ballparks, and cities you originally hoped to. Keep in mind that pennant contenders may sell out late-season games or even a midseason series against division rivals. Once you've determined that a trip is practical, making sure you've allowed enough time for travel between cities, decide which tickets will have to be ordered in advance. You may want to play it safe and order all of your tickets immediately. Ordering all your tickets in advance leaves very little room for error or for spontaneous adjustments, but it also assures that you won't be left on the outside looking in.

I generally order only those tickets that I think will sell well—rivalries, potentially good pitching matchups, opening day, weekend, or holiday games. So far, I haven't miscalculated and been shut out of a game I wanted to see. I would have, if not for an early morning call to the box office from our hotel when Nolan Ryan was unexpectedly scheduled to be on the hill for his last game ever at Oakland Alameda Stadium. Unfortunately, we ended up with seats on the stadium's very top level, about a mile from the pitcher's mound (for a few innings, anyway).

On the other hand, often I have saved a bunch of money and gotten spectacular seats that I would not have been able to get through advance order, or even gotten free tickets, just by waiting until before game time and buying my tickets in front of the park.

It is generally helpful to consult a travel agent or travel club. Travel agents can help with flight arrangements, hotels, and rental cars. Their services are free, and if you get one who really works hard for you, he or she can be a godsend. At the very worst, the information they provide can serve as a good starting point. Travel clubs often provide quite a bit more than emergency roadside assistance. The good ones offer route maps, tour books, and free traveler's checks, as well as discounts at hotels, restaurants, and attractions. Because nothing ruins a trip like car trouble, it's nice to know that if you do break down, help is only as far away as the nearest phone. If you are renting a car, be certain that the rental car company provides free roadside assistance as part of your rental agreement.

You may also want to contact the convention and visitors bureau of the cities you're heading to. Most will mail information to help you plan your trip if you take the time to call or write. This information ranges from a few pamphlets to an entire visitors' kit, with maps and discounts for area hotels and attractions. I've included the address and phone number for each city's convention and visitors bureau, including a toll-free number where available.

Internet resources I've found worthwhile include Travelocity, Expedia,

MapQuest, and hoteldiscounts.com. I've also included Web sites for each city, team, and visitors bureau where possible.

Your local library should have quite a few travel guides available. There are guides for specific cities, states, and particular regions of the country. Also available at most libraries are newspapers of many major cities, which can be helpful in finding local hotel specials and upcoming shows and concerts.

It generally pays to do a little advance research. One year I found myself in Chicago reading about sold-out shows by comedian Jerry Seinfeld and blues legend Buddy Guy. If I had known about them two weeks earlier, I might have been able to get tickets. Since then, I've discovered that many newspapers and entertainment weeklies are willing to send you a copy if you call or write the circulation manager in advance. Most daily newspapers have an entertainment section that runs on Friday or Sunday, so be sure to ask for it.

Another important thing to do once you've decided on a trip is to talk to friends and acquaintances. You never know who might know about the city or cities you're traveling to. A large number of the places I've come across were the result of somebody saying, "Don't miss this restaurant," or "Be sure to stay at this particular hotel," or "Check out this nightclub." You'll be surprised at how willing people are to help or to offer suggestions. It has been my experience that nothing is more reliable than a firsthand recommendation. People often go beyond that and even offer to contact friends in the city, locate places to stay, or even secure tickets to area sights.

To help you plan your trip, I've divided America's major league cities into three regions: East, Midwest, and West. I've tried to include what I consider to be each city's best sights and attractions, my favorite places to eat, drink, and be merry, as well as the attributes and drawbacks of the individual ballparks. The information is as accurate as I could make it, but over the course of time it took to gather, some things are bound to have changed. Please write to let me know if a place does not live up to your expectations, or if I missed a place that should be included. My e-mail address is fieldofdreams@mind spring.com. For updates and additional ballpark information, visit www.mind spring.com/~fieldsofdreams.

Speaking of change, some of baseball's newest parks, Comerica Park, Camden Yards, Pacific Bell Park, and Jacobs Field, are shining examples of ballparks that offer nostalgia and charm as well as all the modern amenities a fan could ask for. Since I'm something of a traditionalist, I place these new parks right behind Fenway Park and Wrigley Field as my favorite parks in "The Show." New outdoor ballparks are also anticipated in San Diego, Cincinnati, and even Boston. With any luck, they will follow the direction of these four new parks and we will witness the extinction of domes, artificial turf, and multipurpose cookie-cutter stadiums.

THE EAST

The main entry plaza of Turner Field during an exhibition game against the Yankees. (Photo by Author)

◆ ATLANTA ◆

I can see a little bit of Camden Yards, a little bit of Jacobs Field. . . . It's beautiful, not one of those homer havens. With the deep power alleys it's really a very fair ballpark.

JOE TORRE

TURNER FIELD

If you have ever taken a road trip to Atlanta to see a ball game, you know how badly the Braves needed a new ballpark. The Braves' old home, Fulton County Stadium, was built in 1965 as a multisport facility for both baseball and football. In order to accommodate both sports, the field of play was much bigger than was needed for a baseball diamond, and it never really served baseball fans well. To add insult to injury, *Sports Illustrated* rated Fulton County Stadium's concessions as some of the worst in the big leagues in 1996.

To the Braves' credit, they never demanded a new place to call their own or held Atlanta hostage by threatening to move to another city. Three factors led to the Braves' new home: The Falcons left for an indoor football stadium, the Braves played better than any other team in the '90s, and on September 18, 1990, the city of Atlanta learned that it would host the 1996 Summer Olympics. Not wanting to leave behind any "white elephant" buildings, the Atlanta Olympic Committee entrusted the Ellerbe Becket architecture firm to build an 85,000-seat track-and-field venue that could be retrofitted as a ballpark for the Braves after the Olympics. The conversion began on August 26, 1996, and continued day and night until game time on May 29, when the Braves faced the Yankees for an exhibition rematch of the 1996 World Series. The entire stadium project cost $242.5 million, with the Braves footing the bill for the $35.5 million conversion.

The finished product is a park the Braves and the city of Atlanta can be proud of. Turner Field has all the amenities a fan could ask for, a natural grass playing field with asymmetrical dimensions, and one of the smallest foul territories in the league.

Even before you enter the ballpark, you start to feel the park's "baseball atmosphere." A monument grove, just in front of the ticket windows, offers a nice picnic area on the center field side of the stadium and features handsome statues of Ty Cobb, Hank Aaron, and Phil Niekro. Within the main entrance is a one-of-a-kind entry plaza with a food court, a kids' baseball arcade area called Scout's Alley, a team souvenir shop with a dozen TVs out front showing every MLB game in progress, a museum and Hall of Fame, and the Chop House restaurant. One of my favorite views in the park is from the walkway beside the Chop House, overlooking the Braves' bullpen out onto the playing field.

Once inside the ballpark, you can appreciate the extent to which the Braves have supplied the fans with every possible convenience. There are plenty of restrooms, cup holders at every seat, more and wider aisles, awning-covered escalators to take you to the upper levels, more spacious concession areas that allow fans to watch the game as they stand in line, comfortable slatted seats, seven ATMs throughout the park, and a phone and water fountain at every restroom location. A canopy over the very back rows of the upper deck provides welcome shade in those sections. Seats behind home plate and along the third baseline are also in the shade, later in the afternoon.

Fans seated near the infield appreciate the bigger scoreboard, video replay screen, and matrix message-board above the batter's background in center field that make it easier to follow the action. Unlike many older stadiums, all seats are angled toward home plate so you don't have to crane your neck for the entire game. The Braves brought along a few relics from the old stadium, including the out-of-town-scoreboard that sits above left field stands, the auxiliary scoreboards along the first and third baselines, and the game-in-progress board on the right field fence.

Many fans don't care for the fact that the stadium was named after Ted Turner instead of Hank Aaron, as was once proposed, but it's Turner's team, and I suppose the name Turner Field is no worse than Wrigley Field, Comiskey Park, Jacobs Field, or Busch Stadium. And it's infinitely better than the corporate monikers of major-league stadiums like Pacific Bell Park, Bank One Ballpark, or Qualcomm Stadium. Fans can take solace in the fact that Hank Aaron, one of the Braves' few heroes as a ballplayer, and the team's current senior vice president, is all over the stadium. A silhouette of Hammerin' Hank's home run swing is at the end of each aisle of seats, and a 100' x 100' billboard of the ball he hit for his 715th career home run greets fans as they enter the stadium. The Hall of Fame features a 1940s club/sleeper railroad car like those Aaron used to travel in before teams began traveling by plane, Aaron's 715th home run ball and bat, and equipment and uniforms ranging from 1871 to 1996. Tours of the ballpark, which include admission to the museum, are $7 for adults.

Concessions at Turner Field are much better than they were at the old stadium albeit a little pricey. Food stands in the West Pavilion feature a rotating menu of food from the visiting team's home city. For example, when the Orioles visit, Maryland crabcakes are served; when the Rockies are in town, it is bison burgers; and when the Braves host the Phillies, expect cheesesteaks. Elsewhere in the park, at the stadium's sixty stands and sixty-four pushcarts, you find pizza and other Italian specialties, hot dogs, ice cream, fajitas, tacos, and specialty chicken. The Chop House restaurant, which is open to everyone, offers a limited menu of barbecue chicken, ribs, and pork sandwiches, as well as bottled microbrew beers. If your seats are less than ideal, you may want to consider getting to the park early and snagging a table with a view of the field. As long as you are eating and drinking, you are welcome to stay.

Turner Field is a more intimate park than Fulton County Stadium—only 50,528 seats versus 52,013—but it has plenty of seating options with prices ranging from $30 for dugout-level seats to just $1 for skyline seats. On the day of the game, 178 skyline tickets are sold, and fans are limited to six per person in order to discourage scalping. Field pavilion seats, which are where bleacher seats are located at most stadiums, are remarkably close to the action and a bargain at $15 each. The Coca-Cola Sky Field is a picnic area that is open to all fans. It has misting fans, a pair of Coke bottle cannons, and giant baseball cards. The first fan to catch a home run ball in this section, 435 feet from home plate and 75 feet above the left field wall, will win $1 million.

I spent two days looking for this park's flaws and came up with very little to complain about. Fans are allowed to bring in their own food and drinks as long as their cooler fits under their seat, or you can picnic in the monument grove before and after the game. Tailgating is also allowed in area parking lots as long as all grilling is done in grassy areas and not in parking spaces. In most areas ticket prices are higher by $3–5 than Fulton County Stadium, but considering the overall appearance of the park, the added amenities, and the proximity of the seats to the playing field, they are well worth it. Purists will fuss that the outfield dimensions are only slightly asymmetrical, and the outfield fence is eight feet high from foul pole to foul pole, with no funky variation of heights or odd bounces created by fences meeting at an angle. The park also lacks any real sense of nostalgia, but it attempts to make up for that with its theme park atmosphere.

Considering that the ballpark was converted from an Olympic track-and-field stadium, Turner Field is an excellent place to take the family to see a game. The designers have gone to great lengths to provide fans with every convenience while keeping the park small enough so that there really isn't a bad seat in the house. Turner Field may not rank up there with other newer parks like Camden Yards, Coors Field, The Ballpark In Arlington, or Jacobs Field, nor does it compare to classic yards like Fenway Park, Wrigley Field, or Yankee Stadium, but it is a vast improvement over the Braves' old home and is a welcome addition to a great sports city.

Be wary of scalping tickets as Georgia law prohibits resale of tickets for more than the face value, and both buyer and seller may be prosecuted.

GETTING TO TURNER FIELD
521 Capitol Avenue, SW

Traffic in Atlanta can be maddening if you don't make plans to avoid major arteries during rush hour. I have not encountered any major delays on my way to the stadium, but I generally get to the stadium early or take advantage of mass transit. The ballpark is conveniently located at the intersection of interstates 75 and 20, just south of downtown, making it easily accessible by car. Parking spaces are limited unless you don't mind walking a few blocks, and prices range from $7–10 per car. Your best bet may be to take a MARTA shuttle from the Five Points station. The shuttle costs just $1.50 or a free transfer ticket for MARTA train riders.

One place that stands to benefit greatly from the city's new ballpark is **The Bullpen**, formerly known as B-Champs Sports Bar & Grill. It's located just across the street from the new ballpark, at 735 Pollard Avenue. Otherwise, the neighborhood surrounding the park does not offer many places to grab a bite to eat so plan on taking advantage of the outdoor picnic areas, tailgating at your car, or eating inside the park.

WHAT TO DO AND SEE IN ATLANTA

Atlanta offers a good deal to do in the way of attractions, nightlife, and culture. The city's mass transportation system, **MARTA**, is one of the most convenient and affordable in the nation. At just $1.25, with free transfers good on buses and trains, it's easy to see all or most of the city in a short period of time. MARTA is so good in fact, that if you fly into town, I recommend foregoing the rental car, staying at a downtown hotel near the MARTA line, and taking the fifteen-minute train ride to downtown from the airport. If you have a lot of luggage, or a group of people to split a cab ride, you might want to consider taking the $15 cab ride to a downtown hotel.

Anybody who has ever been to a ballgame in Atlanta has heard about **The Varsity**. Legend has it that a Georgia Tech business student was told by his professor that he was so incompetent that he couldn't operate a hot dog stand. So he decided to prove his professor wrong, and The Varsity has since become an Atlanta institution. These days the place does a tremendous business and serves up some of the best burgers, dogs, and onion rings on the planet. You'll find it overlooking the Georgia Tech campus at 61 North Avenue.

One of the city's more popular attractions is the **CNN Center/CNN Studio Tour**, which offers an inside look at TBS' world headquarters. It's located on the MARTA route (get off at the Omni Center), in the heart of downtown Atlanta. The tour takes a little less than an hour and costs $6 for adults, with discounts available for senior citizens and children. Reservations are recommended.

Atlanta has several fine museums. Two of my favorites are the **High Museum of Art** and the **Sci/Trek—The Science and Technology Museum of Atlanta**. The High has an impressive collection of twentieth-century art and photographs, as well as a good number of European and African works. Open Tuesday–Sunday, it's free after 1 PM on Thursdays. Otherwise, admission is $5 for adults. Discounts are available for students, seniors, and children. Sci/Trek is a hands-on museum that is a big hit with kids. Ranked in the top ten among science museums in the United States, Sci/Trek features more than 100 interactive exhibits that change regularly. It's open Tuesday through Sunday and adult admission is $6.50.

Another up-and-coming attraction is the **World of Coca-Cola**. It's adjacent to Underground Atlanta, at 55 Martin Luther King Jr. Drive, and is open seven days a week. Expect to spend about an hour on a self-guided tour of the history of the world's most famous soft drink. Tickets are just $3.50 for adults, and reservations are recommended.

NIGHTLIFE IN ATLANTA

One way that Atlanta lives up to the moniker of "Hot-lanta" is with its nightlife. Your best bet for up-to-date entertainment news is to pick up Atlanta's weekly entertainment magazine *Creative Loafing*. The **Buckhead** area, north of downtown, offers a multitude of restaurants and nightclubs, many within walking distance of each other. Two unusual clubs in the area include **BAR Atlanta**, where for no apparent reason customers and staffers will occasionally jump up on the bar and tables and start dancing while bartenders and waitresses pour tequila down customer's gullets, and **Lulu's Bait Shop**, where the drinks are served in giant ninety-six-ounce fishbowls accented with rubber alligators. Tables on Lulu's patio are highly coveted and offer a great view of revelers as they pass by on the street. My favorite restaurant in the Buckhead area is the **Three Dollar Cafe**, where the food is good, affordable, and piled high on your plate, and the beer selection is outstanding and inexpensive.

Perhaps Atlanta's best known club is **The Masquerade**, a bizarre multilevel

dance club, located at 695 North Avenue NE. It's really three clubs—
"Heaven," "Hell," and "Purgatory"—and features dancing and live music of all
kinds. The cover charge varies nightly, depending on the act billed, but the
place alone, not to mention the crowd it attracts, is generally worth the price
of admission. Another Atlanta institution is **Blind Willie's**, at 828 North Highland Street. It's about as good as a blues club gets. The place has a classic
feel, great sightlines and acoustics, and books legendary blues talent just about
every weekend. Seats are limited, so get there early. Nearby you'll find the
Highland Tap. This dark basement bar is a great place to grab a cold beer,
but don't overlook the restaurant. For the money, it's tough to beat their
steaks.

ESPN Zone, at 3030 Peachtree Street, has become one of the premier
places to go in Atlanta before and after a big game. Like the original locales
in Baltimore and New York, this massive sports bar features plenty TVs, loads
of sports memorabilia, decent bar chow, and hundreds of interactive games.
There's even an outdoor patio. If you prefer something not quite so huge, one
of Atlanta's finest sports hangouts is **Frankie's** in Sandy Springs. The emphasis here is on good chow, fun atmosphere, sports trivia, and wall-to-wall sports
memorabilia. There are more than 150 TV monitors, indoors and out on the
patio, so no matter where you sit, you'll have a good view of whatever games
are being shown.

WHERE TO STAY IN ATLANTA

My favorite areas to stay are near Lennox Square Mall, Buckhead, or Virginia
Highlands.

Moderately Priced and Near Ballpark

Comfort Inn   101 International Boulevard (800) 535-0707 or (404) 524-5555
   Minutes to the ballpark, blocks away from CNN Center and the Underground.

Days Inn   2910 Clairmont Road (800) 325-2525 or (404) 633-8411   Very
   affordable hotel with a decent location at exit 32 off I-85.

Hampton Inn   759 Pollard Boulevard (800) 426-7866 or (404) 658-
   1961   Inexpensive hotel across the street from the ballpark.

Holiday Inn   101 International Blvd. (800) 535-0707 or (404) 524-5555
   Minutes to the ballpark, blocks away from CNN Center and the Underground.

Regency Suites Hotel   975 West Peachtree Street (800) 642-3629 or (404)
   876-5003   Reasonably priced hotel adjacent to MARTA and three miles
   from the ballpark.

TEAM HOTELS

Marriott Marquis   265 Peachtree Center Avenue (800) 352-0764 or (404) 521-0000   Reds, Rockies, Marlins, Expos, Mets, Padres, Phillies, and Giants.

Westin Peachtree   210 Peachtree Street NW (800) 228-3000 or (404) 659-1400   Astros, Cubs, Dodgers, Pirates, and Cardinals.

GOOD TO KNOW

- For schedule information or tickets to Braves games, call (800) 326-4000 or (404) 522-7630. For group tickets call (404) 577-9100. You can also write to **Atlanta Braves Ticket Dept.**, P.O. Box 4064, Atlanta, GA 30302-4064. The Braves official Internet address is www.atlantabraves.com.
- Braves games can be heard on **WSB 750 AM**.
- For additional information on Atlanta sights and attractions, write to the **Convention & Visitors Bureau** at 233 Peachtree Street, Suite 2000, Atlanta, GA 30303. Or call (404) 521-6600 or (404) 222-6688.
- For information on mass-transit options write to **MARTA**, 2424 Piedmont Road, NE Atlanta, GA 30324 or call (404) 848-4711.

Closest major league cities (and drive times): Tampa—462 miles (8 hours and 25 minutes); Cincinnati—474 miles (8 hours and 10 minutes); Saint Louis—573 miles (10 hours and 40 minutes).

IN THE VICINITY

The Masters at Augusta National Golf Club   The tournament itself has been closed to the general public for years, but the practice rounds are open on a lottery basis. The tournament is scheduled so that it ends each year on the second Sunday in April. Tickets for the following year's tournament must be ordered in advance. They begin accepting official requests postmarked on June 1 of the year prior to the practice round(s) you hope to see (Monday–Wednesday). Write to Augusta National Golf Club, 2604 Washington Road, Augusta, Georgia 30904, or call (706) 738-7761 or (706) 667-6000 for more information.

◆ BALTIMORE ◆

*It's a combination of 100 years of baseball and it's
baseball in the '90s. This is the whole ball of wax right
here. I've never seen a nicer park.*

TONY LARUSSA

ORIOLE PARK AT CAMDEN YARDS

This may very well be the nicest park in the majors. As soon as it opened,
Camden Yards became the standard to which all new ballparks would aspire.
The Inner Harbor area, where the ballpark is located, underwent a huge
transformation in the last few years and has become a great place to hang out
before and after a game. The ballpark itself offers the old-world charm of
places built eighty years ago, while at the same time providing all the modern
amenities a fan could ask for. A wide-open outdoor plaza behind right field has
a number of unique concession stands and specialty carts. One worth mentioning is former O's slugger Boog Powell's **Boog's Barbecue**.

Fans may bring their own food and drink into the park as long as they are
in coolers that fit under the seat (no more than eighteen inches tall). No cans,
bottles, or alcoholic beverages are allowed, and fans with containers should
enter in gates C, E, or G. Even if you decide to pack a lunch or snack, you may
want to sample the park's crabcake sandwiches, which get my vote as the *single
best ballpark food item available* in the major leagues.

Highlights contributing to the old-time feel of the park include an analog-
style clock atop the center field scoreboard, ornate ironwork throughout the
park, a deep center field corner 410 feet from home plate, and, of course, the
now-famous warehouse wall beyond right field. The out-of-town scoreboard
in right field is easy to read from just about any vantage point in the park
except the right-center field bleachers. You can also see the Bromo-Seltzer
clock tower in downtown Baltimore, beyond the left-center field stands.

Center field scoreboard of Oriole Park at Camden Yards. (Photo by Author)

In a tribute to Baltimore's baseball past, HOK Sports kept the foul poles from Memorial Stadium and installed them at Camden Yards. Another throwback feature is the *Sun* sign promoting the local newspaper atop the scoreboard, which doubles as a hit/error indicator. If a play is a hit, the letter *H* illuminates. If the official scorer determines the play was an error, the letter *E* lights up. Just below the scoreboard on the outfield fence, an old-style "Hit it Here" sign with a hand pointing to the letter *L* refers to the state lottery that helped finance the stadium.

If the park has any negatives, it's the rather large foul territory around home plate, pushing even front-row seats a good distance from the action, and the fact that seats along the outfield baselines don't face the infield. Neither problem keeps this from being an excellent place to see a ball game.

Tickets for weekend games are very difficult to come by, so order early. As with anything new, there is a premium on good seats—$18–25 for the best seats in the house—but the terrace boxes (sections 15–55) are a good value at $16. The right-center field bleachers are also a good deal at $5. The $16 left field boxes (even-numbered sections 66–86) offer your best chance to snag a home run ball. The $9 box seats (odd-numbered sections 73–87) directly behind the first tier of left field boxes are a bargain if you can get them.

HISTORY

Few moments in baseball compare to Cal Ripken surpassing Lou Gehrig's stretch of 2,130 consecutive games. On September 6, 1995, Ripken became the game's all-time Iron Man playing in his 2,131st straight game. His victory lap around the stadium, as the number of games was unfurled on a banner occupying the right field warehouse wall, was one of the most memorable and inspiring celebrations in all of sports. Exactly one year later, Eddie Murray hit his 500th home run into the right field stands at Camden Yards and joined Hank Aaron and Willie Mays as the only players in major league history to have 3,000 hits and 500 home runs over their careers.

On July 13 of that same year, Camden Yards hosted the sixty-fourth All-Star Game—the city's first since 1958. The thirty-five-year span was the longest any major league city had gone between All-Star games. In that year's home run hitting contest, July 12, Ken Griffey Jr. became the first player to hit the warehouse wall on the fly with a home run ball.

Getting to Camden Yards
333 West Camden Street

Take I-95 to exit 52 or 53. There is some parking just off the highway right next to the stadium, but it is limited, so if you don't want a 10–15 minute walk to the park, get there early. A few good deals can be found from vendors in the stadium lots—snacks to bring into the game and Orioles' merchandise after the game. There is also more expensive parking in the Inner Harbor area, with your best bet being the local garages.

One suggestion is to hit the Inner Harbor area early. Take in the sights or fuel up at an area restaurant or tavern and wander over to the game at your convenience. **ESPN Zone** is located in the Power Plant Building at 601 East Pratt Street. This massive sports bar/restaurant is loaded with televisions, interactive games, and sports memorabilia. Be sure to check out the original Etch-A-Sketch drawing of Lou Gehrig and Cal Ripken. Other, more indigenous, places that pack them in before the game, **Sliders Bar and Grill** and **Pickles Pub**, are located across the street from the stadium on Washington Boulevard. Neither place is very fancy, but they offer a wide selection of local microbrews, the food is quick and good, and the crowd loves their baseball. Part of the beauty of the Inner Harbor is that these are but two of many fine bar/restaurants within walking distance of Camden Yards.

Another possibility is to stay at a suburban hotel near the Light Rail System (which may save you a bunch of money compared to the hotels in the heart of the Harbor area) and take the 10–15 minute trip directly to the Inner Harbor/Stadium area for $1.25 each way. For more information on mass-transit options, call (800) 543-9809 or 539-5000 once you get to town.

A third option, and my favorite, is to drive to the **Fells Point** area well before the game and take a **water taxi** across the harbor. It drops you off within an easy three-block walk to the park and picks you up at the same spot after the game. The view of the Harbor as you approach it is fantastic, the fare is a bargain (only $3.25 per person, unlimited use all day), and it helps you avoid the postgame traffic crush. Water taxis generally stop running shortly after night games let out, so be sure to ask when the last one returns before you buy your ticket. Before and after the game, the entire Fells Point area is alive with activity. Its shops, galleries, pubs, and eateries are a lot less trendy and commercial than those in the Inner Harbor area and their prices tend to reflect that.

WHAT TO DO AND SEE IN BALTIMORE

The **National Aquarium**, one of the best in the nation, is located in the Harbor area and features 5,000 creatures large and small. The aquarium has become the state's most popular tourist attraction and is visited by more than 1.5 million visitors each year. One of the aquarium's most impressive displays is a deep racetrack-shaped tank that is home to numerous large sharks that swim around you as you descend a winding ramp. Admission is $11.50 for adults, but worth every penny. Tickets to the aquarium must be bought in advance and are good only for a specific time frame.

The **Baltimore Museum of Art** on Charles Street houses the Cone collection of twentieth-century art and features an impressive group of works by Picasso, Matisse, and Cezanne, among others. Open Wednesday–Sunday, there is an admission charge every day except Thursday. Farther south on Charles Street there are a number of shops, galleries, and cafes within sight of Baltimore's **Washington Monument** in Washington Square. Built more than 150 years ago, the monument offers a great view of the city, provided you are willing to ascend its 228-step spiral staircase. Also nearby is the **Walters Art Gallery**, an outstanding museum exhibiting over 30,000 works of art spanning 5,000 years. The monument requests a $1 donation to climb to the top, and the gallery asks for a $4 donation; both are worth the price of admission.

The **Babe Ruth Birthplace and Baseball Center** is America's second largest baseball museum. A tribute to the "Sultan of Swat" as well as Maryland's baseball past, it's open daily until 5 PM during the season. The museum is open until 7 PM on game nights. The center occupies four row houses at 216 Emory Street just a few blocks west of Camden Yards. Admission is just $4.50.

Baltimore Trolley Tours board every half hour at twenty stops in and around downtown, between 10 AM and 4 PM every day. At a cost of $9, it can be a great way to see the sights and get a feel for the history of the area. You can get on and off as often as you like for the entire day. Ask your hotel concierge for tour schedule and ticket information. One of the most interesting stops on the trolley route is **Fort McHenry**, the star-shaped fort that inspired Francis Scott Key's "Star Spangled Banner," as he saw the American flag still flying above it the morning after a British bombardment during the War of 1812. The fort is a short drive southeast of the downtown area.

NIGHTLIFE IN BALTIMORE

For information on Baltimore area clubs, pick up a copy of the *City Paper*, the area's free entertainment weekly. You may want to call (410) 523-2300 and ask for a copy a few weeks before your trip. The Inner Harbor area surrounding Camden Yards has a wealth of restaurants and bars, although many of the newest additions to the Inner Harbor area are expensive, franchise-type establishments. There are a few notable exceptions. **Hammerjacks** is a huge club at 1101 South Howard Street that has been bringing heavy metal and nationally known rock and roll acts to the area for years. A few blocks away, just below the Washington Monument, you'll find **Buddie's Pub** at 313 North Charles Street. Buddie's offers live jazz and blues bands on the weekends in a smaller, less radical atmosphere. Directly across from Camden Yards, at 204 West Pratt Street, is the **Wharf Rat**, a spin-off of the Fells Point dive that serves everything from a quick lunch to lavish seafood dinners in a warm, comfortable atmosphere. A selection of their made-on-site Oliver beers is also served at the ballpark. They also have live music on the weekends. It gets packed on game days, so come by early.

Overlooking the harbor, you'll find a wealth of casual and fine dining opportunities. My favorite is **Wayne's Bar-B-Que**, a casual place with a patio overlooking a busy sidewalk, outstanding barbecue, and a beer listing of over 100 choices. Other choices in Light Street Pavilion include **Phillips**, an upscale place that offers an all-you-can-eat seafood buffet, and **City Lights**, an upscale restaurant and lounge overlooking the **Harborplace Amphitheatre**, which hosts free concerts Friday through Sunday evenings.

Not actually in the Inner Harbor area, but nevertheless a welcome addition to the Baltimore nightlife scene, is the **Baltimore Brewing Company**. BBC is a huge state of the art brewpub, at 104 Albemarle Street, featuring beer made in huge copper kettles by a member of the Grolsch family. The brewery features a tremendous selection of hand-crafted lagers and ales, as well as a surprisingly diverse menu featuring traditional pub and German fare. One of the area's biggest and best sports bars is the **Downtown Sports Exchange**. Not far from the stadium, at 200 West Pratt Street, the Sports Exchange offers three levels of sports and spirits with twenty-six TVs, a sidewalk patio, and rooftop deck.

The **Fells Point** area offers a nightlife scene more indigenous to Baltimore. The entire area takes on a festival atmosphere at night, on weekends, or after ball games during the week. My favorite Fells Point establishment is **The**

Horse You Rode In On Saloon, at 1626 Thames Street. It's the quintessential old-style pub with little more than a few TVs showing ball games scattered about the place, good beer, and an enthusiastic pregame crowd. After the game, they generally have live acoustic acts. The original **Wharf Rat**, tucked away just around the corner, is a classic dive—short on amenities, but long on fun. Live music fans will want to check out the **Cat's Eye Pub** at 1730 Thames Street. It offers live music, ranging from folk to jazz, blues to Cajun, seven days a week. They do not offer food, but have more than thirty types of beer to choose from. Another great Fells Point live-music venue is **Bohager's Bar and Grill** at 515 South Eden Street, whose Boathouse Crab Deck is a haven for Maryland blue crab fans.

If you're looking for a great place to eat before a night out in Fells Point stop by **John Steven Ltd.** at 1800 Thames Street, which offers a varied menu of seafood, steaks, and pasta in an unassuming atmosphere. Other areas with outstanding nightlife include **Federal Hill** and **Water Street**.

WHERE TO STAY IN BALTIMORE

With the addition of Oriole Park at Camden Yards to an already bustling area, the Inner Harbor area has become the place to stay; the hotels are elegant, and you can walk to most of the area attractions. The downside is that you can expect to pay dearly for that convenience. If you hope to stay in the immediate vicinity of the ballpark, book reservations as soon as you have secured tickets to a game.

INNER HARBOR AREA

Clarion Hotel   612 Cathedral Street (800) 292-5500 or (410) 727-7101
   A newly renovated European-style hotel near Washington Square.
Days Inn Baltimore Inner Harbor   100 Hopkins Place (800) 325-2525 or
   (410) 576-1000   One of the Inner Harbor's few inexpensive hotels also
   happens to be one of the closest to Camden Yards.
Radisson Plaza Lord Baltimore Hotel   Hanover and West Baltimore Streets
   (800) 333-3333 or (301) 539-8400   Within walking distance of Camden Yards.
Sheraton Inner Harbor Hotel   300 South Charles Street (800) 325-3535 or
   (301) 962-8300   Just two blocks from Camden Yards.
Tremont Plaza Hotel   222 St. Paul Place (800) 873-6668 or (410) 727-
   2222   One of the area's more reasonably priced hotels, just five blocks
   from the Inner Harbor and a short walk to Camden Yards.

MODERATELY PRICED ON THE OUTSKIRTS OF DOWNTOWN

Best Western Baltimore East   5625 O'Donnell Street (800) 528-1234 or

TEN FAVORITE BIG LEAGUE CITY SPORTS BARS

10 Fourth Base   Milwaukee, Wisconsin

9 Stan's Sportsworld   Bronx, New York

8 Frankie's/Jocks and Jills   Atlanta, Georgia

7 Bobby Valentine's Sports Gallery and Cafe   Arlington, Texas

6 Chappell's Restaurant & Sports Museum   North Kansas City, Missouri

5 Sneakers/F.X. McCrory's   Seattle, Washington

4 Wayne Gretzky's   Toronto, Canada

3 ESPN Zone   Anaheim; Atlanta; Baltimore; Chicago; New York

2 Hockeytown   Detroit, Michigan

1 Murphy's Bleachers   Chicago, Illinois

---

(410) 633-9500   Just three miles from the Inner Harbor. Courtesy shuttle to Inner Harbor attractions including Camden Yards.

Comfort Inn Airport   6921 Baltimore-Annapolis Boulevard (800) 4-CHOICE or (410) 789-9100   Conveniently located across the street from the Light Rail Station.

Courtyard by Marriott   1671 West Nursery Road (800) 443-6000 or (410) 859-8855   Inexpensive accommodations near BWI Airport.

Inn at the Colonnade   4 West University Parkway (800) 222-TREE or (410) 235-5400   Adjacent to Johns Hopkins University, only 3½ miles from the Inner Harbor.

TEAM HOTELS

Renaissance Harborplace   202 East Pratt Street (800) 872-6338 or (410) 547-1200   All the visiting American League teams except the Rangers.

Marriott Inner Harbor   Pratt and Eutaw Streets (800) 228-9290 or (410) 962-0202   Rangers.

GOOD TO KNOW

- For schedule information or tickets to Orioles games call (410) 481-7328. The Orioles official Internet address is www.theorioles.com.
- Orioles games can be heard on **WBAL 1090 AM**. The leading all-sports radio station is **WTEM 570 AM**.
- To tour Camden Yards on non–game days call (410) 685-9800.

- For more information on Baltimore sights, attractions, and hotels call the **Visitors Center** at (800) 282-6632 or the **Convention and Visitors Bureau** at (800) 343-3468. The city's official Web site is www.baltconvstr.com.

Closest major league cities (and drive times): Philadelphia—102 miles (2 hours); New York—203 miles (4 hours and 30 minutes); Pittsburgh—292 Miles (5 hours and 20 minutes).

IN THE VICINITY

The Preakness, the second jewel of horse racing's Triple Crown, is run the third weekend in May (two weeks after the Kentucky Derby) at Pimlico Race Course. The track is located about ten miles from the Inner Harbor in northwest Baltimore. The Preakness offers all the pageantry and excitement of the Kentucky Derby and generally attracts a crowd of more than 80,000. Tickets, which are $20 and up, are generally available until a few weeks before the race. For race information or to order tickets, call (410) 542-9400.

Despite its traffic, **Washington, D.C.**, may very well be the most tourist-friendly city in the United States. Barring any serious traffic snarls, D.C. is just forty-five minutes from Baltimore. Almost all of the city's best attractions are within walking distance, once you find a parking spot near the Mall, and most of the sights are free.

◆ BOSTON ◆

Fenway Park, in Boston, is a lyric bandbox of a ball-park. Everything is painted green and seems in curiously sharp focus . . .

JOHN UPDIKE

FENWAY PARK

Located about two miles south of downtown, in Kenmore Square near Boston University, Fenway Park is far and away my favorite park in the big leagues. I'm reluctant to the say it's the best in the majors because I know the fact that I'm a lifelong Red Sox fan taints my objectivity. One thing I will say is that there is no more intimate park in baseball; only Wrigley Field comes close. Like Wrigley Field, Fenway offers almost no added amenities. What it lacks in frills, however, it more than makes up for with one-of-a-kind quirks, atmosphere, and nostalgia.

Until its most recent remodeling effort, Fenway was the only single-deck stadium in the majors. It still seats a mere 33,925 fans. Almost every one of them has a great seat. Because of that limited seating capacity and a scarcity of luxury skyboxes, there's talk of tearing the place down in the next few years and replacing it with a newer, "more economically feasible" ballpark. If you are at all inclined to see a game here, you'd better do it soon.

Fenway's famous left field wall, the Green Monster, is much more daunting in person than it is on TV. As a hitter, your first impression must be one of utter disbelief. It seems completely out of place, almost dominating the entire outfield. A ladder, which allows groundskeepers to retrieve balls from the net above the Green Monster, runs up the wall in fair territory just to the left of the scoreboard, adding to the woes of a left fielder attempting to play a carom off the wall. The outfield fence goes from a height of over 37 feet in left, 18 feet in left center, 8.75 feet in right center, to a low of 3.25 feet in right. The

18

Big Mo takes aim at the Green Monster in Fenway Park against the Yankees.
(Photo by Author)

angles formed by the meeting of these varying heights make for some bizarre
bounces, as do a number of recessed doorways, also used by the grounds crew.
The stadium's scoreboards are not exactly state-of-the-art, but they are more
than sufficient. In addition to the manually operated scoreboard at the base of
the Green Monster, there's a giant replay board behind the center field
bleachers and auxiliary boards along both foul lines.

There is no place in the world I'd rather be than in the right field bleachers
when the Yankees are at Fenway. As one of the best rivalries in all of sport,
tickets for these games sell out months in advance, and the atmosphere is pure
pandemonium. The bleachers are the least expensive, most readily available
seats in the park at $9 and tend to be occupied by an inordinate number of
Yankee fans. As the game goes on, the taunting between Sox fans and the
Yankee faithful can become pretty intense. Definitely not for the faint of heart.

Another great place to see a game at Fenway is from the infield roof seats.
They may not sound ideal, but for just $20 you'll get a great view of the
Boston skyline as well as the action on the field below.

The park's two shortcomings are that a few seats in the reserved grandstand have views obscured by support columns, and upper box seats along the
foul lines in the outfield have very little leg room and don't actually face the
diamond, forcing you to turn your head for the duration of the game. How-

ever, the park's best seats, along either baseline and behind home plate, are a bargain at $23 because Fenway's foul territory is the smallest in the majors.

The concessions at the ballpark are above average with one major flaw— there are no vendors wandering in the stands. All the concession stands are located indoors and do not offer closed circuit TV to allow fans on line to follow the game. So there's a good chance of missing a big play while you stand there. Fenway franks are right up there with Dodger dogs as the best ballpark hot dogs in the majors and are certainly worth the trip to a concession stand. In 1995, chicken sandwiches, fruit juices, and clam chowder from **Legal Seafood**, one of the city's best seafood restaurants, were all added to the menu. As a result, Fenway Park had the league's second highest volume of concession sales for the 1995 season.

Outside the park, on the third base side of the stadium, there are quite a few street vendors who sell everything from peanuts, souvenirs, and programs to fresh-cooked food. Be sure to try one of the outstanding sausage and pepper hoagies. Fenway is one of the few major league stadiums that still allows you to bring in your own food and drink, provided it is not alcoholic or in cans or bottles.

HISTORY

The big leagues' oldest park in use has certainly seen its share of milestones and individual accomplishments. On June 23, 1917, Fenway was the site of one of baseball's strangest no-hitters. Babe Ruth started the game by walking the Washington Senators' first batter. He was ejected immediately afterward for arguing the call and was replaced by Ernie Shore. Shore proceeded to set down the next twenty-seven batters as the Red Sox won 4–0.

On September 28, 1960, Ted Williams put an exclamation point on a splendid career by homering in his last ever at-bat. October 21, 1975, provided a moment that few baseball fans will forget as Carlton Fisk's twelfth-inning home run won Game 6 of the World Series. Fisk's waving at the ball with both hands, pleading with it to stay fair, is one of the most memorable moments in baseball and one of very few recent postseason successes for the Red Sox and their fans.

Three years later, on October 2, Bucky Dent broke New England's heart as he homered to win a one-game playoff for the Yankees. On September 12, 1979, Carl Yastrzemski got his 3,000th hit with a base rap off the Yankees' Jim Beattie. Seven years later, on April 29, Roger Clemens struck out a major league record 20 batters against the Seattle Mariners.

On July 8, 1994, Red Sox shortstop John Valentin made an unassisted triple play against the Mariners. Remarkably, an unassisted triple play had happened only nine times in major league history before Valentin's. On June 6, 1996,

Fenway Park was the place to be as Valentin went 4 for 4 to hit for the cycle in the same game that his teammate, Tim Naehring, hit into a triple play. This marked just the second time in major league history that the two feats occurred in the same game.

GETTING TO FENWAY PARK
4 Yawkey Way

Parking at Fenway is very limited, so get there early and expect to pay $10–15 for a spot near the park. As Fenway does not have its own public parking, you will need to drive up and down streets in the area looking for people to direct you to a parking lot. Boston's efficient mass-transit system, known as the "T," is a great alternative to Boston's narrow, confusing roads, especially at rush hour. From downtown Boston, you can take the green line to Kenmore Square Station, just across from Fenway.

If you fly into town, you can catch a free MTA bus at the baggage-claim area, which takes you to the airport subway station. From there you can take the subway to downtown Boston. Money-saving passports for the T are available for one, three, or seven days. Call (617) 722-3200 for sales locations and prices.

WHAT TO DO AND SEE IN BOSTON

Boston's streets are quite confusing, and parking is scarce. If you bring a car into the city, consider leaving it at your hotel. You can also park it at one of the large public parking lots at **Quincy Market** or under the **Boston Commons**, and take the **Beantown Trolley** to see the sights. The trolley allows you to get on and off as often as you like for $14. You'll see most of Boston's landmarks while the driver tells you about their history. There are quite a few places to board the trolley, but one of the most convenient is at Quincy Market.

One of the not-so-historic stops on the route is the **Bull & Finch**, the pub that inspired the TV show "Cheers." It's a nice, cool place to have a beer but is much smaller and darker than its TV likeness, and the prices for drinks and souvenirs are not cheap. Directly across the street is the **Boston Commons**, New England's oldest public park. The **Public Garden**, the country's oldest botanical garden, is best known for its legendary swan boats and is located right beside the Commons.

Other historical highlights include **Beacon Hill**, an area of quaint row houses, most of which were built in the early 1800s. The **Old North Church**, sight of Paul Revere's famous "one if by land, two if by sea" signal of the British invasion, is located on Salem Street at Paul Revere Mall. The church is open to the public from 9 AM–5 PM daily. The church was built in 1723 and still has Sunday services. The **Paul Revere House**, Boston's oldest house, is located at 19 North Square in the North End area off Hanover Street and is open for viewing Tuesday–Sunday; admission is $2.50 for adults.

Faneuil Hall, an important meeting hall during the Revolutionary War, was built in 1742 and expanded in 1805. These days at Faneuil Hall you'll find a massive public market on the street level. All told, there are more than 60 restaurants, bars, and cafes, and 125 shops and galleries to choose from.

North of downtown, across the Charlestown Bridge, is the **Bunker Hill Monument**, a twenty-two-story granite obelisk marking the site of the Revolution's first great battle. Visitors can take the spiral staircase to the top for a great view of the Greater Boston area. Admission is free.

Another free attraction north of downtown is the **U.S.S. *Constitution***, the oldest commissioned ship in the Navy. It was built at a cost of over $300,000 in 1797 and can be viewed at the Charlestown Navy Yard, north of downtown, along the Boston Inner Harbor. Guided tours are available. The **U.S.S. *Constitution* Museum** is on shore next to the ship and has some fascinating exhibits, including one that simulates a battle with you at the helm of the U.S.S. *Constitution*. Admission is just $3 for adults.

The **Museum of Fine Arts** has a tremendous collection of paintings and sculpture from all over the world with an emphasis on American art. The museum building itself is a work of art, and you should expect to spend several hours to see it all. Admission is $7 for adults Thursdays through Tuesdays, but free to everyone on Wednesdays. The **Museum of Science**, located in Science Park, is one of the country's best science museums, featuring hands-on exhibits and displays that are particularly fun for kids. At $7 for adults it is not cheap, but like the Museum of Fine Arts, it is free to everyone on Wednesdays.

The **New England Aquarium**, located not far from Faneuil Hall, has become one of Boston's most popular attractions. It is home to more than 2,000 marine animals, many of which live in a unique 187,000-gallon cylinder-shaped tank that you can view from different levels and perspectives as you wind around it. Admission is $9.50 for adults.

The **John Hancock Tower**, at Saint James Avenue and Trinity Place, presents a terrific panoramic view of the city from its sixtieth-floor observatory. At sixty-two stories tall it's the tallest building in New England. Admission is $3 for adults. Samuel Adams Boston Lager, one of the United States' most highly acclaimed beers, is produced in Boston at the **Samuel Adams Brewery**. Tours of the brewery are open to the public three times a week, Thursdays at 2 PM, and Saturdays at noon and 2 PM, for a cost of $1. The proceeds go to local charities. Tours of the brewing process last about an hour and a half; then free tastings are offered to those of legal drinking age.

Fans of the Red Sox, Celtics, Bruins, and Patriots may want to check out the **Sports Museum of New England**, in the CambridgeSide Galleria. The museum features the largest collection of sports memorabilia in New England and is open seven days a week. Baseball fans may also want to stop by the **Jacob Wirth Company Restaurant** at the intersection of Tremont and Stuart streets. The oldest German restaurant in America, this place has been a favorite of Red Sox players since the days of Cy Young. Plaques of several Hall of Fame players, who ate and drank here regularly, hang on a wall, as does a vintage photo of Babe Ruth. With or without the baseball connection, this is a great place for dinner.

NIGHTLIFE IN BOSTON

There are quite a few nightclubs, restaurants, and watering holes in the immediate vicinity of Fenway Park. **The Cask & Flagons**, a popular tavern with the Boston University crowd on the third base side of the park, is standing room only on game days. **Who's On First** is a sports bar with occasional live bands, on Yawkey Way, just outside the park. **Boston Beer Works** is a huge restaurant and microbrewery offering an excellent selection of ales, lagers, and porters, as well as a diverse dinner menu. My personal favorites are the Boston Victory Bock and the Fenway Pale Ale.

There are about a half dozen outstanding clubs along Lansdowne Street, across from Fenway Park, just beyond the Green Monster. For something completely different, check out **Modern**, a martini and sake bar at 36 Landsdowne Street.

One of the area's best live rock and roll clubs is the **Rathskellar**, in Kenmore Square at the corner of Commonwealth Avenue and Beacon Street. Since 1972 this club has featured the best in up-and-coming alternative and progressive bands. Another Boston nightlife institution is the **Black Rose**, a traditional Irish pub/restaurant that features live music nightly. It's located behind the Quincy Market at State Street near Atlantic Avenue. **Mr. Dooley's**, at 77 Broad Street, is another of the city's outstanding Irish pubs. In Cambridge's Harvard Square, about ten minutes across the river from downtown Boston, you'll find the now famous **House of Blues** at 96 Winthrop Street, which is equal parts blues bar, restaurant, and blues museum. Call ahead for band information, and expect a line out front on weekends.

Boston has several outstanding comedy clubs, all featuring top-notch comedians. The **Comedy Connection**, located in the Quincy Market Food Court on the second level of Faneuil Hall, is one of the city's oldest and best comedy clubs. You can almost always count on seeing nationally known acts, especially on the weekends. Cover charges and show times vary.

For more information on places to eat, drink, and be merry, pick up a copy of the *Boston Phoenix*, the area's free weekly entertainment magazine. It's available at many area restaurants, newsstands, and retail establishments.

WHERE TO STAY IN BOSTON

Boston is another one of those cities where you will have to pay a good deal of money for a decent hotel in the middle of downtown. Weekend packages can be found, as can an occasional ballgame package, so be sure to ask about either before making any reservations. There are also a few hotels on the outskirts of town that offer slightly less expensive rooms, but if they are not convenient to mass transit and you have to pay to park downtown, they may not turn out to be much of a bargain.

DOWNTOWN HOTELS

Boston Park Plaza Hotel   64 Arlington Street (800) 225-2008 or (617) 426-2000   A historic hotel just one block south of the Boston Commons. Also home to one of seven area branches of **Legal Seafood.**

Copley Square Hotel   47 Huntington Avenue (800) 225-7062 or (617) 536-9000   One of Boston's better bargains, close to many downtown attractions.

The Lenox Hotel   710 Boylston Street (800) 225-7676 or (617) 536-5300   Nice accommodations within walking distance of Fenway Park and other attractions. The Lenox is also home to the **Samuel Adams Brewhouse,** which has six styles of Sam Adams on tap and a fine pub menu. Call (617) 536-BREW for more information.

Howard Johnson Lodge/Fenway   1271 Boylston Street (800) 446-4656 or (617) 267-3100   Basic accommodations with the advantage of free parking adjacent to Fenway.

The Midtown Hotel   220 Huntington Avenue (800) 343-1177 or (617) 262-1000   Economy lodging by Boston standards.

TEAM HOTELS

Marriott Copley Square   110 Huntington Avenue (800) 228-9290 or (617) 236-5800   Angels, White Sox, Royals, and Brewers.

Sheraton Boston   39 Dalton Street (800) 325-3535 or (617) 236-2000 All other visiting American League clubs.

GOOD TO KNOW

- For schedule information or tickets to Red Sox games, call (617) 267-1700. The Red Sox official Internet address is www.redsox.com.
- Red Sox games can be heard on **WEEI 590 AM,** which is also the area's leading all-sports station.
- For more information on Boston sights, attractions, and hotels, call the **Convention & Visitors Bureau** at (800) 888-5515, (617) 536-4100 or (617)

424-7664. Or you can write them at Prudential Tower, P.O. Box 990468, Boston, MA 02199-0468. For those with access to the Internet, the city's official web site is www.bostonusa.com.

- For a listing and direct access to some of the area's attractions, hotels, restaurants, and nightlife, call **Boston by Phone** at (800) 374-7400.

Closest major league cities (and drive times): New York—220 miles (4 hours and 30 minutes); Philadelphia—320 miles (7 hours); Montreal—335 miles (5 hours and 40 minutes).

IN THE VICINITY

The Naismith Memorial Basketball Hall of Fame is in Springfield, about two hours from Boston. If you happen to be heading to Cooperstown to see the Baseball Hall of Fame, the Basketball Hall of Fame is actually not far out of your way, off Interstate 90. There are interactive exhibits including a shootout gallery, three theaters, basketball memorabilia, video footage of the game's greatest moments, and tributes to all your favorite players from the past. A proposed $80 million expansion and remodeling promises to put it on a par with the baseball, football, and hockey halls of fame. Admission is $6 for adults. Call (413) 781-6500 for more information.

✦ CLEVELAND ✦

We are now arriving in Cleveland. Set back your watches forty-two minutes.

TIM McCARVER

JACOBS FIELD

Since 1994, the Jake's inaugural year, Indians fans have made this one of the toughest tickets in baseball. You get within two blocks of the place and begin to feel the baseball atmosphere. When you see it for the first time, you'll swear it belongs there, as if it's been there forever. If you've seen the Indians play at Municipal Stadium, a.k.a. "the mistake by the lake," you know how overdue this park is.

Fortunately, the folks who built Jacobs Field seem to have taken care of every detail. The ballpark blends in perfectly with the surrounding neighborhood, and every possible creature comfort has been provided. The seats and aisles are wider than they are at most parks; seats on the outfield side of either dugout are angled toward the infield, allowing for much more comfortable viewing, and the bleacher seats in left field, just above a 19-foot high "mini green monster," are nearly 100 feet closer to home plate than those at the old Municipal Stadium. The scoreboard directly behind the bleachers measures 220 feet wide and 120 feet tall and is one of the biggest in the majors. It features a giant game-in-progress scoreboard, a replay screen, and a color message board. In play just below the bleachers, taking up the entire left-center field portion of the outfield wall, is an out-of-town scoreboard.

Other impressive features include asymmetrical outfield dimensions, a four-tiered picnic area with a view of the field near the Indians' bullpen in center field, and wide-open concession areas with plenty of seats and tables. All three decks offer shade and protection from rain at the very back of each level. There is also a restaurant, called the Terrace Club, on the second level along the left field foul line, just above the wide-open Eagle Avenue entrance area. Standing-room-only bleachers, just beyond the outfield fence down the left field line, are sold on the day of the game.

I knew the stadium was a hit with the locals when I saw the line of about 200 people waiting to get into the souvenir store. I have been to Municipal Stadium on sunny days and wondered if there were 200 people in the entire upper deck. If Jacobs Field has any drawbacks, they are minor. The score and replay boards almost get lost among the advertising on the giant scoreboard behind the left field bleachers. The visitor's bullpen occupies some prime home run territory, just inside the right field foul pole, keeping the fans from going home with a souvenir. And the exterior of the stadium with its lime-stone, granite, and yellow brick facade is not quite as impressive as the interior. On the whole, though, it's a fantastic place to watch a ball game, especially when you consider the most expensive game seat you can buy is only $23. The $18 lower boxes and $10 bleacher seats are also exceptional values. Because the Indians have been so successful on the field, tickets are said to be sold out for the upcoming season. They can only be bought through ticket agencies, scalpers, and package deals, so expect to pay dearly for them if the Indians maintain their level of play.

Tours of Jacobs Field are available during the season on non–game days. Tours cost just $5 for adults, last about an hour, and leave from the Indians Team Shop on Ontario Street. Call (216) 420-4400 in advance for more information.

HISTORY

Jacobs Field opened in April of 1994, and the Indians have certainly enjoyed playing in their new digs ever since. The season-ending strike of 1994 may have prevented them from visiting the playoffs that year, but the very next year they won their division, the pennant, and played in their first World Series in forty years. Despite a relatively short history, the ballpark has also been the scene of several big baseball moments.

On July 8, 1995, Kenny Lofton stole home against Seattle Mariners pitcher Chris Bosio. On September 30, 1995, Albert Belle hit his fiftieth roundtripper of the season off Kansas City hurler Melvin Bunch. Belle also hit 50 doubles that season, making him the first player in history to accomplish such a 50-50.

Jacobs Field's first-ever playoff game, on October 3, 1995, was a classic that set the tone for the entire series against Boston. Tony Pena hit a two-out solo homer off Zane Smith in the 13th inning, to beat the Red Sox. The Indians went on to sweep the Red Sox and then beat the Seattle Mariners in the ALCS to advance to the World Series against the Braves. On October 24 of that same year, Eddie Murray singled home the game-winning run in the

View of Jacobs Field from the upper deck behind home plate. (Courtesy of the Cleveland Indians)

eleventh inning of Game 3 to give Cleveland their first World Series game win in forty-seven years. The Indians' World Series woes continued, however, as the Braves ended up winning the Series in six games.

GETTING TO JACOBS FIELD
2401 Ontario Street

Gateway Sports Complex, of which Jacobs Field is part, is situated in downtown Cleveland, just off I-90 or I-77, at East Ninth Street. Parking is sufficient, but more than one fan has told me that the train is the best way to get to and from the park if you don't have access to the season ticket holder's parking garage. The Regional Transit Authority or RTA has a stop within a five-minute walk of the park, via an enclosed walkway from the Tower City Center Station. The RTA has three rail routes running from the airport through Tower City Center to East Cleveland. For specific route and schedule information, call (216) 621-9500.

There are several bars and restaurants in the immediate vicinity, so another option may be to come early and grab something to eat or drink before the game. Tailgating is neither convenient nor encouraged at area parking lots.

WHAT TO DO AND SEE IN CLEVELAND

The **Rock and Roll Hall of Fame** opened to rave reviews Labor Day Weekend of 1995. The lakeside hall of fame was designed by famous architect I. M. Pei and was built at a cost of $84 million. Your first question is probably "What the hell is the Rock and Roll Hall of Fame doing in Cleveland?" The committee who decided on Cleveland took into account the city's central location and the fact that Cleveland doesn't have that many other attractions that would overshadow the Hall of Fame. But the city's trump card was the fact that back in 1952, Cleveland disc jockey Alan Freed is credited with being the first person to use the term "rock and roll."

The 150,000-square-foot museum features a permanent collection of instruments, photos, clothing, art, recording equipment, lyric sheets, and memorabilia of all kinds, donated by seemingly every rock and roll legend dead or alive. This collection is rotated into the museum's massive display space, so each visit can be a new experience. The actual Hall of Fame is magnificently done, with inductee's signatures etched in glass along the walls of a silent chamber that can only be reached via a circular staircase.

Next door to the Rock and Roll Hall of Fame you'll find one of the city's newest attractions. The **Great Lakes Science Center** is a fun place to take the kids, with hundreds of hands-on exhibits that focus on the history of the Great Lakes, their effect on the region, and the lakes' many shipwrecks. There's also an IMAX theater, which has a separate admission price.

The **Cleveland Museum of Art** has a collection of paintings and sculpture by a number of renowned artists, including Rembrandt, Picasso, Monet, Renoir, and van Gogh. There's also an impressive collection of Asian and medieval European art. The museum is located in University Circle at 11150 East Boulevard, overlooking the **Fine Arts Gardens of Wade Park**. Admission to the museum and gardens is free, except for special exhibits.

The **Cleveland Museum of Natural History** in University Circle is perhaps best known for being home to "Lucy," one of the oldest complete skeletons of early mankind. There are also dinosaur and fossil displays, as well as geological exhibits. The museum is open daily, from 10 AM–5 PM Tuesday–Saturday and 1–5:30 PM on Sundays. It's also open Wednesday evenings, 5–10 PM, during the spring, winter, and fall. Admission is $6 for adults and $4 for children.

The **Cleveland Metroparks Zoo** is spread out over 165 acres in the Brookside area, about 5 miles south of downtown. The zoo is home to over 3,300 animals including big cats, monkeys, bears, kangaroos, and rhinos. A two-story, two-acre rain forest exhibit features more than 600 animals, representing 118 species, and 10,000 plants from the jungles of Africa, Asia, and South America. Admission to both the zoo and rain forest exhibits is $7 for adults.

The **U.S.S.** *Cod* is a World War II submarine docked at 1089 Marginal Way, not far from Municipal Stadium. Thirty-minute tours are offered daily. The fact that between 50 and 100 men would be aboard one of these subs for weeks or months at a time is remarkable. If you've never seen one from the inside, try to find the time. Admission is only $4.

NIGHTLIFE IN CLEVELAND

A number of places have opened up in the Gateway area surrounding the ballpark. **Panini's** is a long fly ball from the park at 840 Huron Road. They specialize in giant sandwiches stuffed with french fries. **Ferris Steakhouse**, just around the corner on Fourth Street, features an open-air bar overlooking the street and a fun atmosphere on game days.

For the most part, Cleveland nightlife can be summed up in two words: **The Flats**. That's not to say that The Flats district is the only place to go, but if you're looking for a variety of clubs, cafes, and pubs, all within walking distance, the area really does have something for everyone. Located on both sides of the Cuyahoga river, there's a great selection of sports bars, comedy clubs, dance places, restaurants, and simple watering holes.

My favorites are on the east bank, but on either side you are certain to find a few places to your liking. The **Basement** has a steady, young crowd, plays progressive dance music, and features a decor that somehow reminds you of a friend's basement or college apartment. Complete with beat-up furniture and blacklight posters, the place is a throwback to the late 1970s and early 1980s. **Slam Jam** is a good-sized sports bar featuring a roomy patio overlooking the river, pool tables, one-on-one basketball court, batting cage, air hockey tables, and a number of sports-related video games. They also offer a limited menu of sandwiches and burgers. **Heaven and Earth** is a two-story, live music concert club and is just up the street at 1059 Old River Road.

Across the river, on the west bank of The Flats, is the **Nautica Entertainment Complex**, which is home to about a dozen different places, including the **Improv Comedy Club**, **Grand Slam Sports Grille**, **Howl at the Moon Saloon**, and **Jillian's Billiard Club**. The complex is also home to several restaurants, a giant video arcade, and the **Nautica Queen Cruise Ship**, which offers lunch and dinner cruises. Reservations are recommended.

Not far from The Flats, at 1360 West Ninth Street (where it meets Saint Clair) is an obscure blues joint known as **Wilbert's**. You probably won't see any ads for the place, but it's generally packed with locals seeking hot blues music and great food. Wilbert's is very likely to have a legendary blues act playing the night(s) you are in town, especially on weekends.

Cleveland's premiere brew pub is the **Great Lakes Brewing Company**, located in an 1860s saloon at 2516 Market Street. It features a restaurant downstairs and a number of fine beers brewed on site, including a Dortmunder named after football player John Heisman. Tours are available on request, and lunch and dinner are served Monday through Saturday.

WHERE TO STAY IN CLEVELAND

Cleveland Indians games have become a hot ticket, but they may be easier to come across than a nearby hotel room. Much to our surprise, we were told that on Indians home dates, hotels in the area are sold out weeks in advance. This is partially because Indians games at Jacobs Field are selling out, but also because there is a serious lack of hotels in the downtown area. With that in mind, you may want to call and book a room as soon as you have secured tickets.

DOWNTOWN HOTELS

Embassy Suites 1701 East 12th Street (800) 362-2779 or (216) 523-8000 Nice accommodations within a short drive of the ballpark. The two-room suites are convenient for families and small groups looking to keep expenses down.

Holiday Inn Lakeside 1111 Lakeside and 12th (800) HOLIDAY or (216) 241-5100 About five minutes from Jacobs Field. Free shuttle within the downtown area.

Radisson Gateway 651 Huron Road (800) 333-3333 or (216) 377-9000 Upscale hotel within walking distance of Jacobs Field.

Ritz Carlton 1515 West 3rd Street (800) 241-3333 or (216) 623-1300 Deluxe accommodations within walking distance of the ballpark and other area attractions.

Sheraton City Centre 777 Saint Clair Avenue (800) 325-3535 or (216) 771-7600 A short walk to the ballpark, nice accommodations in the heart of downtown.

TEAM HOTELS

Embassy Suites Hotel 1701 East 12th Street (800) 333-3333 or (216) 523-8000 Orioles, Red Sox, Angels, White Sox, and Tigers.

Marriott Society Center 127 Public Square (800) 228-9290 or (216) 696-9200 Royals, Brewers, Twins, Yankees, Mariners, and Blue Jays.

Renaissance Tower City 24 Public Square (800) 468-3571 or (216) 696-5600 Oakland A's.

OTHER AREA HOTELS

Baymont Inn 4222 West 150th Street (800) 428-3438 or (216) 251-8500 Inexpensive accommodations just north of the airport, about twelve miles from downtown.

Cleveland Airport Marriott   4277 West 150th Street (800) 228-9290 or (216) 252-5333   Affordable accommodations about fifteen minutes from downtown.

Holiday Inn   4181 West 150th Street (800) HOLIDAY or (216) 252-7700   Affordable accommodations just north of the airport, about fifteen minutes from downtown.

Intercontinental   8800 Euclid Avenue (800) 327-0200 or (216) 707-4300   Luxury accommodations about four miles from Jacobs Field.

GOOD TO KNOW

- For schedule information or tickets to Indians games, call (216) 241-5555. The Indians official Internet address is www.indians.com.
- Indians games can be heard on **WKNR 1220 AM**, which is also the area's leading all-sports station.
- For a free guide on upcoming events and what to do in Cleveland call the **Visitor's Center** at (800) 321-1001 or (800) 321-1004.

Closest major league cities (and drive times): Pittsburgh—157 miles (3 hours); Detroit—178 miles (3 hours and 15 minutes); Cincinnati—253 miles (4 hours and 30 minutes).

IN THE VICINITY

Canton, Ohio, less than seventy miles from Cleveland, is home to the **Football Hall of Fame**. Occupying 5 buildings and more than 82,000 square feet, at 2121 George Halas Drive, the Hall of Fame is a shrine to giants of the gridiron. It does a wonderful job of documenting the changes in the game with an awesome collection of football memorabilia, film footage, and photos from more than seventy-five years of professional football. No matter what your favorite team is, you are sure to find this a fascinating place to spend an afternoon.

In 1995 the Hall of Fame underwent an $8.6 million renovation and extension that added greatly to its display space. Among the additions is a 360-degree theater that plays larger-than-life video footage of football's greatest plays and players. Admission is just $7 for adults. Every summer the Football Hall of Fame hosts an NFC–AFC exhibition game to kick off the NFL preseason. Induction ceremonies are held that same weekend. For more information on the game or the Hall of Fame, call (216) 456-8207.

✦ MIAMI ✦

I couldn't imagine how they'd make a ballpark out of it. But it looks great. And the ballplayers will tell you this is the best, truest infield in baseball.

DON ZIMMER

PRO PLAYER STADIUM

Built in 1987, Pro Player is one of the newest, sleekest, and best football arenas in the NFL. It's set up perfectly for a rectangular football field, and despite a capacity of 73,000 fans, every seat has a great view of the gridiron. However, because it was not designed with baseball in mind, the Marlins' ownership had to spend $10.6 million converting it into a baseball facility.

Some of the more innovative changes include the installation of a retractable section of 6,400 seats in left field, field-level seats on the third base side that are removed for football games, tarpaulins covering the entire outfield upper deck seating area, and a pitcher's mound that sits on a motorized platform, allowing it to be raised into position for baseball games. Your first impression is likely to be one of pleasant surprise, as none of the renovations look at all temporary. These changes result in reduced seating capacity for ball games to 47,662, by no means intimate, but certainly better than playing in a half-empty football stadium.

Pro Player sits on an island of grass, surrounded by a huge parking lot, just south of the Snake Creek Canal. Smatterings of palm trees, reminiscent of Dodger Stadium, are located near the entrance ramps and ticket booths. The stadium's most impressive feature is the manual scoreboard with a 5-foot diameter analog clock that sits along the fence in left field. It starts 32 feet from the foul pole and runs more than 200 feet toward center field. At its highest point, the scoreboard is 33 feet tall; on either end it's 22 feet high. A ball must clear the scoreboard in order to count as a home run, and a ball that

Aerial view of Pro Player Stadium. (Courtesy of the Florida Marlins)

strikes any part of the scoreboard, including the clock, is considered in play.

The playing field is natural grass, and the outfield dimensions are slightly asymmetrical. An indentation in the left-center field power alley makes for one of the deepest outfields in the league, at 434 feet. Two giant scoreboards sit atop the stadium; the larger one, with a message board and a 27 x 36 foot JumboTron video screen, is above the right field stands, and the other is directly opposite it along the third base line. There are also a number of well-positioned, narrow auxiliary scoreboards that allow you to keep track of the count, outs, score, and who is batting.

Because Pro Player is so new, it has all the conveniences you might expect from a modern sports venue. The stadium's forty concession stands, on both the upper and lower concourses, are situated so you don't have to walk more than a section or two in either direction before finding one. Each stand has a TV monitor, allowing you to follow the action while you wait on line. Several stands offer spacious seating areas and a theme decor. In addition to typical ballpark fare, Dominos Pizza is available on the third base side on both levels and Carvel ice cream is available near both outfield corners on the lower concourse only. There is also a nice selection of ethnic food. JR's, a bar/restaurant on the club level, offers stools with a view of the field and waitress service of typical pub food in air-conditioned comfort.

Two twenty-five foot wide, circular entrance ramps are situated at each corner of the stadium, making it easy to enter and leave the stadium. There are also two reversible escalators located in each corner. The will call window is located at Gate G along the first base side of the stadium. Other ticket windows are located at each corner of the stadium, in front of the circular ramps. Reselling tickets on stadium grounds is prohibited, although there are generally a few folks looking to part with their extra seats at face value.

While the finished product at Pro Player Stadium may be something less than nostalgic, it's by far the most accommodating multisport arena used by a major league baseball team today.

HISTORY

The Marlins won their first ever home game 6–3 over the Dodgers on April 5, 1993. That same season, Jeff Conine hit the stadium's first grand slam off Rockies pitcher David Nied on May 1, 1993. Three years later, on May 11, 1996, Al Leiter threw the Marlins' first ever no-hitter at home, in what was then known as Joe Robbie Stadium, against the potent lineup of the Colorado Rockies.

On April 17, 1997, Cardinals' catcher Mike Difelice pulled off a straight steal of home plate against the Marlins. It was Difelice's first stolen base in the big leagues and the first theft of home by a Cardinal since Vince Coleman pulled it off in 1990. On October 18, 1997 the Marlins hosted their first World Series game. They won the game 7–4 and went on to win the series 4 games to 3 over the Cleveland Indians as Edgar Renteria hit an RBI single in the eleventh inning of game seven on October 26, 1997. It was just the Marlins' fifth year as a franchise, making them the youngest World Champions in MLB history. Barry Bonds hit his 400th home run on August 23, 1998, to become the first player with 400 home runs and 400 stolen bases.

GETTING TO PRO PLAYER STADIUM
2269 N.W. 199th Street

Parking and traffic are, for the most part, a breeze, as the stadium parking lot covers 140 acres and originally had nearly 15,000 parking spots for cars. Some parking lots open two and a half hours before game time, others open two hours prior to the game. Despite the fact that parking is plentiful, it's somewhat pricey, costing as much as $15. Leaving the parking lot and finding the right highway home can be a little tricky, but if you pay attention to the signs, you'll end up exactly where you want to be.

Mass transit is not really an option, as Pro Player is located in the middle of a residential area, well outside of downtown. No trains or local shuttles run to the stadium. There is, however, a "Marlins/Max Bus" which runs from the Martin Luther King Bus Station, at N.W. 62nd Street and N.W. 27th Avenue, in Miami. Other park and ride sites are also available for $7 or less. For more information on public transportation within Dade County, call (305) 638-6700.

WHAT TO DO AND SEE IN MIAMI

Miami is not so much a city as it is a collection of neighborhoods. Each neighborhood has its own distinct identity and makeup, from the elegance and prestige of Bal Harbour, to the beaches and nature walks of Key Biscayne, and the urban ethnic festivals of Little Havana. Most peoples' impression of Miami is derived from the **Art Deco Historic District**, a one-square mile area located in South Miami Beach. Located between 6th and 23rd streets, from Ocean Drive to Lenox Avenue, the Art Deco district has been featured as the backdrop for a number of movies and TV shows. It's also home to many of the city's sights and attractions, including **South Beach**, also known as SoBe, one of Miami's most prolific nightlife and dining sections.

The **Bass Museum of Art** is in the northeast corner of the Art Deco district, at 2121 Park Avenue. The museum features a relatively small permanent collection of Old Masters paintings and sculpture, as well as traveling exhibits.

Miami's premiere attraction is, of course, the beach. **Miami Beach** offers a 300-foot wide beach that stretches for more than 10 miles along the Atlantic Ocean. Dozens of pastel-colored, luxury oceanfront hotels are situated on Collins Avenue. A 2-mile boardwalk overlooking the beach was recently added between 21st and 46th streets. South of that, both above and below **Lummus Park**, are a number of public beaches. For $15 (plus tip), many beaches offer the use of a pair of chairs and a good-size umbrella. I enjoyed the beaches between 10th and 15th Streets. They had plenty of volleyball nets, public restrooms, concession stands, and a good crowd. I've been told that certain beaches are reserved for nude sunbathing, but you are likely to see some topless tanning no matter where you go, although there is supposedly a pretty hefty fine for women caught without both halves of the suit on!

The **Coconut Grove** neighborhood offers some of the Miami area's most impressive attractions. The **Vizcaya Museum** is located on the bay, in what was once the 70-room winter home of industrialist James Deering. The 30-acre grounds include over 10 acres of gardens and fountains. The museum itself has 34 rooms of antique furnishings and decorative arts that span more than 300 years. Admission is $8 for adults. The **Miami Museum of Science** is across the street and features over 150 hands-on technology exhibits and displays. The Museum of Science is also home to the **Space Transit Planetarium**, which has an observatory as well as astounding multimedia astronomy and laser shows. Combined admission to the museum and planetarium is $8.50 for adults.

The entire Coconut Grove area is littered with upscale shops, outdoor cafes, and elegant restaurants. But nowhere is this more evident than at the open-air shopping and entertainment center known as **CocoWalk**. Located where Main Street meets Grand Avenue, you'll find an abundance of shops, galleries, and restaurants by day, and a wealth of nightlife options at night.

Coral Gables, with its stately entrance gates, Spanish Mediterranean architecture, tree-lined roads, and miles of waterways, is the country's first planned community. It's also home to two of the Miami area's most picturesque attractions. The **Venetian Pool** is a tropical lagoon carved out of a coral rock quarry, featuring caves, stone bridges, and waterfalls, surrounded by palm trees. In its day, it hosted jet-setting Hollywood stars, but it is now open to the public Tuesday through Sunday. It's located at 2701 DeSoto Boulevard in Coral Gables. Admission is $4 for adults.

Miami is renowned for horse racing and is home to two of the most beautiful thoroughbred racetracks in the country. **Hialeah Park** is a magnificent track that also happens to be home to the largest colony of American flamingos. It's located at 2200 East 4th Avenue, off I-27, a few miles northwest of downtown Miami. Races are Wednesday to Sunday, from mid-March through the end of the baseball season. Admission and parking are free. **Gulfstream Park** is just off US1, at Hallandale Beach Boulevard, north of Miami in Broward County. It closes just before baseball's opening day, but is open every day except Monday through all of spring training. This is truly a gorgeous, state-of-the-art facility that horse racing fans should go out of their way to check out. Admission ranges from $2–4, depending on whether you prefer to sit in the grandstand or the air-conditioned clubhouse.

NIGHTLIFE IN MIAMI

The *Miami New Times* is an excellent free source for area nightlife and restaurant options. Complete club listings can also be found on their Web site, www.miaminewtimes.com. Bear in mind that things don't really get hopping in Miami until after eleven at night, so you may want to grab a late dinner before heading out to spend a night on the town.

South Beach is one of the area's hottest tourist draws. A multitude of restaurants and nightclubs, most within walking distance of each other along

Ocean Drive or Washington Avenue, makes this a great place to sample Miami's unique brand of nightlife. There are countless open-air nightclubs and restaurants along Ocean Drive, where the people-watching could last all night. My personal favorites are the **Delano**, a funky hotel and bar with a hip, sophisticated crowd at 1685 Collins Avenue, and **Wet Willie's**, an open-air club and great place to people-watch at 760 Ocean Drive. A few blocks away, at the corner of 10th Street, you'll find an **All-Star Cafe** in the Edison Hotel at 960 Ocean Drive.

If you're more in the mood for a dance club, and dance clubs are what Miami nightlife is known for, the South Beach area offers a wealth of options. A premiere dance place is **Shadow Lounge**, an elegant 2-story club at 1532 Washington Avenue. This upscale spot is open Thursday through Saturday until 5 AM and has a fairly strict dress code. There is a cover charge on Fridays and Saturdays. **Cristal** offers an incredible display of lights and music in a posh setting. The crowd dresses to impress, and there's almost always a line to get in the place, despite the cover charge. **Cristal** is located at 1045 Fifth Street and occasionally features live music.

In downtown Miami, between Biscayne Boulevard and Biscayne Bay at 4th Street, is the **Bayside Marketplace**, which features more than 30 bars and cafes overlooking the bay. In addition to free nightly concerts, several of the clubs offer live entertainment. Two of the marketplace's newest tenants include the **Hard Rock Cafe** and **Crocodile Cantina**. You're not likely to miss the Hard Rock located on the waterfront at the southern end of the marketplace, as the exterior boasts a 65-foot guitar with neon strings running up the neck.

Another outstanding collection of nightclubs can be found at **CocoWalk** in Coconut Grove. CocoWalk is home to a number of night spots including the **Improv Comedy Club**, **TuTu Tango**, and **Fat Tuesdays** in the Mayfair Marketplace at 3390 Mary Street. There's also a multiplex cinema and a **Planet Hollywood** just around the corner.

WHERE TO STAY IN MIAMI

Pro Player Stadium, located near the Dade County/Broward County lines, is actually closer to downtown **Fort Lauderdale** than it is to downtown Miami. With that in mind, you may want to look into the possibility of staying in Fort Lauderdale. For more information on Fort Lauderdale hotels and attractions, call the Fort Lauderdale Convention and Visitors Bureau at (800) 22-SUNNY or (305) 765-4466.

The Stadium is northwest of Miami, a good way from most of the area's sights and attractions. While there are a few hotels in the vicinity, you may be better off staying a little closer to Miami Beach or even the airport, which is centrally located. Generally, hotels on the beach are going to cost a good deal more than inland locations, but some deals can be found and most hotels in south Florida cut their rates in half after May 1. Below is a partial list of area hotels.

MIAMI BEACH HOTELS

Days Inn North Beach   7450 Ocean Terrace (800) 325-2525 or (305) 866-1631   Economy accommodations in the heart of Miami Beach.

Comfort Inn   6261 Collins Avenue (800) 654-4656 or (305) 868-1200   Affordable hotel directly on the beach with a pool, restaurant, and bar.

Radisson Deauville   6701 Collins Avenue (800) 327-6656 or (305) 865-8511   Nice oceanfront accommodations with pool, tennis courts, fitness center, and pool bar.

Sol Miami Beach Resort Hotel & Spa   3925 Collins Avenue (800) 336-3542 or (305) 531-3534   Oceanfront hotel with two restaurants and lounges, pool bar, and poolside grill.

OTHER AREA HOTELS

Bay Harbor Inn   9660 East Bay Harbor Drive (305) 868-4141   Clean, convenient, and affordable, the inn is a short drive from the beach and within walking distance of a few worthwhile restaurants.

Courtyard by Marriott   15700 NW 77th Court (800) 443-6000 or (305) 556-6665   One of the hotels closest to Joe Robbie Stadium.

Crown Sterling Suites   3974 NW South River Drive (800) 433-4600 or (305) 634-5000   Reasonably priced two-room suite hotel near the airport.

Doubletree Hotel at Coconut Grove   2649 Bayshore Drive (800) 222-TREE or (305) 858-2500   Located one block from Biscayne Bay, within walking distance of most Coconut Grove attractions, including CocoWalk and the beach.

La Quinta Inn   7401 NW 36th Street (800) 221-4731 or (305) 599-9902   Nice accommodations at a reasonable price, located just south of Joe Robbie Stadium.

Wellesey Inn   7925 NW 154th Street (800) 444-8888 or (305) 821-8274   Very affordable, nice accommodations not far from Joe Robbie Stadium in Miami Lakes.

TEAM HOTELS

Boca Raton Marriott   5150 Town Center Circle (800) 228-9290 or (407) 392-4600   Cardinals.

Don Schula's Hotel and Golf Resort   6842 Main Street (800) 247-4852 or

(305) 821-1150   Pirates when they are in town, and one of the closest Dade County hotels to Pro Player Stadium.

Ft. Lauderdale Marriott Marina   1881 SE 17th Street (800) 228-9290 or (954) 463-4000   Braves, Cubs, Reds, Rockies, Astros, Dodgers, Expos, Mets, Phillies, and Padres.

Sheraton Bal Harbour   9701 Collins Avenue (800) 325-3535 or (305) 865-7511   Giants.

GOOD TO KNOW

- For schedule information or tickets to Marlins games, call (305) 350-5050. The Marlins official Internet address is www.flamarlins.com.
- Marlins games can be heard on **WQAM 560 AM**, the area's leading all-sports station.
- For more information on Miami sights, attractions, and hotels call the **Convention & Visitors Bureau** at (800) 283-2707 or (305) 539-3100. For those with access to the Internet, the city's official Web site is www.miamiand-beaches.com.
- South Florida has a 24-hour activity line, that is available in 6 languages. In Miami, call (305) 557-5600 or (305) 527-5600 from Fort Lauderdale.

Closest major league cities (and drive times): Tampa—285 miles (5 hours and 15 minutes); Atlanta—665 miles (12 hours and 20 minutes).

IN THE VICINITY

Baseball's most prolific hitter has his own restaurant/radio station, the **Pete Rose Ballpark Cafe**, in Boca Raton, just a little more than an hour north of Miami. Rose's radio show is broadcast weekdays between 6 and 8 PM from this better-than-average sports bar with plenty of TVs, a game room, and two bars. Speaking of hitters, the **Ted Williams Hitters Hall of Fame** is located in Hernando, between Tampa and Ocala, about six hours northwest of Miami.

Key West, about 150 miles from Miami, is the southernmost point of the 48 contiguous states. The drive southwest on U.S. 1 takes about three and a half hours, crosses 44 bridges linking the islands of the Gulf of Mexico, and is one of the most scenic and unique in the country. Key West is famous for its sunsets viewed from Mallory Square, and its laid-back yet lively nightlife. It also offers some of the country's best snorkeling, scuba diving, and deep-sea fishing.

◆ MONTREAL ◆

Because then there'd be two languages
I couldn't speak—French and English.

CASEY STENGEL
On why he never visited Montreal

OLYMPIC STADIUM

This stadium has everything there is to dislike about a modern-day ballpark: artificial turf, a hideous orange ceiling, symmetrical outfield dimensions, a 12-foot high wall all the way around the outfield, seats that don't quite face the diamond, and rotating signs (in French, no less); even the announcements are done in French first. Nevertheless, I found myself muttering to my friends, "There's something about this place that I can't help but like."

When fans sensed a rally, they would get off their folding seats and bang them together in unison and a bell would clang every time an Expo pitcher struck out an opponent as if to imply they were "ringing 'em up." Seat banging and bell ringing must be unique to Montreal fans, as I've never seen it done in any other ballpark.

The park's more pleasing attributes include wide-open concession areas with plenty of tables and seating, better-than-average scoreboards, and giant replay screens spanning the entire outfield. The concessions are exceptional and very reasonable (especially when you consider you're paying Canadian dollars). One unusual offering was the mixed-drink vendors; they mix a drink for you right at your seat. The park is very clean and the ushers unusually polite. There is also a small but handsome statue of Jackie Robinson, who played with the Montreal Royals before he played for the Dodgers, just outside the main gate and ticket area.

Some of Olympic Stadium's pitfalls, in addition to those already mentioned, are that the seats are cramped and the area behind the center field fence, underneath the scoreboard, looks more like a high school gym or auditorium than a ballpark. The will-call and ticket windows are indoors in a very hot, crowded area where the main gate, Expos' team store, and Metro ramp all converge, making it very difficult to get around. If you are meeting people before the game, a better place might be at the Jackie Robinson statue. The roof, which is supposed to come on and off like a giant umbrella, no longer works, and it is rumored that it will cost $300 million to repair it.

Olympic Stadium was built for the track-and-field competition of the 1976 Olympics, so it is not well suited for viewing baseball, as all of the seats face straight ahead and not necessarily toward the diamond. The best seats are the V.I.P. boxes, downstairs near the diamond. They are a little pricey, but very much worth the few dollars more than the regular boxes. If you must sit upstairs, try to get directly behind home plate, as the seats there are considerably closer to the field than those down the foul lines.

HISTORY

The first regular season major-league game played at Olympic Stadium, a loss to the Phillies, was played on April 15, 1977. Four years later, on May 10, 1981, Expos pitcher Charlie Lea threw a no-hitter to beat the Giants 4–0. The Expos won the '81 NL East division, their first title in history, and faced the Dodgers in the NLCS. On October 19, the Expos World Series hopes were dashed in the fifth and final game of the series when Rick Monday hit a two-out home run in the top of the ninth inning to give the Dodgers a 2–1 lead they never relinquished.

The first time the All-Star Game was ever played outside the United States was July 13, 1982, and Olympic Stadium hosted the midseason classic. On May 23, 1991, Phillies pitcher Tommy Greene beat the Expos 2–0 with his first career no-hitter.

GETTING TO OLYMPIC STADIUM
4549 Avenue Pierre-de Coubertin

Montreal's version of the subway, called the Metro, is very convenient for getting to and from the games. One of the best-kept secrets at the park is the parking deck directly underneath the stadium, with room for a few thousand cars at a cost of only $8. Parking elsewhere is cheaper, and should allow you to get out of the post-game traffic a little quicker.

WHAT TO DO AND SEE IN MONTREAL

Montreal is as European a city as I've seen on this side of the Atlantic. It has a nice blend of old and new, with almost no end to the fascinating architec-

Fans exiting Olympic Stadium. (Photo by Author)

ture, sights, and nightlife. People were more than willing to help us find our way around town despite our inability to speak much French.

One of Montreal's most visited attractions is the **Old Port**, located in northeast Montreal on the banks of the Saint Lawrence River. The parks and wharves in the area make this a popular place to walk around, eat, shop, and take in some of the city's sights. Montreal is one of North America's most historic cities, and you can really get a good sense of its European influence here along the banks of the Saint Lawrence River. Or if you prefer, you can take a tour of the port by glass-roofed boat, ferry, amphibious bus, or even a jet boat.

Basilica of Notre Dame, completed in 1829, is one of North America's grandest cathedrals. It has magnificent stained-glass windows, twin spires, and one of the world's largest organs. The Basilica is open daily, and admission is free. Other attractions in the Old Port area include *Le Pelican,* a full-size replica of a seventeenth-century three-masted French warship, and **EXPOTEC**, an interactive science exhibition featuring a seven-story IMAX theater.

The **Montreal Museum of Fine Arts** has an outstanding permanent collection and plays host to many fine traveling exhibits as well. At the time I was there, the museum featured an exhibition of Roy Lichtenstein's work, sponsored by the Solomon Guggenheim Foundation. The museum is open until 9 PM on Wednesdays, when they offer a discounted admission price of $4.50 for adults.

One of the most scenic attractions in Montreal is the **St. Joseph's Oratory** on the side of Mount Royal. The Oratory is the largest sanctuary devoted to St. Joseph and is crowned by a massive copper dome, which is second in size only to St. Peter's in Rome. Not far from St. Joseph's you'll find **Mount Royal Park**, laid out by Frederick Law Olmstead, designer of New York's Central Park. The park offers miles of running, walking, and cycling trails, as well as a respite from Montreal's hectic urban pace.

Right next to the stadium you'll find the **Montreal Biodome**, equal parts environmental museum, indoor rain forest, aquarium, and zoo. The Biodome bills itself as "four ecosystems under one roof" and is home to a remarkable diversity of wildlife. Admission is $8.50 for adults.

One of Montreal's newest attractions is the **Casino de Montreal**. The casino opened in October of 1993 and is housed in a stunning structure on Notre Dame Island, about twenty-five minutes from downtown. They offer 86 gaming tables featuring blackjack, roulette, baccarat, keno, and more than 1,500 slot machines.

NIGHTLIFE IN MONTREAL

The nightlife in Montreal is absolutely incredible—unlike anything I've seen since visiting New Orleans. **Crescent Street**, a strip of cafes and nightclubs centered by the **Hard Rock Cafe**, is a great place to start. Our favorite, by far, was **Sir Winston Churchill's** at 1459 Crescent Street. Referred to by the locals as Winnie's, the place is dark yet lively, with a great patio overlooking Crescent Street. Inside, you'll find a decent-sized dance floor, danceable rock music, a friendly staff, reasonable drinks, and a handsome, adult crowd.

Another area with a wealth of nightlife options is Saint-Laurent Boulevard. A highlight is **A Gogo Lounge**, a dance club at 3682 Saint-Laurent Boulevard. This place is open daily and features music from the '60s, '70s, and '80s. Expect a modest cover charge and a line out the door on weekends. Nearby you'll find **Barfly**, a jazz place, **Cigaremporium**, a cigar bar, and several dance places including **Kokino's** and **Polly Esther's**.

Sherlock's at 1010 Sainte-Catherine West, is another outstanding dance club with jazz, dancing, and alternative tunes as well as billiards. Admission is free every day except Saturday.

WHERE TO STAY IN MONTREAL

The area known as **Place des Arts**, around Sherbrooke Street West, offers a number of hotels in every price range. Most area hotels are within walking distance of many of the city's better museums, as well as the restaurants and cafes of Saint Laurent Street. More important, it's just a few blocks from several Metro stations. Listed below are a few of the hotels in Place des Arts and other parts of Montreal.

PLACE DES ARTS HOTELS

Delta Montreal   450 Sherbrooke West (514) 286-1986   Very nice accommodations for a reasonable price in a great location.

Holiday Inn Downtown   420 Sherbrooke West (514) 842-9381   Convenient location, nice rooms, and plenty of shops, cafes, and nightlife in the area.

Hotel La Citadelle   410 Sherbrooke West (514) 844-8851   A reasonably priced hotel with nice rooms, great location, and a friendly, helpful staff.

Westin Mont-Royal   1050 Sherbrooke West (800) 228-3000 or (514) 284-1110   Luxury hotel in the heart of the arts district.

OTHER MONTREAL HOTELS

Le Meridien   4 Complexe Desjardins (800) 543-4300 or (514) 285-1450   Luxury hotel near Old Montreal and Old Port, just twenty-five minutes from Olympic Stadium.

Le Nouvel Hotel   1740 Rene-Levesque Boulevard West (800) 363-6063 or (514) 931-8841   Affordable downtown hotel near the subway.

Ramada Inn Downtown   1005 Guy Street (800) 567-0880 or (514) 938-4611   Affordable accommodations in the heart of the shopping district.

TEAM HOTEL

Le Centre Sheraton   1201 Rene-Levesque Boulevard (800) 325-3535 or (514) 878-2000   All National League clubs when they are in town playing the Expos.

GOOD TO KNOW

- For schedule information or tickets to Expos games, call (514) 846-3976. The Expos official Internet address is www.montrealexpos.com.
- Expo games can be heard on **CIQC 940 AM** or in French on **CKAC 730 AM**.
- For a complete listing of area attractions, restaurants, and hotels, call the **Quebec Department of Tourism** at 1-800-363-7777.

Closest major league cities (and drive times): Boston—333 miles (5 hours and 40 minutes); Toronto—340 miles (6 hours and 10 minutes); New York—382 miles (7 hours and 45 minutes).

IN THE VICINITY

Canada's capital, **Ottawa**, is an incredibly clean and lush city located between Montreal and Toronto, along the border of Ontario and Quebec. Despite being in the Province of Ontario, it's just a little over two hours' drive from Montreal. Like most capital cities, Ottawa features a number of fascinating government buildings and monuments, but it is also home to a number of fine parks and museums. The **National Gallery of Canada** is one of the country's finest art museums, with works by such masters as Rembrandt, Cézanne, Degas, Picasso, van Gogh, and Monet, among others. The museum is located at 380 Sussex Drive in Major's Hill Park. Admission is $5 for adults, except Thursdays, when admission is free. For more information, call (613) 990-1985.

Ottawa's premiere tourist attractions, however, are the three gothic, copper-roofed **Parliament Buildings** which sit atop Parliament Hill. At ten every summer morning, visitors can witness the traditional changing of the guard. For more information on sights, attractions, and lodging in Ottawa, call the Ontario Ministry of Tourism and Recreation at (800) 905-2746.

◆ NEW YORK ◆

The only thing worse than a Mets game is a Mets double-header.

CASEY STENGEL

The best solution for overcrowding in New York would be to combine Nickel Beer Night with a baseball bat promotion at Yankee Stadium.

NEIL J. LISS

SHEA STADIUM

I made my first trips to Shea as a kid back in the early '70s. The park is adjacent to the grounds of the 1964 World's Fair and doesn't really have the feel of a ballpark. It looks like it came from another era, perhaps the same era that brought us automobile tail fins and avocado-colored kitchen appliances. The Mets were actually playing good ball at that time. Having won the World Series just a few years earlier, they managed to keep most of that team intact and were contenders throughout the early to mid-seventies. But I remember thinking it was a shame they had to play in that park.

Fortunately, when I returned a few years ago, I was pleased to see that Shea had been remodeled since my childhood visits. Despite the noise of planes taking off and landing at nearby La Guardia Airport, Shea has become a relatively nice park and a decent place to see a ball game. The giant scoreboard in right center field is one of the best in baseball, showing scores around the league, and batting orders for both teams, as well as balls, strikes, and outs. There is also a huge Sony DiamondVision TV in left-center for replays and individual batter statistics. If you are fortunate enough to be there

47

when a Mets batter hits a home run, a "big apple" appears out of a hat just beyond the fence in center field.

Considering that Shea was built as a multiuse park (the Mets used to share it with the NFL's Jets before the Jets followed the Giants to the Meadowlands in New Jersey) it has something of a baseball-only feel to it now. Unfortunately, the outfield dimensions are completely symmetrical, as is the height of the outfield fence. There are four levels of seating down each foul line and behind home plate, as well as a small bleacher section overlooking the opponent's bullpen in left-center field. The field-level box seats offer the best view, as well as your best chance for snaring a foul pop-up. Most of the second and third-level seats on the first base side offer some afternoon shade, as do the the very back rows of those levels all the way around the diamond. The downfall of those back-row seats is that you tend to lose sight of towering fly balls and the odds of a foul ball coming your way are slim.

Concessions at Shea are above average, and we found the vendors to be attentive and entertaining. Deli sandwiches, knishes, and Carvel ice cream are some of the park's highlights.

HISTORY

Shea Stadium opened on April 17, 1964, with a 4–3 loss to the Pittsburgh Pirates. Five years later, on September 24, 1969, the Mets clinched their first division title by beating the St. Louis Cardinals. On October 16 of that season, the Miracle Mets won their first World Series championship by beating the heavily favored Baltimore Orioles in five games.

Willie Mays joined the Mets on May 14, 1972, and celebrated his first game in the Big Apple by hitting a home run against his former teammates, the San Francisco Giants. Mays' solo homer provided the difference in the game as the Mets won 5–4. On October 8, 1973, Pete Rose started a brawl with Mets shortstop Buddy Harrelson with a hard slide into second base during the NLCS. The Mets went on to win the game and the series, but came up short against the Oakland A's in the World Series.

The Mets pulled off one of the greatest comebacks in World Series history on October 25, 1986. One out from losing the series to the Red Sox, the Mets were behind 5–3 in the bottom of the tenth inning. They managed to hit three straight singles to make it 5–4. Then with runners at the corners, Bob Stanley came in to relieve Calvin Schiraldi and uncorked a wild pitch, allowing Kevin Mitchell to score the tying run and Ray Knight to advance to second base. Next was the error that made baseball history. Red Sox first baseman Bill Buckner let a Mookie Wilson ground ball escape between his legs, and Knight scampered around third to win the game. The Mets went on to win game seven two days later for their second World Series championship.

View from the nosebleed seats at Shea Stadium. (Photo by Author)

GETTING TO SHEA STADIUM
126th Street at Roosevelt Avenue

The drive between downtown Manhattan and the Flushing Meadows area of Queens can be the longest six miles you'll ever drive in your life if you don't plan ahead. During the week, afternoon games let out at rush hour, so you may want to tailgate after the game. The same problem can occur with the traffic before night games, as the city's rush hour back to Long Island may make you miss an inning or two if you don't head for the stadium before five. For the most part, Shea is pretty easy to find and parking is adequate, although not all of the parking is right next to the stadium, or in the nicest part of Queens. Plan to get there early if you don't want to walk more than a few blocks. If you'd rather avoid the hassle, the best way to get to Shea is by taking the No. 7 train out of Manhattan or the L.I.R.R. from Long Island to the Willets Point/Shea Stadium station. Rush-hour trains can be very crowded and you might want to avoid them.

YANKEE STADIUM

In direct contrast to Shea Stadium, "The House That Ruth Built" has always had that classic feel of a baseball-only park. Built in 1923, Yankee Stadium was tailor-made for baseball. Foul territory on either side of home plate is surprisingly small for such a large ballpark, with first and third bases even closer to the stands than home plate. The upper deck and center field bleachers are a long way from the action but offer nice views of the entire field.

No matter where you sit, the scoreboards do a nice job of keeping you abreast of the action on the field as well as of scores from around the league. A left-center power-alley board shows the time, inning-by-inning scoring, plus runs, hits, and errors. In straightaway center field, a board shows who's batting (by number), his updated batting average, home runs and RBIs for the season, the ball/strike count, and how many outs there are. Official scoring decisions, such as errors, hits, passed balls, and wild pitches, are flashed on this same screen, as are the lineup of the team at bat, and fielding positions.

Field-level boxes down either baseline are the most expensive in the park at $23. Those not directly behind home plate offer the best view. Bleacher seats are a bargain at $6. The right field bleachers are much closer to the playing field than the ones in left, giving you a better chance at grabbing a home run ball. Right field bleacher seats are not recommended for everybody though. Yankee bleacher creatures tend to tilt back many a brew and are some of the harshest fans in the nation. Some of these folks make European soccer fans look like pansies, and the profanity and vulgarities spewed here could make a longshoreman blush. Fans of the opposing team might do well to sit in another section, especially if they care to show off their colors or openly root against the Yankees. Personally, I thoroughly enjoyed a day in the bleachers as Ken Griffey Jr. taunted New York's crudest and beat the Yankees almost single-handed.

The most unique feature of the stadium is a small memorial park behind the center field fence, with a group of plaques, statues, and monuments of former Yankee greats like DiMaggio, Mantle, Ruth, Gehrig, and others. The statues, along with a flagpole, were once part of the playing field. Since the 1975 remodeling, this section is no longer in play. Fans can tour this area up to forty-five minutes before game time.

My single biggest disappointment at the park was the bland, overpriced concessions; nothing was exceptional other than the prices. Another downfall is the attitude of the ushers and vendors at the park, who can be incredibly obnoxious, even by New York standards. If you are not sitting in the bleachers, your best bet for ballpark food at Yankee Stadium is the Sidewalk Cafe at section 15 on the field level. This area offers the park's best selection of food, as well as a nice patio area to enjoy your meal.

HISTORY

Yankee Stadium opened on April 22, 1923, for a game against the Boston Red Sox. The Yankees won that game and, perhaps equally predictable, Babe Ruth hit the park's first home run. On September 30, 1927, Babe Ruth hit his record-setting sixtieth home run of the season at Yankee Stadium.

On October 8, 1956, Yankee Stadium was the site as Don Larsen pitched the first and only perfect game in World Series history. On October 1, 1961 Roger Maris hit a home run to break Ruth's record with his sixty-first round tripper of the season. Yankee fans got to see Mickey Mantle hit his 500th career home run on May 14, 1967.

View of Yankee Stadium from the East River. (Courtesy of the New York Yankees)

On October 18, 1977, Reggie Jackson earned the nickname "Mr. October" by hitting three consecutive home runs on three straight pitches in game six of the World Series. Independence Day, 1983, saw Dave Righetti victimize the Red Sox again with his first career no-hitter. That same month, on July 24, the famous George Brett pine tar incident took place as Yankee skipper Billy Martin protested Brett's apparent game-winning two-out home run because pine tar on his bat extended more than 18 inches up the handle. Brett was called out, and the Yankees won 4–3. Brett went berserk, nearly assaulting the home plate umpire, but Kansas City successfully appealed the decision and eventually won 5–4 when the rest of the game was replayed on August 18.

On May 17, 1998, David Wells tossed the second perfect game in Yankees team history, a 4–0 victory over the Twins. The very next year, on July 18, David Cone duplicated the feat with a 6–0 win against the Expos. It marked the first time in history a team had pitchers toss perfect games in consecutive seasons. All told, Yankee Stadium has been the site of three perfect games, more than any other park in baseball.

GETTING TO YANKEE STADIUM
161st Street and River Avenue

Traffic around Yankee Stadium is a nightmare, perhaps the worst in the majors. I actually spent more time in traffic before and after one game than I did at the stadium. Parking is limited, and as I mentioned earlier, the neighborhood is not exactly plush. Plan on getting there early if you want to park in one of the fenced lots, and consider tailgating after the game. Better yet, take the No. 4, D, or C subway to the 161st Street station in the Bronx. The platform is just a short walk from the ballpark. There are generally plenty of "New York's finest" near the park on game days, so few problems occur. It may also help to stick with the crowd upon exiting the stadium. Before and after Yankee games the place to be is **Stan's Sportsworld**, a string of souvenir shops and sports bars on River Street, near the entrance to the right field bleachers.

WHAT TO DO AND SEE IN NEW YORK

To a first-time visitor, New York City can be somewhat overwhelming. The city's five boroughs occupy just 301 square miles, yet are inhabited by more than 7 million people. There are 712 miles of subway lines and nearly 12,000 taxi cabs, so you might as well leave the car behind. Your options include 17,000 places to eat, hundreds of hotels, more than 150 museums, 35 Broadway theaters, thousands of shops, and a nightlife that never stops.

If you're driving into the city, your best bet is to park your car either on the street or in a lot and get around via subway or cab. The subway system in Manhattan is not as bad as you might think. It is old, and in some places rundown, but most of it is well maintained, convenient to area attractions, and affordable. Free easy-to-read maps are available at token booths and are also posted inside most subway cars. If you don't look for trouble, subways are generally safe and easy to use, especially during the day. If you decide to check out the city's nightlife, it might be wise to take a cab back to your hotel.

I won't waste time pointing out the obvious, but a few of the things in New York that should not be missed are the **Empire State Building**, the **World Trade Center**, **Ellis Island**, and the **Statue of Liberty**.

Another way to get an up close look at the Statue of Liberty and the entire island of Manhattan is to take a **Circle Line Cruise**. The trip takes about three hours and features a narrated tour and view of New York's waterfront landmarks, including the World Trade Center, United Nations Building and Ellis Island. Cruises depart from Pier 83, where West 42nd Street meets the Hudson River. Call ahead for departure times and cost.

The Brooklyn Bridge, built in 1883, is the first steel suspension bridge ever built and is certainly a sight worth seeing on its own, but even more impressive is the spectacular view of the lower Manhattan skyline from the bridge itself (especially at sunset). Take the pedestrian walkway at least halfway across for the best camera angle. While you're in the vicinity, the **South Street Seaport** offers eleven waterfront blocks of nineteenth-century atmosphere with a cobblestone marketplace featuring shops, restaurants, and a maritime museum. Also available at South Street Seaport is an abbreviated version of the Circle Line Cruise called the "semi-circle." The trip takes only ninety minutes and does a loop around the southern tip of Manhattan.

Central Park, occupying more than 850 acres between 5th Avenue and Central Park West and 59th and 110th Streets, is remarkable because as you get toward the heart of it, you can almost forget that you are in the middle of the world's busiest city. Some of the highlights include the two-and-a-half-acre Strawberry Fields, a tribute to John Lennon who was shot across the street at the Dakota apartment building. A 1903 carousel featuring massive hand-carved horses is located on the south end. The park is a haven for athletes of all sorts, so you're bound to come across soccer and softball games, as well as frisbee players, in-line skaters, and skateboarders.

The **Metropolitan Museum of Art** is the single largest museum in the United States and certainly one of the world's best art museums. It's the permanent home to more than two million works of art, spanning over 5,000 years of culture, and includes work by Monet, Renoir, Manet, Gauguin, and van Gogh, among others. The museum is located on the eastern edge of Central Park, between 80th and 84th streets on 5th Avenue. Suggested contribution is $10 for adults.

The **American Museum of Natural History**, just west of the park between 79th and 81st streets, is one of the largest and best of its kind. You could easily spend a few days here and still not see the entire collection of more than thirty million artifacts. Suggested donation for adults is $10. Admission to the theater and planetarium is separate. The **Museum of Modern Art** (MOMA) is just a few blocks south of the park on 53rd Street, between 5th and 6th Avenues. For years MOMA was one of the most controversial museums in the country. It seems to have lost that reputation, but gained one as home to some of the world's greatest artwork, including Monet's *Water Lilies,* Van Gogh's *Starry Night,* and Matisse's *Dance.*

The **Solomon R. Guggenheim Museum**, the only building in New York City designed by Frank Lloyd Wright, is quite possibly the most user-friendly museum in the world. The bulk of the museum's collection is housed in the Great Rotunda, a spiral-shaped building that allows you to take the elevator to the top and walk down a wide spiral ramp as you view the art. The museum's collection of nineteenth and twentieth-century art is one of the best in the nation and includes works by Picasso, Chagall, Manet, and many others. The museum is located on the Upper East Side at 575 Broadway. Admission is $12 for adults.

One of the city's more unique museums is the ***Intrepid*** Sea-Air-Space Museum. Most of the museum's airplanes and spacecraft are located aboard the *Intrepid*, a World War II U.S. aircraft carrier, docked at Pier 86, on the Hudson River. The *Intrepid* served in World War II and Vietnam and had a vital role in the space program. Also docked at the pier, and included in the admission cost, are a destroyer and guided-missile submarine. Admission is $12 for adults.

Not far from Yankee Stadium is **The Bronx Zoo**, now known as the International Wildlife Conservation Park. It's the oldest and largest city zoo in the United States and at $5.75 for an adult ticket, still a bargain by New York City standards. The zoo is spread out over 256 acres and is home to over 3,600 animals. In recent years, it has undergone major reconstruction, making the settings more open and natural. The Bengali Express monorail and Skyfari cable car, which cost extra, make it easy to get around. Open seven days a week, admission is by donation on Wednesdays.

NIGHTLIFE IN NEW YORK

The diversity of New York nightlife is incomparable. On any given day, you are likely to see a dozen major musical acts in town as well as the nation's best comedians and magicians. Broadway is, of course, home to the world's best musicals and dramas, and off-Broadway hosts many future Broadway hits. The best source for entertainment news in the city is the *Village Voice*. Most of the major music and comedy clubs list upcoming shows in the *Voice*. If possible, pick one up midweek and plan ahead for the weekend. Better yet, get one several weeks in advance to acquire tickets to the hottest shows and concerts. They also have a Web site at www.villagevoice.com. Listed below are some of the city's more consistent night spots, but by no means is this a complete list.

MUSIC SCENE

B.B. King's Blues Club & Grill 243 West 42nd Street (212) 997-4144 Blues legends and classic rock bands perform nightly at this 500 seat club.

Bitter End 147 Bleecker Street (212) 673-7030 This club is to folk music what CBGB's is to punk music. Many of folk music's greats got their start here, including Bob Dylan, Joni Mitchell, Tracy Chapman and more.

Birdland 2754 Broadway at 105th Street (212) 749-2228 One of the city's better jazz clubs. No cover Sunday to Thursday—$5 minimum bar tab or $10 at a table. Friday and Saturday $10–20 cover and a $10–20 minimum.

The Blue Note 131 W. 3rd Street (212) 475-8592 Perhaps the Village's best-known jazz club; pricey but generally has top-rate talent. There's a $5 drink minimum. Shows start at 9 and 11 PM during the week, and 9 and 10:30 on Friday and Saturday.

The Bottom Line 15 West 4th Street (212) 228-6300 The city's ruling rock club can be counted on for a massive crowd and top-notch entertainment. Lately, however, the Bottom Line has strayed from its rock and roll roots, booking blues, jazz, and even country acts. Cover charge is usually $15, with no drink minimum.

CBGB's 315 Bowery Street (212) 982-4052 Beginning its third decade, CBGB's is the birthplace of American punk. The place is dark, graffiti-ridden, bizarre, and part of rock and roll history. Located on Manhattan's Lower East Side. Cover varies.

China Club 268 West 47th Street (between Broadway and 8th Avenue) (212) 398-3800 For more than fifteen years this place has been one of the city's hottest rock clubs. As it's only open Monday, Friday, and Saturday nights, it can be extremely difficult to get in. More than a few Yankees players frequent the VIP deck, and don't be surprised if one of your favorite bands does an impromptu jam on stage.

Kenny's Castaways 157 Bleecker Street (212) 473-9870 A hot spot for Village regulars, this club features rock bands on the rise.

Lone Star Roadhouse 240 West 52nd Street (between Broadway and 8th) (212) 245-2950 New location for a New York institution, that at one time received the W.C. Handy Blues Club of the Year Award. The bands range from blues to country to rock. Cover varies and there is generally a two-drink minimum unless you have dinner.

Manny's Car Wash 1558 Third Avenue (between 87th and 88th) (212) 369-BLUES Despite the name, all blues bars should be like this one; small, crowded, smoky, and loud. Manny's showcases the best in blues nightly, but the best night to see the more legendary blues acts seems to be Thursday. The free Sunday Night Jam Session is a rare treat in New York City.

The Ritz 254 West 54th Street (212) 541-8900 Perhaps a little past its prime, but still a major player in the New York City music scene. Shows often sell out early. Expect a line and steep cover charge at the door.

The Wetlands 161 Hudson Street (212) 966-4225 A throwback to the '60s featuring a psychedelic atmosphere with music ranging from blues and pop to disco and zydeco. Call ahead for lineup.

COMEDY CLUBS

No city in the world offers the diversity of comic talent that you'll find in New York. In addition to the comedy clubs listed below, comedians are often in town for *Saturday Night Live* and the *Late Show with David Letterman*.

Caroline's 1626 Broadway (between 49th and 50th streets) (212) 757-4100 Odds are you've seen this place on TV. A plush Midtown club featuring top-name comedians. Generally has a two-drink minimum and pricey cover for better-known acts.

Catch a Rising Star 1487 1st Avenue (212) 794-1906 Another New York club featured on the Comedy Channel, it's one of the city's oldest and best comedy clubs. Top-notch comedians are still booked on a regular basis.

Dangerfield's 1118 1st Avenue (between 61st and 62nd streets) (212) 593-

1650   A New York City institution since 1969 that regularly hosts established and up-and-coming comedians.

The Improv   358 West 44th Street (212) 765-8268   The original Improvisation is the city's first comedy club. Richard Pryor and Rodney Dangerfield started out here, and the list of big name comedians who have appeared on stage here is endless.

SPORTS BARS

New York seems to have a "sports bar" on every other corner. The majority of them are little more than holes in the wall with a television or two and no cover charge. There are a few sports bars that are worth going out of your way for.

Broadway Joe Steakhouse   315 West 46th Street (212) 246-6513   Emphasis here is definitely on red meat and seafood. In its day, it was popular with celebrities.

Charley O's   162 West 34th Street (212) 563-7440   In the Madison Square Garden complex. Before, during, and after Garden events this is the place to be.

ESPN Zone   1472 Broadway (212) 921-3776   Beside the subway station in Times Square, this sports bar/restaurant offers two floors of dining, a third-floor interactive game room, two 14-foot large screen TVs, and a dozen 36-inch televisions. Baseball fans will appreciate the Jackie Robinson stained glass portrait on the first floor and the Babe Ruth photo mural made up of more than 2,000 baseball cards located between the first and second floors.

Mickey Mantle's Restaurant   42 Central Park South (212) 688-7777   Just what you'd expect. Tons of sports memorabilia and art. Healthy portions of good food at a fair price and plenty of TVs.

Polo Grounds   1472 Third Avenue (212) 570-5590   One of the East Side's premiere sports bars. If a local team is playing a big game or if they've sold out a home game, you're likely to find a big crowd here.

Rusty Staub's on 5th   575 Fifth Avenue (near 47th, 5th and Madison) (212) 682-1000   One of the classiest members of the Miracle Mets operates this great place for steaks, ribs, and seafood. Not inexpensive but worth it.

WHERE TO STAY IN NEW YORK

New York has nearly as varied a selection of hotels as it does restaurants and nightlife. No matter where you stay, you are going to spend a good deal of money. Unfortunately, that doesn't always mean you'll be enjoying luxury accommodations. Ideally, you'll want to stay at a place that's near a subway station, and if you are driving into the city, you'll want a place that offers reasonably priced, secure parking. That might not sound like a lot to ask for, but in New York City, finding a hotel with either, let alone both, is a chore. Your best bet is to stay in Manhattan and commute to the ballgames, as both stadiums are easily accessible by subway. Some of the better-known, reasonably priced hotels are listed below.

MANHATTAN HOTELS

Hotel Beacon 2130 Broadway at 75th Street (800) 572-4969 or (212) 787-1100 Reasonably priced hotel on the Upper West Side near Central Park.

Edison Hotel 228 West 47th Street between Broadway and 8th Avenue (800) 637-7070 or (212) 840-5000 Reasonable accommodations just west of Broadway.

Fitzpatrick Manhattan Hotel 687 Lexington Avenue (between 56th and 57th Streets) (800) 367-7701 or (212) 355-0100 Nice accommodations on the east side of Midtown.

Herald Square Hotel 19 West 31st Street (800) 727-1888 or (212) 279-4017 Budget hotel near Empire State Building, Madison Square Garden, and Penn Station.

Holiday Inn Downtown 138 Lafayette Street (800) HOLIDAY or (212) 966-8898 Nice accommodations near Greenwich Village and Statue of Liberty.

Hotel Wolcott 4 West 31st Street (212) 268-2900 Bargain hotel located in the heart of Midtown.

Milford Plaza 8th Avenue and West 45th Street (800) 221-2690 or (212) 869-3600 Reasonably priced hotel in the heart of the theater district.

Paramount Hotel 235 West 46th Street (800) 225-7474 or (212) 764-5500 Affordable hotel in Midtown Manhattan. Near subways and theater district.

Park Savoy Hotel 158 West 58th Street (212) 245-5755 Budget hotel one block from Central Park and walking distance of several area museums

Quality Hotel by Journey's End 3 East 40th Street (800) 4-CHOICE or (212) 447-1500 Relatively affordable hotel on Midtown's east side.

Salisbury Hotel 123 West 57th Street (800) 223-0680 or (212) 246-1300 A comfortable hotel located near Carnegie Hall and Central Park.

TEAM HOTELS

Grand Hyatt Park Avenue at Grand Central (800) 233-1234 or (212) 883-1234 All American and National League clubs.

GOOD TO KNOW

- For schedule information or tickets to Mets games call (718) 507-8499.
- For schedule information or tickets to Yankee games call (718) 293-6000. The Yankees official Internet address is www.yankees.com.
- Mets games can be heard on **WFAN 660 AM**, which is also the area's lead-

ing all-sports station (not to mention one of the nation's best). Yankee games can be heard on **WABC 770 AM**.

- For more information on New York City sights, attractions, and hotels call the **Convention and Visitors Bureau** at (212) 484-1200. For those with access to the Internet, the city's official Web site is www.nycvisit.com.

Closest major league cities (and drive times): Philadelphia—100 miles (2 hours and 30 minutes); Boston—222 miles (4 hours and 30 minutes); Baltimore—203 miles (4 hours and 30 minutes); Pittsburgh—403 miles (7 hours and 45 minutes).

IN THE VICINITY

Cooperstown, New York, is not exactly "in the vicinity" of anything, but more than 400,000 people a year make the trek through beautiful upstate New York, between the Adirondacks and Catskill Mountain area, to see **The Baseball Hall of Fame**. The drive is about as scenic as you'll find anywhere, especially the miles of rolling farmland and lakes in the area immediately surrounding Cooperstown. The town itself, with a year-round population of 2,100, has one stoplight, no franchise establishments of any kind, and is a throwback to days gone past.

Cooperstown is about equidistant from New York City and Boston, so it's appropriate that the first thing you see as you walk in are life-size statues of Babe Ruth and Ted Williams. Both are carved out of single pieces of oak and painted to look just like the "Babe" and the "Splendid Splinter" at bat. It only gets better from there. The Grandstand Theater presents a multimedia show about baseball's legacy, while the hall itself displays memorabilia, such as uniforms, equipment, and old film footage from its early days through the current season. No matter who you grew up rooting for, you are bound to enjoy a few hours strolling through the hall's many changing exhibits. There are sections dedicated to baseball writers and announcers, a display of early baseball cards, a gallery of baseball art, and of course, a room full of brass plaques enshrining baseball's greatest players.

Outside the Hall of Fame is Doubleday Field, where two major league teams play the Hall of Fame Game each year. The field seats 10,000, and on any given day you are likely to find a little league or American Legion game being played on it.

Admission to the Hall of Fame is just $6 for adults. Plan to spend at least three hours, and don't be surprised if you end up spending a good deal more time. For more information, call (607) 547-9988 or write to National Baseball Hall of Fame, Cooperstown, NY 13326.

TEN FAVORITE PLACES TO SIT
AT A MAJOR-LEAGUE BALLPARK

10 **Infield roof box seats at Fenway Park.** These upstairs seats offer a great view of the field of play and the downtown skyline, as well as your own separate rest rooms and concession stands.

9 **Behind home plate at Dodger Stadium.** Blue all around you and nothing but arid hills and palm trees beyond the outfield wall. The best seats in the house are the dugout level seats along either baseline, but they're virtually unattainable.

8 **First base box seats at Jacobs Field.** Right on top of the action with a sweeping view of the scoreboards and city skyline. One of the toughest tickets in the big leagues.

7 **Lower box seats behind the Red Sox on-deck circle at Fenway.** What could be better than an up close view of the battle between pitcher and batter with the Green Monster as a backdrop.

6 **The left field bleachers at Pacific Bell Park.** Just under the giant glove is a great place to snag a home run ball; not far from Orlando's Barbecue and Red Stripe beer stand, but far enough away from Gilroy's Garlic Fries.

5 **Lower level behind visitor's on-deck circle at Yankee Stadium.** The stadium was built with these seats in mind. Close to the action with an awesome view of the outfield facade.

4 **First base box seats at Coors Field.** A great new stadium with a tremendous view of the Rocky Mountains beyond left field. A row of purple seats encircling the stands marks the stadium's mile-high point.

3 **Lower level behind the net at Camden Yards.** Right on top of home plate with the warehouse wall, Bromo Seltzer clock tower, and scoreboard spread out before you.

2 **Skybox seats at Comiskey.** A stocked fridge, hot dogs with all the trimmings, official scoring decisions piped into the box, and a dessert cart wheeled in during the late innings. A once in a lifetime experience. Try it if you get the chance.

1 **Bleacher seats at Wrigley Field, Fenway Park, or Yankee Stadium.** All three offer rowdy yet knowledgeable fans, having fun, and giving the opposing team hell. Perhaps not ideal for a family outing, but always a fun day at the ballpark.

◆ PHILADELPHIA ◆

*Once I was picked up by a squad car at 4 A.M. on a
Philadelphia street. They fined me $75 for being intox-
icated and $400 for being with the Phillies.*

BOB UECKER

VETERANS STADIUM

Over the years, Philadelphia fans have gotten a reputation for being somewhat surly. If I had to watch baseball in this park, I might be surly too. Philly
is a great town, in fact I was born there, but it has the dubious distinction of
being home to the longest consecutive "cellar dweller" teams in both leagues.
The Philadelphia A's set the American League record by being a last-place
team for seven straight years, and the National League Phillies held a grip on
last for five years. To add insult to injury, Veterans Stadium is one of the worst
outdoor parks in the big leagues.

Built as a multisport complex in 1971, Veterans Stadium is home to the
Phillies and Eagles, while the Flyers and 76ers play at the Spectrum, just to
the south of the park. It would appear that the Flyers and 76ers got the better
deal. The stadium is a cold, dull gray, and has all the charm of a parking lot.
The colors inside are faded and washed out, especially the artificial turf, which
is by far the worst in the majors. Not only can you see its seams, but in the
outfield, the football markings are as plain as day.

Most ballparks of the past had a few individual quirks that made them
unlike any other. The designers of Veterans Stadium seem to have gone out of
their way to make sure the Vet doesn't have any. There are far too many bad
seats, foul territory around the infield diamond is huge, and the outfield
dimensions are completely symmetrical; even the outfield fence, which is 12
feet high all the way around, wipes out any chance of a player robbing an
opposing batter of a home run.

The park does have a few redeeming qualities. It's right off I-95 in south Philadelphia, making it one of the most easily accessible big-league ballparks. There is plenty of inexpensive parking right beside the stadium, and because the park seats more than 62,000 people, tickets are generally easy to come by. Prices range from $8–24. Many of the seats in sections 500 and up are a long way from the action, so avoid them if you can.

Concession selections are best at the stadium's two food courts, located on the 200 and 500 level. Choices there include sub sandwiches, Mexican food, french fries, fried chicken, imported beers, and of course, Philly cheese steak sandwiches, in addition to standard ballpark fare. There are no vendors walking around the stands, so the only way to get something to eat or drink is to go to the concession stands. Bear in mind that if you go on a beer run, you're limited to two per trip.

Veterans Stadium also offers a **Stadium Restaurant** with a view of the field, near the right field corner. It's located on the Super Box (400) level; reservations are suggested. Call (215) 271-2300 for reservations and more information. The **Hall of Fame**, located behind section 224, consists of a series of plaques honoring former greats with the Phillies and Athletics. The stadium's most impressive feature is the large center field scoreboard, which is very

View from center field of Veterans Stadium in Philadelphia. (Photo by Author)

informative, providing player stats, game-in-progress information, and has an animated replay board two sections to the right. Out-of-town scores are shown on smaller sideboards. A neon Liberty Bell sits atop the upper deck in straight-away center field.

Tailgating is not allowed in the Phillies' parking lots, but there is a lot south of Zinkoff Boulevard where tailgating is encouraged. The Phillies do allow you to bring food and drink (nonalcoholic) in small coolers into the park.

Be careful dealing with scalpers, because reselling tickets on Veterans Stadium property is illegal. Tickets involved may be confiscated, so you may want to buy tickets in advance or at one of the ticket booths located on the podium level.

HISTORY

Philadelphia baseball franchises have been playing the national pastime since the 1880s, and until moving to Veterans Stadium, they won just one league pennant and no World Series. The Phillies began playing at Veterans Stadium on April 10, 1971, and won three straight division titles from 1976–78. But it wasn't until October 20, 1980, that they won their first World Series championship as Tug McGraw struck out the Royals' Willie Wilson to end the game.

On April 29, 1981, Hall of Famer Steve "Lefty" Carlton struck out Tim Wallach for his 3,000th career strikeout. August 10 of that same year, Pete Rose singled to break Stan Musial's NL record of 3,630 career hits. In Veterans Stadium's twentieth season, on August 15, 1990, Terry Mullholland beat the Giants 6–0 by pitching the park's first no-hitter.

GETTING TO VETERANS STADIUM
Broad Street and Pattison Avenue

As I mentioned earlier, Veterans Stadium is easy to get to from I-95, and parking is convenient and quite reasonable. The mass transit system in the Philadelphia area is also very efficient. It consists of a network of buses, trolleys, subways, and commuter trains, called SEPTA. The Broad Street subway line and bus routes 17, 68, and C go directly to and from Veterans Stadium. Express subways run before and after games up until midnight; after that, shuttle buses are available. For more information on the SEPTA system call (215) 580-7800.

WHAT TO DO AND SEE IN PHILADELPHIA

Most of the city's historical attractions are located in the vicinity of **Independence National Historical Park**. Your best bet may be to stop by the Visitors

Center at 3rd and Chestnut or to ask one of the costumed, bell-clanging town criers for a free map of the area attractions. The best-known and most-visited attractions within the park are the **Liberty Bell Pavillion,** home of the Liberty Bell, on Market Street between 5th and 6th streets, and **Independence Hall,** which is directly across the park from the Liberty Bell, on Chestnut Street. **Congress Hall,** where the U.S. Senate and Congress met for eleven years, is on one side of Independence Hall, while **Old City Hall,** which served as the home of the Supreme Court, is on the other side of Independence Hall. All of the park's buildings are open from 9–5 and are free to the public.

If you build up a thirst walking around the area, you may want to stop by the **City Tavern,** a colonial-style pub and restaurant dating back to 1773, at 2nd and Walnut. The **Norman Rockwell Museum** is at the corner of 6th and Sansom, not far from Independence Hall.

Along the waterfront, between Market and South streets, is **Penn's Landing,** a beautiful riverfront park that's home to several of Philly's larger festivals, including the **Jambalaya Jam,** held during Memorial Day weekend, and **Riverblues,** one of the East Coast's best blues festivals, held the weekend before Memorial Day weekend each year. Aside from the festivals, the area's principal attraction is the marina, which is home port to a number of historic ships.

The **Philadelphia Museum of Art** is the country's third-largest art museum, boasting a collection of more than 300,000 works of art. Admission is $6 for adults, except Sundays when admission is free. Located in Fairmount Park at 26th Street and Benjamin Franklin Parkway, the museum is open Tuesday through Sunday.

The Barnes Foundation is home to a remarkable collection of more than 1,100 works of art belonging to the late Dr. Albert C. Barnes. It's located at 300 North Latches Lane, in Merion, about a half hour outside Philadelphia.

The Franklin Institute Science Center was built in honor of one of the country's greatest thinkers, Benjamin Franklin, and is home to many of his personal effects. The museum is made up of the Mandell Futures Center, the Fels Planetarium, the Tuttleman Omniverse Theater, and the Science Center itself. One of the pioneers of hands-on displays and exhibits, the museum features a walk-through human heart, interactive computer displays, and an Air Force jet you can actually sit in. An adult combination ticket allowing you to visit all four venues is available; a ticket for the Science Center, Futures Center, and either the planetarium or theater is $12. The museum is located at 20th Street and Benjamin Franklin Parkway and is open daily.

Catty-corner to the Franklin Institute, at 1900 Benjamin Franklin Parkway, is the **Academy of Natural Sciences Museum.** Its primary exhibit is the Discover Dinosaurs display, which features more than a dozen dinosaur fossils including a Tyrannosaurus Rex. It is open daily.

The **Rodin Museum** at 22nd Street and Benjamin Franklin Parkway has the largest collection of Rodin sculptures and drawings outside of France. The museum is open Tuesday through Sunday, and admission is by donation.

Across the Schuylkill River is the **Philadelphia Zoo**, which is the country's oldest zoo. It features America's only white lions and more than 1,500 other animals from all over the world.

NIGHTLIFE IN PHILADELPHIA

To see what's going on in Philadelphia pick up a copy of *Welcomat*, the area's free entertainment weekly. The premiere nightlife district is the **South Street** area, between Front and 10th Streets. All told you'll find more than seventy-five restaurants and a number of nightclubs all within a short walk of each other right on South Street, as well as the area a few blocks above and below South Street. A few that you may want to look out for are listed below.

Theatre of the Living Arts (a.k.a. T.L.A.), at 334 South Street is one of the area's hippest live music venues and showcases up-and-coming, as well as nationally known, rock and roll acts. **Khyber Pass Pub**, at 56 South Second Street, is the best place to see indie rock and local bands. **The Tin Angel Acoustic Cafe** which features, as the name implies, acoustic music is located at 20 South Second Street.

Another spot with a concentration of clubs (albeit mostly trendy ones) is the waterfront area along Christopher Columbus Boulevard (formerly known as Delaware Avenue). Some good ones are **KatManDu** at Pier 25, a bar and restaurant that's only open during baseball season, and the **Rock Lobster** between Piers 13 and 14 at Vine Street, a riverfront bar with live music and a casual outdoor patio. **Babylon**, at 1001 North Delaware, is one of the more happening local dance clubs, and **Dave and Buster's** at Pier 19 is a bar and restaurant with a huge game room.

Not unlike the people of Pittsburgh, Philadelphians tend to favor their own local joints. One of the more popular ones is the **North Star Bar** which features local original bands and occasional national acts. You'll find it at 27th and Poplar streets. The **Samuel Adams Brew House** serves several varieties of their own microbrewed beer and has occasional live music. It's located above the Sansom Oyster House at 1516 Sansom Street. Another good choice is **Dr. Watson's Pub**, at 216 South 11th Street, a sit-down club hosting local original bands that has three floors of fun, food, games, and a friendly, intimate atmosphere.

Speaking of brew pubs, the **Dock Street Brewing Company**, in Logan Square at the corner of Eighteenth and Cherry streets, is one of the city's best restaurants and nightspots. Their Amber and Pilsner brews are two of the finest in the nation, and are complemented by a rotating selection of ales, stouts, and porters. An added bonus is the food selection, which is outstanding, yet surprisingly affordable.

One of the better live music venues is the **Tower Theater** at 69th and Ludlow, in Upper Darby. It features nationally known acts at reasonable prices in a medium-sized hall. Philadelphia also has a number of outstanding jazz clubs. The reigning king among jazz clubs is **Zanzibar Blue**, at 301 South 11th Street. **Ortlieb's Jazz Haus** is a cozy place at 847 North Third Street.

WHERE TO STAY IN PHILADELPHIA

There are just a few hotels in the area around Veteran's Stadium, which is well south of the city's historic attractions and nightlife districts. Your best bet may be to stay in the area around Penn's Landing or in the heart of the historic district, as hotels there are most centrally located. With that in mind, the following is a partial list of Philadelphia hotels.

AREA HOTELS

Comfort Inn Penn's Landing   100 North Columbus Boulevard (800) 424-6423 or (215) 627-7900   Within walking distance of Independence National Historical Park, Penn's Landing, and Columbus Boulevard area nightclubs.

Embassy Suites Hotel Center City   1776 Benjamin Franklin Parkway (800) EMBASSY or (215) 561-1776   Near Fairmount Park, close to most of Philadelphia's museums.

Holiday Inn-Independence Mall   400 Arch Street (800) THE-BELL or (215) 923-8660   Within two blocks of Independence National Historical Park and other area sights.

Holiday Inn Philadelphia Stadium   10th Street and Packer Avenue (800) HOLIDAY or (215) 755-9500   Adjacent to Veteran's Stadium and the Spectrum.

Travelodge Hotel-Stadium/Airport   2015 Penrose Avenue (800) 255-3050 or (215) 755-6500   Recently renovated budget hotel about a mile from the stadium.

TEAM HOTELS

Doubletree   Broad Street at Locust Street (800) 222-8733 or (215) 893-1600   Reds.

Ritz Carlton   10 Avenue of the Arts (800) 241-3333 or (215) 735-7700   Braves.

Sheraton Society Hill   2nd and Walnut Streets (800) 325-3535 or (215) 238-6000   All National League clubs except the Braves and Reds.

GOOD TO KNOW

- For schedule information or tickets to Phillies games, call (215) 463-1000.
- Phillies games can be heard on **WGMP 1210 AM**. **WIP 610 AM** is the area's leading all-sports radio station.
- For more information on Philadelphia sights, attractions, and hotels, call the **Philadelphia Visitor's Center** at (800) 537-7676.
- For schedule information or tickets to events at the **Spectrum**, call (215) 336-3600.

Closest major league cities (and driving times): Baltimore—102 miles (2 hours) New York—100 miles (2 hours and 30 minutes); Pittsburgh—319 miles (6 hours); Boston—320 miles (7 hours).

IN THE VICINITY

Atlantic City and its famous boardwalk, beaches, and casinos are less than an hour away from Philadelphia by car. Atlantic City has become best known for its casinos, but you can also stroll along four miles of oceanfront beaches and the nation's oldest boardwalk, or check out one of the amusement parks if gambling is not your forte. Call the Atlantic City Visitors Authority at 1-800-BOARDWK for more information on Atlantic City attractions, hotels, and packages.

In Camden, New Jersey, a short ferry ride away from Penn's Landing, is the **New Jersey State Aquarium**, which features an underwater shipwreck and daily dive shows inside its 760,000 gallon tank. More than 2,500 aquatic animals representing 175 species are on display. Admission is $9 for adults.

◆ PITTSBURGH ◆

Some parks have those games where you guess the number of people in the park. Here, you have to identify them, too.

LEE MAZZILLI

PNC PARK

The Pirates' new ballpark changes everything for baseball fans in Pittsburgh. A tribute to Forbes Field and other classic yards, PNC Park offers a healthy dose of the nostalgia and tradition that Three Rivers Stadium lacked. The two-tier, baseball-only stadium seats just 38,127 fans, making it the most intimate new ballpark in the big leagues. With the ballpark situated along the Allegheny River, a 450-foot home run shot to right field could land in the river, reminiscent of McCovey Cove at Pacific Bell Park in San Francisco.

Just as Houston's Enron Field incorporates the old Union Station Train Depot into the stadium design, PNC Park utilizes the historic, rebuilt Martin Building as a ticket and administrative office on the left field corner of the park. A statue of Willie Stargell looms nearby at the corner of Federal and General Robinson streets. Statues of Roberto Clemente and Honus Wagner were brought over from Three Rivers Stadium. Clemente is at the base of the bridge at 6th Street and Wagner is outside the Home Plate Rotunda, the park's main entrance plaza.

Located at the foot of the Roberto Clemente Bridge, PNC Park was constructed with fan convenience and comfort in mind. The highest seat in the park is just 90 feet above the field. More than two thirds of the seats are on the lower level, and nearly every seat, except those in the bleacher sections, offers a sweeping view of the riverfront and downtown skyline. On the first base side of the main concourse, an open terrace area known as "Tastes of Pittsburgh" offers a variety of local fare and a great view of the river. Culinary highlights include Primanti Brothers sandwiches, Mineo's pizza, and Benkovitz's fish sandwiches. Fans are also allowed to bring small coolers (no cans or bottles) to the ballpark. Feel free to eat your meal in the terraced picnic area beyond right center field, which accommodates more than 250 people.

The park also features a natural grass playing field and asymmetrical outfield dimensions. The deepest point of the field is 410 feet in center field, where a six-foot wall allows outfielders the opportunity to snag would-be home runs. The right field corner is just 320 feet from home plate, but a 21-foot wall (not coincidentally Clemente wore number 21) keeps low line drives from leaving the yard. The left field corner may be more inviting, just 325 feet away from the plate with a six-foot fence. The bullpens are terraced in straight away center field.

An Outback Steakhouse, which is open to the public year round, sits underneath the scoreboard in left center field and offers an outdoor party deck overlooking the field. "Kiner's Corner" is another common area in left field, where fans can get a good look at the playing field.

Pittsburgh has always been a family-oriented franchise, offering some of the most affordable tickets in the game. Bleacher seats are just $12 and may be the best family value in the park. The front rows of the outfield bleacher sections are just five feet from the field of play—a great spot to catch souvenir home run balls. Another family option might be the outfield grandstand seats, just $9 each, but they are a long way from the field.

HISTORY

PNC Park opened for regular season play on April 9, 2001, with a game against the Reds, so the lion's share of the park's historical moments remain to be seen. Over the years, however, Pittsburgh fans have witnessed quite a few landmark games since the Pirates began playing National League baseball in 1891.

Remarkably, a Major League or Negro League no-hitter was never pitched at Forbes Field in its sixty-two-year history. On August 14, 1971, during Three Rivers Stadium's first full season of hosting big league ball, the Bucs were victims of a Bob Gibson no-hitter, losing 11–0. Despite that setback, the Bucs won their division, the NLCS, and the World Series in 1971. On October 13, the Pirates beat the Orioles 4–3 in the World Series' first-ever night game.

On August 9, 1976, John "The Candy Man" Candelaria tossed a no-hitter against the Dodgers for a 2–0 victory. Early in the '79 season, on April 18, Phillies first baseman Greg "The Bull" Luzinski hit the longest home run in Three Rivers history, a 483-foot missile off Pirates pitcher Don Robinson. Exactly eight years later, on April 18, 1987, Luzinski's teammate Mike Schmidt

The Pirates' new home. An aerial view of PNC Park. (Courtesy of the Pittsburgh Pirates)

hit his 500th career home run, also off Don Robinson. On July 12, 1997, Pirate hurlers Francisco Cordova and Ricardo Rincon beat the Astros in the first tandem extra inning no-hitter in major league history.

GETTING TO PNC PARK
600 Stadium Circle

PNC Park, just east of the former site of Three Rivers Stadium, is most easily accessed by car. There is a fair amount of reasonably priced parking in the vicinity, although not all of it is right next to the stadium. Traffic can be rough for heavily attended games, as the park is in a fairly congested area and there is only one way in and out. Your best bet is to get there early to tailgate or visit some of the area bars and restaurants. The area's best pre- and postgame spot is the **Clark Bar & Grill**, just a short walk from the new park. The place can get packed before and after games, so get there early if you can. **Hi-Tops Sports Bar** is a new place on Federal Street within walking distance of PNC Park. It has a 50-foot bar, eight 10′×10′ TVs, a dance floor, and sixty-five TVs scattered throughout the bar.

For most games you can take the **Gateway Clipper**, a riverboat, from **Station Square**. The price includes a ticket to the game, a ninety-minute cruise with a baseball-style buffet dinner, and roundtrip service to and from the stadium. Parking is free at Station Square, an area of renovated warehouses that offers a hotel and several nightlife options, as well. For more information call (412) 355-7980.

WHAT TO DO AND SEE IN PITTSBURGH

Pittsburgh has a number of sights and attractions spread all over town, but a good number of them can be found about fifteen minutes east of downtown, in the Oakland and Shadyside areas. The left field wall and the original home plate from **Forbes Field**, which was torn down in 1970, remain intact on the grounds of the University of Pittsburgh. Home plate is in its original position, displayed under glass in the lobby of the Forbes Quadrangle Building, while part of the left field wall stands behind the Law School Building. A plaque indicates where Bill Mazeroski's famous home run landed, to beat the Yankees in game 7 of the 1960 World Series

While you are in the area, you may want to stop by **The Carnegie**, a museum complex at 4400 Forbes Road. The Carnegie was a gift to the city from Andrew Carnegie in 1890. What Carnegie referred to as the "noble quartet" of art, science, music, and literature are represented by the Museum of Natural History, Museum of Art, the Music Hall, and Library all under one roof. The **Museum of Natural History** is home to the nation's third largest collection of dinosaur fossils, including the skeletal remains of a Tyrannosaurus Rex, and is the sixth largest museum of its kind. The **Museum of Art** is right next door and is made up of two larger galleries, sculpture and architecture halls, as well as an outdoor sculpture court. As you might expect, the museum's collection consists of an extensive display of paintings and sculpture by the Old Masters, complemented by a good deal of contemporary work, housed in the newer Scaife Gallery. One entry fee allows you to see both museums, so plan to spend a good part of the day.

The Frick Art Museum is located at 7227 Reynolds Street in Point Breeze and displays a small but impressive group of paintings, sculptures, and tapestries from the collection of industrialist Henry Clay Frick and his wife. His Victorian estate, **Clayton**, is adjacent to the museum and recently underwent a $6 million renovation. It features the Frick's original decor and furnishings as well as a carriage museum with a number of carriages, sleighs, and automobiles of the era. The museum is free, but guided tours of the home are $5. Farther to the northeast you'll find the **Pittsburgh Zoo and Aquarium**, which is located in Highland Park and is home to more than 6,300 animals kept in natural settings spread out over 77 acres. The new $16 million aquarium features a rain forest setting, sharks, and Amazon River dolphin. The zoo and aquarium are open every day, except Christmas, from 10 AM to 6 PM.

On the north side of town, occupying seven floors of a converted warehouse not far from the stadium, you'll find the **Andy Warhol Museum**. The museum opened in 1994 and features more than 700 pieces of the artist's work including paintings, prints, drawings, sculpture, and films. The museum, located at 117 Sandusky Street, is open Wednesday through Sunday and costs just $5 for adults. Nearby, at the corner of Troy Hill Road and Vinial Street, you'll find the **Penn Brewery**. This beautifully restored nineteenth-century brewery offers short informative tours of its brewing facility and serves genuine German cuisine. Tours are free, but advance reservations are recommended.

The **Carnegie Science Center** is next to Three Rivers Stadium at One Allegheny Avenue. Calling itself "an amusement park for the mind," the center features more than 250 interactive exhibits. Some of the highlights include working robots, laser demonstrations, a World War II submarine, the Pacific Coral Reef Aquarium, a miniature train exhibit with 2,300 feet of track, as well as a planetarium and OmniMax theater. A combination ticket which allows you into the museum, planetarium, and OmniMax theater is $12 for adults, the museum alone is just $5.75 for adults.

Downtown Pittsburgh is where the transformation from a smoky industrial town to an up-and-coming, white-collar city is most apparent. The towering skyscrapers, enormous parks, scenic bridges, and Point State Park's giant fountain make for as pretty a downtown skyline as you'll find. **Point State Park** is at the confluence of the Monongahela and Allegheny Rivers and is home to the **Fort Pitt Museum**, with historical focus on Western Pennsylvania's role in the French and Indian War, as well as the important events that led to the founding of Pittsburgh. Fort Pitt, built by the British in 1758, was at one point the largest and most extensive outpost in North America. The museum is a reproduction of one of its original bastions and is open Tuesday through Sunday. Admission is just $4 for adults.

Across the Monongahela River there are two inclined trolley cars that offer spectacular views of the city skyline from a mountainside observation deck. They are both open until late in the evening for night viewing, cost $1 each way, and are well worth the short trip. The **Duquesne Incline** is at 1197 West Carson Street, while the **Monongahela Incline** is across from Station Square, also on West Carson Street.

NIGHTLIFE IN PITTSBURGH

Pittsburgh is one of the few big cities in the United States where small, local pubs and taverns still prevail. The **Strip District**, formerly the produce district at Smallman and 10th Street, is an up-and-coming nightlife area on the riverfront. **Banana Joe's Sports Bar & Grill** is a massive place with two giant screen TVs, five big screen TVs, and small TVs at every booth. Live bands also perform occasionally on the bar's backstage. Other clubs in the area include **Donzi's**, an upscale dance club overlooking the water, **Area 51**, **Rosebud**, and **Metropol**. Other than the Strip District, the Clark Bar and Grill, and Hi-Tops, your best bet may be **Station Square**, a good-sized shopping and entertainment complex with a number of restaurants and nightclubs, including the **Funny Bone Comedy Club**, **Bucca di Beppo**, and **Chauncy's**. Call in advance for information on upcoming acts and cover charge at the Funny Bone.

Outside the downtown area, in Bloomfield, check out **Church Brew Works** at 3525 Liberty Avenue. This former church, replete with stained glass windows, has been converted into a popular microbrewery and restaurant. **Dave & Busters**, a giant bar and game room, is housed in a former steel mill in Homestead, not far from downtown along the Monongahela River.

As I mentioned earlier, there are countless small taverns around town and you may want to ask your hotel concierge for the best ones near you, or pick up a copy of *In Pittsburgh*, the city's free entertainment magazine.

WHERE TO EAT IN PITTSBURGH

Ask a dozen Pittsburgh natives where to go for a meal that's indigenous to the area, and you're likely to get a dozen different responses. Listed below are some of the places I came across.

Benkovitz Seafoods   A Pittsburgh institution with great food at reasonable prices. If you don't get a chance to stop by, try a Benkovitz Fish Sandwich at the ballpark. Their original location is at 23rd and Smallman streets (412) 263-3016.

Gallagher's Pub   An Irish Pub with American and Irish fare and the warm friendly atmosphere typical of countless Pittsburgh neighborhood establishments. Located at 2 South Market Square (412) 261-5554.

Primanti Brothers   I went to the original location, at 46 18th Street, for an after-hours binge. The place is located in an old warehouse district and gets packed at lunch, dinner, and after the bars close. The atmosphere is far from plush, but the sandwiches are piled high and at that time of night, I swore it was the best I ever had. Call the original location at (412) 263-2142 to find out which of their three locations is closest to you.

WHERE TO STAY IN PITTSBURGH

Many of Pittsburgh's better hotels are located in the heart of downtown with easy access to the subway, which offers a convenient free-fare zone in the immediate downtown area. You will, however, have to pay a premium for such convenience during the week, as many downtown hotels cater to business travelers and are somewhat pricey. Many hotels offer weekend packages and a few offer Pirates packages, so be sure to ask about both. If you are driving or have access to a car, you may want to consider staying in one of the less expensive hotels on the outskirts of town. The Oakland area offers a number of sights and attractions and is only a short drive from downtown.

DOWNTOWN HOTELS

Pittsburgh Hilton   600 Commonwealth Place (800) HILTONS or (412) 391-4600   Across from Point State Park in Gateway Center.

Pittsburgh Marriott   112 Washington Place (800) 228-9290 or (412) 471-4000   Between the Civic Arena, where the Penguins play, and Duquesne University.

Ramada Hotel   One Bigelow Square (800) 272-6232 or (412) 281-5800   Across from Steel Plaza and subway station. In the heart of everything downtown.

Sheraton Hotel Station Square   7 Station Square Drive (800) 325-3535 or (412) 261-2000   Across the river from downtown and several nightclubs in the immediate vicinity.

LESS EXPENSIVE HOTELS OUTSIDE DOWNTOWN

Hampton Inn   3315 Hamlet Street (800) HAMPTON or (412) 681-1000   Within minutes of Oakland sights and attractions.

Red Roof Inn   6404 Steubenville Pike (800) THE-ROOF or (412) 787-7870   Inexpensive accommodations just twelve miles south of downtown Pittsburgh.

TEAM HOTELS

Vista International   (412) 281-3700   Cubs, Rockies, Dodgers, Mets, Phillies, Cardinals, Padres, and Giants.

William Penn   (412) 281-7100   Braves, Reds, Marlins, Astros, and Expos.

GOOD TO KNOW

- For schedule information or tickets to Pirates games call (800) BUY-BUCS or (412) 321-BUCS. The Pirates official Internet address is www.pirate-ball.com.
- Pirates games can be heard on **KDKA 1020 AM.**
- The **Pittsburgh Convention and Visitor's Bureau** will send you a complete visitors guide if you call them at (800) 366-0093. For those with access to the Internet, the city's official Web site is www.pittsburgh.net.

Closest major league cities (and driving times): Cleveland—157 miles (3 hours); Cincinnati—298 miles (5 hours); Baltimore—292 miles (5 hours and 20 minutes); Detroit—335 miles (6 hours and 5 minutes).

◆ TAMPA BAY ◆

TROPICANA FIELD

Built with baseball in mind, this 48,000-seat baseball-only facility has traits of both domed and outdoor stadiums. The permanent roof, made of teflon-covered fiberglass, is set at a slight angle, allowing for greater interior height above homeplate than center field. When the Devil Rays win, the translucent roof is illuminated with an orange glow. Once inside the main entrance rotunda, modeled after Ebbets Field in Brooklyn, fans are introduced to twenty-first-century baseball.

The playing field consists of Astroturf 12, a low-bounce artificial turf surface with a full dirt infield similar to those you'd find at outdoor parks. Although it's only 50 feet from home plate to the backstop, there is a good deal of foul territory along the basepaths and down the line in the outfield. The outfield dimensions are asymmetrical and, unlike other domed stadiums, the outfield fence presents a few tricky angles—especially down the left field line and in center field. It is by far the most brightly lit indoor stadium in the big leagues.

Only time will tell, but Tropicana Field should be a hitter's paradise, as the left field corner is just 315 feet from the plate, and the deepest part of the park is 417 feet. Dead center is 410 feet from the plate, and the right field pole is listed at 322 feet.

While the stadium may lack the charm and nostalgia of the league's better parks, it attempts to make up for it by creating an "outdoor atmosphere" with giant murals, lofty concourse areas, and a slew of amenities. More than 300,000 square feet, in the shape of a ring, have been added to the existing dome. This ring gives the dome a much better looking exterior and houses, among other things, the center field mall and a pair of food courts—one along each foul line. One of the dome's most exciting additions is the **Batter's Eye Restaurant**, a three-level sports bar/restaurant/game room with a view of the action from beyond the center field fence. In addition to food and drinks, the bar offers batting cages, pool tables, miniature golf, and video games.

Fans are not likely to have to wait long for food and beer, as there are 260 concession stands throughout the stadium. As fans enter the main center field gates they'll pass through a baseball-oriented pedestrian mall, known as **Center Field Street**, with restaurants, shops, bars, and galleries. In addition to traditional ballpark fare, Center Field Street offers a **Taste of Tampa Bay** with local food specialties such as Cuban sandwiches, deviled crabs, and empanadas. There is also a kids' concession area with lower counters, smaller servings, and lower prices.

The stadium's most unique aspect is the **Scouts Section** situated directly behind home plate. This section of seats provides fans with a radar gun to clock the pitcher's heat and individual TV monitors that show the action from any of nine perspectives around the field. The monitors also present player statistics, show replays from games around the league, offer interactive games, and even allow you to order food, drinks, and souvenirs from your seat. Seats here sell on a game-by-game basis for $195 and are unlike any others in the big leagues.

While the home plate boxes are among the most expensive in baseball, the stadium does offer a decent selection of more affordable seats to choose from. The field boxes are some of the best in the stadium and offer your best chance to snag a foul ball or autograph. They are located along the basepaths and behind home plate, and cost $60. If there is a bargain to be had in the stadium, it's the lower boxes that sell for $20. These seats are directly behind the field boxes and are particularly good in sections 101–126. Terrace boxes, situated behind the lower boxes, are also somewhat reasonably priced at $15 each.

Other seats include the $12 lower reserved seats, which are essentially outfield bleacher seats; the $10 upper reserve seats, located upstairs behind home plate and along the basepaths; and $3 general admission seats, which are a long way from the plate in left field and to either side of the hitters' background.

GETTING TO TROPICANA FIELD
One Stadium Drive

The stadium is actually in downtown St. Petersburg, across the bay from Tampa. From Tampa take I-275 South across the Howard Farkland Bridge into downtown, and get off at the Dome exit. There are no mass transit options other than the city bus. For more information on local bus lines, call (813) 530-9911. Even with the addition of a parking deck and a new parking lot just east of the stadium, parking is very limited. Because the surrounding neighborhood is not particularly conducive to leaving your car unattended you may want to consider using one of the ball game shuttles that run from many of downtown St. Pete's parking lots.

HISTORY

Tropicana Field opened on March 31, 1998, as the Devil Rays lost to the Detroit Tigers 11–6. On April 1 of that season, the Devil Rays had their first victory, as Fred McGriff led the way with four RBIs in an 11–8 win over the Tigers. Jose Canseco hit an unusual ground rule double against the Tigers on May 2, 1999. The ball landed on a cat walk inside the roof and never came down. Wade Boggs got his 3,000th hit in style with a home run off of Chris Haney of the Indians on August 7, 1999. He was only the 23rd player to reach the 3,000 hit mark.

WHAT TO DO AND SEE IN TAMPA

Tampa is the new spring-training home of the New York Yankees. Newly opened **Legends Field** is one of the nicest spring training facilities in Florida, and during the regular season it's also home to the Tampa Yankees of the Single A Florida State League. Legends Field seats 10,387 fans and has outfield dimensions identical to those at Yankee Stadium. Tickets for Tampa Yankee games range from $3–5, and parking is free. Legends Field also hosts major concerts throughout the year. The Devil Rays are the only big league team to play spring training games in their home town. Games are played at **Al Lang Field**, another of the nicest spring-training parks in Florida. Seats along the first base side offer a nice view of the bay and marina as well as the game. The Class A Devil Rays play 70 home games starting in early April. Tickets range from $3–$5.

   Busch Gardens, Florida's other amusement park, is located in northeast Tampa at 3000 East Busch Boulevard. This 335-acre park has a beautiful 80-acre safari park, several intense roller-coasters, dolphin shows, a brewery, the nation's fourth largest zoo, and Adventure Island, a neighboring water theme park. Busch Gardens opens at 9:30 AM every day. The Serengeti Plain features giraffes, zebras, rhinos, antelope, and other wild animals roaming freely as visitors view them from aboard a monorail. The Congo section is home to white Bengal tigers and the River Rapids ride down a quarter-mile section of manmade white water. Admission is $34.95 for adults, with discounts for children and seniors. Expect to spend an entire day.

   The **Florida Aquarium** is home to more than 4,000 species of marine life housed in an $84 million complex at 701 Channelside Drive in downtown Tampa. Built in 1995, the aquarium features several viewing tanks including a half-million-gallon tank with a giant coral reef exhibit. Admission is $13.95 for adults.

   If after Busch Gardens and the Florida Aquarium you still haven't had enough of Florida's abundant wildlife, check out the real thing at **Canoe Escape** on the Hillsborough River. Just minutes from downtown Tampa, this 16,000-acre wilderness park allows you to see alligators, turtles, and birds in their natural habitat as you paddle downstream. Trips are available every day and take anywhere from two hours to a full day.

The **Salvador Dali Museum** is within walking distance of Al Lang Field at 1000 Third Street South, in St. Petersburg. The nation's largest collection of Dali works under one roof is housed in an impressive group of galleries on the banks of the Bayboro Harbor. The museum opens at 9:30 AM Tuesday–Saturday and noon Sunday and Monday. Admission is $8 for adults. Also in St. Petersburg, at 255 Beach Drive, you'll find the **Museum of Fine Arts**, which offers a small but impressive collection of paintings and sculpture by artists such as Renoir, O'Keeffe, and Monet. The museum is open from 10–5 every day except Monday, and costs just $5 for adults.

The **Museum of Science and Industry** is the largest science center in the Southeast, offering 450 hands-on exhibits and displays. MOSI also has a planetarium, OmniMax Theatre, flight and space displays, a learning center, butterfly garden, and a forty-acre wilderness area with a three-mile hiking trail. The museum is located at 4801 East Fowler Avenue, in northeast Tampa, and is open seven days a week. Admission, including entry to the IMAX theatre, is $11 for adults. Monday admission to the museum is by donation.

NIGHTLIFE IN TAMPA

The best source for nightclub and restaurant information in the Tampa/St. Pete area is *The Weekly Planet*, a free entertainment tabloid. *The Planet* is available all over the metro area at bars, restaurants, and retailers. One area that offers a tremendous number of bars, restaurants, and cafes within walking distance of each other is historic **Ybor City** on Tampa's east side. Comparable to Miami's Little Havana area in that it has a distinct Latin American flavor, Ybor City is more tourist-friendly. It also offers a wealth of specialty shops, galleries, and cigar factories.

The **Columbia Restaurant**, at 2117 East 7th Avenue, is an Ybor City institution serving Cuban and Spanish cuisine at this location since 1905. Columbia offers three large dining rooms, an open courtyard, and two stages where the flamenco is performed nightly. A second location—same great food without the atmosphere of the original location—is at the Pier in St. Petersburg. For live blues, check out the **Blues Ship Cafe**, at 1910 East 7th Avenue. The Blues Ship is a classic dive that regularly books the nation's best blues musicians on the weekends and showcases regional acts throughout the week. For more progressive live music, stop by **The Rubb** at 1507 East 7th Avenue, which hosts nationally known acts playing rock, alternative, rockabilly, and pop music. Shows start at 9 PM, and cover charge varies.

The **Tampa Bay Brewing Company**, at 1812 15th Street in Ybor City, offers a list of seven outstanding microbrewed beers. The list ranges from True Blonde Ale to Iron Rat Stout. Their 4–8 PM happy hour is one of the area's best with $2 pints and two-for-one mixed drinks. They also offer a decent pub-style lunch and dinner menu. The **Ybor City Brewing Company** offers hour-long tours of its microbrewery Tuesday through Saturday from 11 AM until 3 PM. The brewery is located in a renovated 100-year-old cigar factory at 2205 North 20th Street. Tours cost $2 and conclude with a tasting in their hospitality room.

Another nightlife area worth checking out is the **Pier** in downtown St. Petersburg. The Pier extends nearly half a mile into Tampa Bay at the base of Second Avenue and has a number of cafes, bars, and restaurants to choose from. The Pier's best watering hole is **Nick's On The Water**, which offers a reasonably priced menu in an upscale setting overlooking the bay. Their deck attracts a handsome young crowd and is a nice place for drinks. A free trolley runs from the parking lot out to the Pier. Parking costs $3.

Before and after a game at Tropicana Field, head to **Ferg's Sports Bar & Grill** at 1320 Central Avenue. Located across the street from the stadium, Ferg's offers an inexpensive menu and pitchers of domestic beer for as little as $4.25. The place gets packed on game days, so get there early. Another sports bar not far from the stadium is **El Cap**, at 3500 Fourth Street North. The walls are crammed with baseball memorabilia, and the burgers are some of the best in the city.

For something completely different, try **Skipper's Smokehouse**, at 910 Skipper Road (at Nebraska) in Tampa. Skippers features live reggae and blues music in an oyster bar setting and a moderately priced yet diverse seafood menu.

WHERE TO STAY IN TAMPA

The Tampa/St. Pete area offers plenty of places to stay within a short drive of the stadium, sights, and attractions. You'll probably want to make a choice based on whether you plan to spend more time seeing area attractions or at the stadium. The area immediately surrounding the stadium in downtown St. Petersburg is unspectacular but does offer some hotel bargains, while the area's better-known attractions are across the bay in and around Tampa.

ST. PETERSBURG HOTELS

Bayfront Hilton   333 First Street South (800) HILTONS or (813) 894-5000   Nice fifteen-story hotel with spacious rooms overlooking Al Lang Field and Tampa Bay.

Comfort Inn   1400 34th Street North (800) 228-5150 or (813) 323-3100 Basic motel accommodations about two miles from Tropicana Field.

Days Inn Marina Beach Resort   6800 Sunshine Skyway Lane (800) 325-2525 or (813) 894-0635   Affordable hotel on the southern edge of town, facing a private beach on Tampa Bay. Fifteen minutes from Tropicana Field.

Days Inn St. Pete Central 650 34th Street North (800) 325-2525 or (813) 321-2958 One of the better bargains in downtown St. Pete. Two miles from Tropicana Field.

La Quinta Inn 4999 34th Street North (800) 531-5900 or (813) 527-8421 Another bargain hotel with handsome rooms, four miles south of Tropicana Field.

TAMPA HOTELS

Amerisuites 4811 West Main Street (800) 833-1516 or (813) 282-1037 Nice accommodations near the airport and I-275.

Best Western All Suites Hotel 3001 University Center Drive (800) 528-1234 or (813) 971-8930 Nice, affordable hotel convenient to Busch Gardens and I-275.

La Quinta Busch Gardens 2904 Melbourne Boulevard (800) 531-5900 or (813) 623-3591 Bargain accommodations conveniently located off I-4.

Marriott-Tampa Westshore 1001 North Westshore Boulevard (800) 228-9290 or (813) 287-2555 Luxury thirteen-story hotel near airport and I-285.

The Wyndham Harbour Island 725 South Harbour Island Boulevard (800) WYNDHAM or (813) 229-5000 Luxury twelve-story hotel near the Florida Aquarium.

GOOD TO KNOW

- For Devil Rays schedule information or tickets call (813) 825-3250.
- Devil Rays games can be heard on **WFLA 970 AM**. The leading all-sports radio station is **WFNS 910 AM**.
- For Tampa tourist information, call (800) 448-2672 or write the Tampa/Hillsborough Convention and Visitors Association at 111 East Madison Street, Suite 1010, Tampa, FL 33601. The city's official Web site is www.thcva.com.
- For St. Petersburg tourist information, call (800) 345-6710, or write the St. Petersburg Chamber of Commerce at 100 Second Avenue North, St. Petersburg, FL 33701.

Closest major league cities (and drive times): Miami—285 miles (5 hours and 15 minutes); Atlanta—462 miles (8 hours and 25 minutes).

IN THE VICINITY

Baseball fans, especially Red Sox fans, may want to spend some time at the **Ted Williams Museum and Hitters Hall of Fame.** The hall dedicates eight

TEN BEST MAJOR-LEAGUE BALLPARKS

10 Kauffman Stadium   The addition of a natural grass playing field makes an already outstanding park that much better. The waterfalls and fountains beyond the right and center field stands provide a great show after games.

 9 The Ballpark in Arlington   As fan-friendly a park as there is in the majors. A great sense of nostalgia and all the amenities, including the Ballpark Grill, a bar/restaurant overlooking the field. Hall of fame murals and frieze sculptures depicting Texas history are a nice touch.

 8 Coors Field   Stadium designers took all the best ideas of Camden Yards, Jacobs Field, and The Ballpark in Arlington, set it down in the heart of baseball-crazy Denver and made sure to provide a great view of the Rocky Mountains.

 7 Comerica Park   The carnival atmosphere, the Ferris wheel, carousel, giant tiger statues everywhere, and the player statues beyond the outfield—my favorite baseball art in the big leagues—add up to one great ballpark.

 6 Jacobs Field   A much needed replacement of Municipal Stadium. The downtown location, modern conveniences, and nostalgic feel add up to a great baseball experience.

 5 Pacific Bell Park   Nostalgic atmosphere, great food, all the amenities fans could ask for, but the effort to involve young kids without trying to dig any further into mom and dad's wallet is what impressed me most about this brand-new park.

 4 Yankee Stadium   "The House that Ruth Built" led the way in 1923 and remains one of the game's true cathedrals.

 3 Oriole Park at Camden Yards   Accomplishes a combination of nostalgia and modern fan amenities unlike any park before or since. If at all possible, sit downstairs along the first base line and be sure not to miss the crabcake sandwiches or Boog's Barbecue.

 2 Wrigley Field   A classic for the very same reasons as Fenway. Wrigley's ivy-covered walls, classic center field scoreboard, and the overall Wrigleyville atmosphere make for a great day at the ballpark.

 1 Fenway Park   A timeless park with great fan support, located in a great baseball neighborhood. The Green Monster, the stands' proximity to the field of play, and the manual scoreboard in left field set Fenway apart.

galleries and an eighty-seat theater to the "Splendid Splinter" and twenty other hitters selected by Williams as the game's best. Visitors will see a permanent collection of Red Sox memorabilia, including Williams' first contract, vintage equipment, film footage, sculpture, paintings, and prints. The museum is a short drive north of Tampa, at 2455 North Citrus Hills Boulevard in Hernando, Florida. It's open to the public every day, except Monday, from 10 AM–4 PM. Admission is just $3 for adults, and discounts are available for seniors and children. For more information, call (904) 527-6566.

For high-flying excitement, check out **Fantasy of Flight** in Polk City, about an hour east of Tampa. More than twenty-five historic aircraft reside here, as well as a number of realistic flight simulators that allow visitors to experience the thrill and drama of an aerial dogfight. There's also a full-scale, multimedia diorama of the interior of a B-17 Flying Fortress during a bombing run. Other aircraft include a B-24 Liberator, an FM2 Wildcat fighter plane, and a Supermarine Spitfire MK16. Fantasy of Flight is open daily from 9–5 and costs $10.95 for adults.

◆ TORONTO ◆

This place is great. It's like something out of 2001.

BRET SABERHAGEN

SKYDOME

The people of Toronto are very proud of their SkyDome. As a marvel of modern technology, they should be; as a ballpark, I'm not so sure. Like Montreal's Olympic Stadium, this ballpark has everything there is to dislike about a modern baseball facility: artificial turf, a retractable roof, symmetrical dimensions, a uniform 10-foot high outfield fence, loads of foul territory, and no real ballpark feel to it.

Unlike my Montreal trip, nothing about my experience at the Toronto game allowed me to get past all that. Our seats were incredibly overpriced considering how far they were from home plate—$25 for second-level outfield "sky club" seats, in front of the Hard Rock Cafe and Windows Restaurant. Despite the fancy name, these seats were nothing more than glorified bleacher seats. Similar seats at Yankee Stadium or Fenway Park, actually much closer to the infield, would cost $6–10. Our seats were a long way from home, but we were a whole lot closer than the unfortunate folks in the $4 sky deck seats. Perhaps the most disturbing part of our visit was the stadium's unenthusiastic atmosphere, despite a sizable crowd.

In fact, the place felt more like a shopping mall than a ballpark. We got there in the middle of the first inning and were pleased to see that the roof was open for the game that night. Aside from the distant playing field, there was almost nothing to indicate that we were at a ballpark. No crowd noise, no vendors hawking programs or souvenirs, not even the smell of hot dogs and popcorn. For all we knew, our cabby could have dropped us off at the wrong place. We got inside the concourse area and it was more of the same. We came across a McDonald's, but no indication of a main gate or how to get to our seats.

The first thing that strikes you is that the place is remarkably clean. Once you get to your seats, you can't help but be overwhelmed by the sheer size of the place. Just as most multiuse parks in the United States come up short in comparison to baseball-only facilities, the SkyDome—which the Blue Jays share with the Toronto Argonauts of the Canadian Football League—is too much of a bad thing. Too big a place, too many seats and gimmicks, not enough charm and character. The problem is only made worse by the fact that CFL fields are 30 yards longer than the NFL's.

Even though the roof was opened, the place didn't have the open-air feeling of a regular outdoor park. The roof weighs 11,000 tons and is made up of four sections, three of which slide inside the fourth. So the roof is at least one-quarter of the way closed at all times. That quarter is in the outfield end of the stadium where we were sitting, so that may have contributed to the sensation of being indoors despite the roof being open.

Some of the things I liked most about the park were the tremendous replay screen in right center and the view from the **Hard Rock Cafe** in right field. General admission to the Hard Rock during a game is $3 (you enter from outside the stadium and do not need to have a ticket to the game); reserved seating starts at $28, but that includes $23 towards your food and drink bill. Tickets go on sale one month in advance at the cafe. Another bar, **Sightlines**, overlooks the playing field as well. The **Windows** restaurant, just beyond right-center field, seemed more like a place to entertain clients or bring a date than a place I'd go to see a ball game. There is also a luxury hotel inside the dome, which is where all-star second baseman Roberto Alomar lived for his first few years with the Blue Jays. Seventy of the rooms have a view of the field. The hotel became somewhat notorious one night a few years ago as television cameras covering a game "accidentally" caught an amorous couple in a compromising position with the curtains open.

HISTORY

The Blue Jays opened the SkyDome with a midseason 5–3 loss to the Milwaukee Brewers on June 5, 1985. Their homefield woes continued as Oakland A's pitcher Dave Stewart fired a no-hitter against them on June 29, 1990. The very next year, the Jays went on to win their first division title and became the first team to draw four million fans in a single season.

Toronto beat the Atlanta Braves 1–0 on October 20, 1992, in the first World Series game played outside the United States. The Jays proceeded to win the series in seven games and brought Canada its first major-league baseball championship.

On October 23, 1993, Joe Carter led Toronto to a second straight World Series championship with a three-run dinger off Phillies pitcher Mitch "Wild

Thing" Williams in the bottom of the ninth inning of game six. Carter's blast gave the Jays an 8–6 victory.

GETTING TO THE SKYDOME
Bremner Boulevard and Blue Jays Way

The stadium is located just off the QEW, right in the heart of downtown, and is also accessible by subway (get on and off at Union Station next to the SkyDome). Right beside the stadium is the CN Tower, the tallest freestanding structure in the world, so if you are traveling by car, it's almost impossible to miss. There are no stadium lots, but parking lots in the vicinity seem to be adequate and not overly expensive (between $5 and $10). The area directly around the stadium, known as the **Harbourfront** area, has a number of restaurants and bars to grab a drink or a bite to eat before and after the game.

One warning though: Be careful if you park on a downtown street. It is illegal to park on many downtown streets on weekdays during rush hour in the mornings or evenings. In order to make the commute easier, all main thoroughfares are cleared of parked cars.

WHAT TO DO AND SEE IN TORONTO

Toronto is clean and new looking, and its people are polite and helpful. There is a vast selection of sights and attractions spread around the city and on the outskirts of town.

The **Royal Ontario Museum** is Canada's largest and, perhaps best, museum. It's unique in that it is a combination art, archaeology, and science museum housed in three buildings at one site. There are more than one million objects on display, from dinosaur skeletons to fine art, so expect to spend at least half a day if you hope to see even half of what's there. The museum is located on the Yonge/University subway line (get on and off at the museum station) at the corner of Bloor Street and Queens Park Avenue. Admission is free to all on Tuesdays between 4:30 and 8 PM; otherwise it is $7 for adults. Free guided tours are available.

A short walk south, in Queens Park, you'll find the **Ontario Parliament Buildings**, which were built in the late 1800s. The Legislative Assembly still holds sessions in the chambers, for which tickets are free. There are several historical displays within the buildings, as well as a number of paintings and sculptures. The buildings are open Monday through Friday at 9 AM. Admission is free.

Aerial view of the Skydome with the roof open. (Courtesy of the Toronto Blue Jays)

North of downtown Toronto, you'll find **Casa Loma**, a 98-room castle built in the early 1900s by Sir Henry Pellatt. It features magnificent, fully furnished rooms, six acres of gardens with a number of sculptures and fountains, and an 800-foot tunnel connecting the medieval-style mansion to the stables. Admission is $8 for adults, and there is an additional charge for parking.

If you prefer things more contemporary, two of Toronto's best attractions are within walking distance of each other right in the heart of downtown. The **Hockey Hall of Fame** recently moved into its new home, a classic structure known as the Great Bell Hall, at 161 Bay Street. The Hall features a number of interactive exhibits, such as a video simulator that allows you to play goalie, taking on one or two puck handlers trying to slide one by you. There is also an area where you can make a few shots on goal or even take a stab at calling your own play-by-play to some of hockey's greatest goals. Of course, you'll also see how players' equipment has changed over the years, and there's a lot of video footage and quite a few photos of the sport's heroes, such as Gordie Howe, Bobby Orr, and Cyclone Taylor. The highlight of a visit to the Hockey Hall of Fame is the octagon-shaped room with a 45-foot high stained-glass dome, that holds all of hockey's major trophies, including Lord Stanley's Cup. The Hall is open daily and costs $6.50 for adults.

If you take a not-so-short walk west on Front Street, you'll find the 1,815-foot **CN Tower**, the world's tallest structure. There are three observation decks, the highest of which is at 1,470 feet. There is also the **Top of Toronto** revolving restaurant and the **Horizons Nightclub**, at 1,150 and 1,135 feet, respectively. On clear days you can see Niagara Falls and the United States from the very highest observation deck. A trip to the top will set you back $12.95, but the view is one of the most impressive in the city.

Ontario Place is an entertainment and amusement complex on three man-made islands in Lake Ontario, just south of Exhibition Park. Highlights include an amusement park, a World War II destroyer, an outdoor concert facility, a six-story IMAX theater, shops, and restaurants. Ontario Place is open daily from 10:30 AM–1 AM from mid-May to Labor Day. Admission varies with special events. Call (416) 314-9899 for a recorded message about upcoming and current events.

The **Metro Toronto Zoo** is a short drive east of downtown in Scarborough. Considered one of the world's best zoos, it has more than 4,000 animals in natural habitat displays spread out over 710 acres. Fortunately, there is a monorail and zoo-mobile to help make it easier to see the entire zoo. Admission is $9 for adults.

NIGHTLIFE IN TORONTO

Toronto has an incredibly vibrant and happening nightlife. At any given time there is likely to be a number of rock, jazz, blues, and reggae superstars playing at area clubs and concert venues. It may help to pick up a copy of one of Toronto's free entertainment weeklies, *Now* or *Eye Weekly*. Both emphasize performing arts and list upcoming live music and comedy shows. A good deal of the nightlife is concentrated in areas not far from the SkyDome in the Harbourfront area or on Yonge and Spadina Streets, making it easy to check out a few clubs in one night. Listed below are a few of the area's more prominent clubs.

Appleby's   2787 Englington Avenue East (416) 266-1969   A sports bar with seven TVs, five pool tables, reasonable drink prices, a decent bar menu, and live music.

Bamboo   312 Queen Way (416) 593-5771   One of Toronto's best-known live music venues. Music runs the gamut from jazz to hiphop.

C'est What   67 Front Street (416) 867-9499   One of the city's premiere jazz clubs, with a casual cellar atmosphere, 30 kinds of beer on tap, and live music seven days a week.

Gretzky's   99 Blue Jays Way (416) 979-PUCK   "The Great One," Wayne Gretzky's nightclub, is just one block north of the SkyDome. The interior is crammed full of Gretzky memorabilia from childhood photos to NHL uniforms and equipment. Upstairs is a rooftop patio.

Horseshoe Tavern   370 Queen West (416) 598-4753   One of the city's most established live music bars, presenting live acts seven days a week.

Jerk Pit (North)   4611 Steeles Avenue West (416) 742-3011   Several locations, all specialize in reggae and blues by major recording artists. Cover varies with act, but expect top-rate talent and a cover between $10–20.

Phoenix Concert Theatre   410 Sherbourne Street (416) 323-1251   Don't let the name fool you. This place is equal parts nightclub and concert hall. The place begins to kick after 11 PM on the weekends and may very well have a line to get in.

WHERE TO STAY IN TORONTO

Because the city's attractions are spread out all around town, making it almost impossible to see them without a car of your own, it may not be so critical to stay in the heart of downtown Toronto. If you are without a car and don't intend to go to the zoo or Casa Loma, then downtown is your best option, as the subway and buses can shuttle you to and from most other attractions. Listed below are a few of the area hotels. For a more complete list, call (800) ONTARIO.

DOWNTOWN HOTELS

Best Western Metropolitan   108 Chestnut Street (800) 528-1234 or (416) 977-5000   Decent hotel with very affordable weekend rates available during the summer.

Beverly Place   235 Beverly Street (416) 977-0077   Historic Bed and Breakfast Inn on the outskirts of Queen's Park with very reasonable rates.

Clarion Essex Park Hotel   300 Jarvis Street (800) 567-2233 or (416) 977-4823   Newly renovated, European-style hotel. A short walk to the Yonge Street subway line.

Comfort Hotel   15 Charles Street (800) 424-6423 or (416) 924-1222   Newly remodeled, inexpensive hotel near the corner of Yonge and Bloor Streets.

Crowne Plaza Toronto Centre   225 Front Street (800) 422-7969 or (416) 597-1400   Nice accommodations at a bargain price, right beside the SkyDome and CN Tower.

Holiday Inn on King   370 King Street (800) HOLIDAY or (416) 599-4000   A short walk to the SkyDome, CN Tower, and the Harbourfront area.

Metropolitan   108 Chestnut Street (800) 668-6600 or (416) 977-5000   Decent hotel with very affordable weekend rates during the summer.

Novotel Toronto Centre   45 The Esplanade (800) 221-4542 or (416) 367-8900   Closest hotel to the Hockey Hall of Fame. Also near Yonge Street nightlife area.

Ramada Hotel & Suites   300 Jarvis Street (800) 567-2233 or (416) 977-4823   Newly renovated, European-style hotel. A short walk to the Yonge Street Subway line.

SkyDome Hotel   1 Blue Jays Way (800) 228-9290 or (416) 341-7100   Not inexpensive, but perhaps worth it to never have to leave your room to see a game.

TEAM HOTELS

Hilton International   (800) HILTONS or (416) 869-3456   Royals, A's, Mariners, and Rangers.

Harbour Castle   (416) 869-1600   White Sox, Indians, Tigers, Brewers, Twins, and Yankees.

Marriott Eaton Centre   (800) 228-9290 or (416) 597-9200   Red Sox.

Sheraton Centre   (800) 325-3535 or (416) 361-1000   Angels.

GOOD TO KNOW

- For schedule information or tickets to Blue Jays games, call (416) 341-1234. The Blue Jays official Internet address is www.bluejays.com.
- Blue Jays games can be heard on **CJCL 590 AM. THE FAN 1430 AM** is the area's leading all-sports station.
- To tour the SkyDome, call (416) 341-1000.
- For free information on sights, attractions, and hotels in Ontario, call **1-800-ONTARIO.**
- U.S. Citizens are entitled to a refund of all G.S.T. taxes they're charged

during their stay in Canada. There are certain conditions, of course, but it is worth your while to save receipts for hotels and purchases other than food and ball game tickets. On your way out of Canada, stop at the duty-free station to find out what expenses qualify for a refund, and get a credit to spend in the store, or U.S. currency.

Closest major league cities (and drive times): Detroit—257 miles (4 hours and 50 minutes); Cleveland—296 miles (5 hours and 30 minutes); Montreal—340 miles (6 hours and 5 minutes).

IN THE VICINITY

The Canadian side of **Niagara Falls** offers the more spectacular view, but the area around it has gotten to be more and more touristy. Nevertheless, the falls are certainly worth seeing. There is no charge to view the falls. If standing beside the top of the falls is not enough of a rush, you can take the *Maid of the Mist*, a boat that takes you out near the base of the falls. Another option is to take the elevator and the narrated tour that takes you behind the falls. There are separate admission charges for each. For more information about the Canadian Niagara Falls area, call (800) 563-2557.

THE MIDWEST

View of The Ballpark in Arlington from upstairs, behind home plate. (Courtesy of the
Texas Rangers)

◆ ARLINGTON ◆

It's breathtaking . . . . The fans here get the conven-
ience of new parks with the old look to it.

NOLAN RYAN

THE BALLPARK IN ARLINGTON

The bigger of 1994's two new ballparks—the home of the Texas Rangers—features a variety of seating choices (with a capacity of over 49,000 on 5 levels,
including suites) and a healthy dose of instant charm and nostalgia. You can
tell the designers of The Ballpark in Arlington did their homework, borrowing
ideas from the best stadiums in baseball and fusing them together to fashion
their own classic ballpark.

Some of those apparently borrowed features include: a two-tiered home
run porch in right field, complete with ceiling fans, reminiscent of Detroit's
Tiger Stadium; a white canopy facade around the inside top of the park a la
Yankee Stadium before its 1975 renovation; a manually operated out-of-town
scoreboard in the left field wall at ground level like Fenway Park's Green
Monster; and a brick exterior that resembles Camden Yards. Curiously, in an
otherwise brand-new park, the foul poles and bleacher seats from Arlington
Stadium were used in the new park. Another oddity is a small section of
ground-level seats in the right field corner where fans view the game through
an opening in the outfield fence.

The more modern conveniences include wide, comfortable seats and
aisles, elevators and reversible escalators to the upper levels, open concession
areas, cup holders at almost every seat, available handicapped seating for 480
wheelchairs, a 17,000 square foot **Legends of the Game** baseball museum,
and a restaurant/bar overlooking the field. The Ballpark also has more
concession stands and restrooms than the Rangers' old home, Arlington
Stadium.

93

The stadium's finishing touches include cast-iron Texas lone stars on each aisle seat, larger lone stars on steel trusses throughout the park, huge sepia-tone murals of sixty-seven individual Hall of Famers outside the entrance of each luxury suite, and four-foot by nineteen-foot frieze sculptures depicting ten different scenes from Texas history. These sculptures are each repeated nine times around the exterior of the park. Also adorning the outside of the park, high above the arched windows, are thirty-five steer heads and twenty-one lone stars cast in sand and concrete. If you can, be sure to stop by early to check out the Hall of Fame murals and "freeze" sculptures.

Among the park's unique quirks are the odd-shaped bullpens that almost look like they were placed as an afterthought. The Rangers bullpen runs parallel to the fence in right center, making for some interesting angles on the outfield wall and pushing the fence to a distance of just 377 feet from home plate. The visitors bullpen is perpendicular to the fence in the left-center field power alley. Both bullpens are raised to make it easier to identify pitchers as they warm up.

There is a good deal of foul territory behind and around home plate making the seats near first and third base the closest to the diamond. Club level tickets are the most expensive in the park at $16. Seats at the front of sections 35–37 are some of the best in the house because they jut out onto the field somewhat closer to first base and are angled toward the pitchers' mound. If you can't sit downstairs, the upper deck seats directly behind home plate are a good value at $10 and offer a nice panoramic view of the park. The first fifteen rows on either level of the right field home run porch, as well as the entire first level of left field stands are better than average outfield seats at $8 and offer a fair chance to snare a home run ball.

The Rangers have also made an effort to make the ball game experience affordable for families, offering discounts for children in the grandstand reserved and bleacher sections. Tickets for kids in those sections are $3 and $2 respectively. On the other end of the spectrum is the **Friday's Front Row Grill** in right field above and behind the home run porch. For $108 you get 4 window seats overlooking the field and $54 credit toward your food and drink expenses.

I have only two minor complaints about my visit to the Ballpark in Arlington. First, there is a little too much neon signage in the outfield. And second, during the seventh-inning stretch they played just one chorus of "Take Me Out to the Ball Game" and broke directly into some square dance music. Perhaps I'm too much of a traditionalist, but that seemed almost sacrilegious. Plus, I felt pretty stupid as I started singing the second verse all by myself. Perhaps you can learn from my mistake and save yourself from similar embarrassment.

HISTORY

The Ballpark in Arlington, opened in 1994, is one of the newest parks in the big leagues and as such does not have too many stories to tell. That may change soon, as the Rangers are a talented young club playing before enthusiastic crowds who expect the Rangers to venture deep into the postseason in the coming years. The stadium's first regular season game was on opening day, April 11, 1994, as the Rangers hosted the Milwaukee Brewers. The Brewers stole the Rangers' thunder by collecting the stadium's first hit and home run and also won the game 4–3.

Jose Canseco, playing for Texas at the time, provided a glimpse of things to come, by blasting 3 home runs and driving in 8 runs on June 13 of the stadium's inaugural season. A little more than a month later, on July 28, Kenny Rogers of the Rangers pitched the park's first-ever no-hitter and just the 12th perfect game in major league history, with a 4–0 victory over the Angels.

GETTING TO THE BALLPARK IN ARLINGTON
1000 Ballpark Way

The Ballpark is located almost halfway between Dallas and Fort Worth just off I-30, less than 20 minutes from either city and even closer to the airport. The original stadium, located right next door, was called Turnpike Stadium at one time, so that should give you an idea of how easy it is to get to. There are no mass-transit options other than hotel shuttles and the city bus.

If you are flying into Dallas, consider yourself warned. The Dallas/Fort Worth airport is the second largest airport in the world. It may also be the most confusing. From the sky, the airport and surrounding roads look like a bowl of spaghetti. The place is so big that you have to take an unmanned shuttle tram and a bus from the terminals to rental car agencies. Several area hotels offer free shuttles to and from the airport. Taking advantage of this may allow you to return your rental car the day before you actually have to leave. Not only will that save you a day's rental fee, but it can also spare you the aggravation of returning your rental car and then trying to find your terminal for an outgoing flight.

WHAT TO DO AND SEE IN AND AROUND ARLINGTON

Arlington offers a few interesting attractions concentrated in the area surrounding the ballpark. **Six Flags Over Texas** is a 205-acre amusement park adjacent to the new ballpark and offers over 100 rides, shows, and midway games. The park's feature ride is the Texas Giant, rated the number 1 roller coaster in the world by *Fast Track* magazine. The park is open daily in the summer and on weekends in early spring and late fall. An all-inclusive admission is $24.95 for adults. **Wet 'n' Wild** is a water-oriented theme park. Like Six Flags, it is open daily in the late spring, summer, and early fall. Admission is $16.95 for adults.

Bobby Valentine's Sports Gallery Cafe is a great place to go before and after games. This sports bar has wall-to-wall baseball memorabilia, offers a free shuttle to and from the ballpark, and has twenty-five television sets on which to watch the game highlights or pregame show. While you're there, be sure to check out the Nolan Ryan room, which features a baseball card of every player he ever struck out. One of the area's more unusual attractions is the **Air Combat School**, which allows you to strap into an actual jet fighter cockpit/flight simulator and dogfight with bogey aircraft. Attending ground school and ejection training, donning your flight gear and the "flight" itself take about an hour and a half and costs $35 per person.

Dallas is where you'll find most of the area's more impressive sights and attractions. **The Sixth Floor Museum**, located in the School Book Depository, from which Lee Harvey Oswald is supposed to have shot President Kennedy, has become Dallas' most visited attraction. An effort has been made to keep the building laid out exactly as it was when Kennedy was assassinated, giving the place an eerie feeling. Admission is $4; for $2 more you'll be given a Walkman-type cassette player that describes what each exhibit is. The audio tour was well worth the extra couple of dollars, as it routes you through what might otherwise be a confusing, haphazard layout. To the museum's credit, it did not completely dismiss theories that there may have been others behind Kennedy's assassination.

Within a few blocks of the museum, before you get to the **West End Historic District**, you'll pass by the **West End Pub** at 211 N. Record Street. There's nothing fancy or trendy about the place, but it does have a friendly staff, excellent bar food, and a genuine pub atmosphere. If it's not your cup of tea, continue on toward the West End Historic District, which has a tremendous selection of eateries and taverns. You'll also find the **West End Marketplace**, an indoor mall with some very unique shops and push carts. I especially liked the hologram art and sculpture store.

At night, the West End area swells with revelers checking out the thirty restaurants and eight nightclubs that offer a variety of live bands playing rock, jazz, R&B, and blues. A few of the places are a little on the touristy side, but nearly all of them have ice-cold Texas beer on tap and serve a mean frozen margarita. **Dick's Last Resort**, a laid-back place on North Market Street, where you're likely to hear a little Dixieland jazz, and the **Dallas Brewing Company**, a handsome microbrewery at 703 McKinney Avenue, were among my favorites. If you are in town in mid-July, you may want to head to the West End Market for the annual **Taste of Dallas** food festival.

A few miles northwest of downtown Dallas, in the city of Irving, Cowboys fans will want to tour **Texas Stadium** for a behind-the-scenes look at the home of "America's Team." You'll see the Cowboy's locker room, a luxury skybox, and if you feel the urge, you can charge out of the tunnel and onto the field, where you are welcome to run a few pass patterns or even kick a field goal or two. Be sure to bring your own ball, though. The tour costs $5 for adults.

Fort Worth's **Kimball Art Museum**, at 3333 Comp Bowie Boulevard in the **Fort Worth Cultural District**, generally has free admission when it's not hosting special traveling exhibits.

The **Fort Worth Museum of Science and History** is located at 1501 Montgomery Street and consists of seven exhibit halls displaying everything from dinosaurs to computers. The museum is also home to the **Noble Planetarium** and the **Omni Theater**, which features an eighty-foot domed screen and state-of-the-art sound system. Admission to the museum is $3 for adults, the planetarium costs another $3, and films in the Omni Theater are $5.50.

The **Fort Worth Stockyards District** is a ten-block historic area that was once one of the largest cattle markets in the world. Today it's a huge entertainment and shopping complex, where you can take a ride on the **Tarantula Steam Train**, down a few cold ones at the **White Elephant Saloon**, or learn how to two-step at **Billy Bob's Texas**, the world's largest country-and-western honky tonk.

NIGHTLIFE IN AND AROUND ARLINGTON

A good source for information on Dallas' nightlife is the *Dallas Observer*, a free alternative tabloid, or call the **Dallas Events Hotline** at (214) 746-6679. The area's premiere nightspots, with a cutting edge flair for alternative, blues, and heavy metal music, are located in the section of town known as **Deep Elum**. The area has a more urban, less touristy, feel to it than the West End and doesn't really get hopping until later in the evening. My favorite nightclubs were **July Alley**, a dark, rowdy place with great progressive music at 2809 Elm Street, and **Club Dada**, down the street at 2720 Elm Street, which has live music nightly. All told, there are about seventeen clubs in the immediate vicinity, including **Adair's Saloon**, **Trees**, and **On the Rocks**. If you get there early and have an appetite for a good, inexpensive meal, consider stopping by the **Deep Elum Cafe** or one of the area's other eateries. For more information about Deep Elum happenings, call the **What's Up Line** at (214) 747-DEEP.

Elsewhere in town, be sure to check out one of the **Dave and Busters**, which feature billiards, no-keeps blackjack casinos, shuffleboard, and video games galore. There's one at 8021 Walnut Hill and another at 10727 Composite. A sports bar owned by ex-Cowboys is the **Cowboy's Sports Cafe** at 9454 North McArthur Boulevard, in Valley Ranch. Owners Tony Dorsett, Everson Walls, Eugene Lockhart, and Alfredo Roberts occasionally stop by.

Blues fans might want to stop by **Blue Cat Blues**, at 2617 Commerce. They generally book regional and nationally known blues acts. **The Improvisation**, at 4980 Beltline Road, is the area's preeminent comedy club.

Another area known for its nightlife is **Greenville Avenue**, between the LBJ Freeway and Ross Avenue, north of downtown. Upper Greenville offers a number of discos and '50s and '60s style clubs, while lower Greenville has a number of neighborhood pubs and sports bars. Below McCommas on Greenville Avenue, check out **Zubar**, an alternative club with a patio overlooking the street that allows for great people watching, or **Milk Bar**, which offers thumping dance music, a nightclub atmosphere, and a rooftop patio.

WHERE TO STAY IN AND AROUND ARLINGTON

The Arlington area, because it is equidistant from Dallas and Fort Worth, presents a number of options in places to stay. If you plan to see the sights of both Dallas and Fort Worth, in addition to a ball game and the other sights of Arlington, it may be a good idea to stay right in Arlington. That way you won't have a commute of much more than twenty minutes in either direction. Hotels near Dallas-Fort Worth International Airport offer a similar benefit, as the airport is conveniently located between all three cities. Below is a partial list of area hotels.

ARLINGTON HOTELS

Best Western 3501 East Division (800) 528-1234 or (817) 640-7722 Just two miles from the stadium and offers a free shuttle to airport Monday–Friday 8 AM–5 pm.

Country Suites 1075 Wet 'n' Wild Way (800) 456-4000 or (817) 261-8900 One mile from the ballpark, twenty minutes from Fort Worth and Dallas.

Courtyard Marriott 1500 Nolan Ryan Expressway (800) 321-2211 or (817) 277-2774 Across from stadium and within walking distance of Six Flags amusement park.

LaQuinta Inn 825 North Watson Road (800) 531-5900 or (817) 640-4142 Half a mile from the stadium, a short walk to Six Flags and Wet 'n' Wild.

DALLAS HOTELS

Best Western Market Center 2023 Market Center Boulevard (800) 275-7419 or (214) 741-9000 Complimentary breakfast, on-site lounge, and shuttle.

Country Suites   4100 West John Carpenter, Irving (800) 456-4000 or (972) 929-4008   One mile from the airport, fifteen minutes from Arlington and Dallas.

Drury Inn   4210 West Airport Freeway, Irving (800) 325-8300 or (972) 986-1200   One mile from DFW Airport. Complimentary buffet breakfast and courtesy van.

FORT WORTH HOTELS

Comfort Inn   2425 Scott Avenue   (800) 424-6423 or (817) 535-2591   Complimentary breakfast, pool, exercise room, and tennis courts.

Courtyard Marriott   3150 Riverfront Drive (800) 321-2211 or (817) 335-1300   Fifteen miles from the stadium. Pool, whirlpool, and exercise room on-site.

Ramada Hotel Downtown   1701 Commerce (800) 272-6232 or (817) 335-7000   Indoor pool and Jacuzzi. Airport transportation available.

TEAM HOTELS

Arlington Hilton   2401 East Lamar Boulevard   (800) HILTONS or (817) 640-0440   White Sox and Indians.

Arlington Marriot   1500 Convention Center Drive East   (800) 442-7275 or (817) 261-8200   All American League teams except the White Sox, Indians, and Yankees.

Hyatt Regency Dallas   300 Reunion Boulevard (800) 233-1234 or (214) 651-1234   Yankees.

GOOD TO KNOW

- For schedule information or tickets to Rangers games, call (817) 273-5100. The Rangers' official Internet address is www.texasrangers.com.
- Ranger games can be heard on **KRLD 1080 AM**. **KTCK 1310 AM** is the area's leading all-sports station.
- For tickets to preseason or early-season **Cowboys** games, call (214) 579-5000. For **Dallas Stars** tickets, call (214) GO-STARS. For **Mavericks** tickets, call (214) 658-7068.
- For more information on Arlington area sights and attractions, call the **Convention and Visitors Bureau** at (800) 433-5374. The city's official Web site is www.arlington.org.
- For information on any of the Fort Worth attractions call (800) 433-5747 or (817) 332-2000.
- The PGA Byron Nelson Classic is held every year in Irving, Texas, in mid-May.

TEN BEST ATTRACTIONS NEAR OR IN A MAJOR-LEAGUE CITY

10 **The National Aquarium**—Baltimore, Maryland   The Inner Harbor's crowning achievement, albeit a bit expensive.

9 **DisneyLand**—Anaheim, California   The world's original theme park is still the best.

8 **Rock and Roll Hall of Fame**—Cleveland, Ohio   A tremendous tribute to America's music heritage that has helped transform the city of Cleveland.

7 **Vietnam Memorial**—Washington, D.C.   Simply the most moving man-made structure I have ever seen anywhere. In a city that is replete with images of power, this simple memorial is an absolute must-see.

6 **Mount Rainier**—Seattle, Washington   On a clear day Mount Rainier is a glimpse of nature at its best. The entire Northwest is a national treasure.

5 **Niagara Falls**—New York/Canadian border near Toronto   A powerful demonstration of nature's might. The sound alone is astounding, especially from tunnels behind the falls or aboard the "Maid of the Mist" which brings you near the base of the falls.

4 **The Gateway Arch**—Saint Louis, Missouri   An awesome sight along the Mississippi River with a sweeping view of the city and ballpark from its apex.

3 **Statue of Liberty**—New York, New York   Another signature landmark with a tremendous view of the surroundings, although the hike to the top is considerably more rigorous.

2 **Golden Gate Bridge**—San Francisco   Walk to the middle and take in the city skyline as yachts, cruise ships, and supertankers pass below you. The surrounding park has miles of walking trails and a wealth of incredible views.

1 **The Grand Canyon**—Arizona   Absolutely awesome. The sunrises and sunsets are the most remarkable I've ever seen. Hike or ride a mule to the basin, take a helicopter ride through the interior, or better yet, traverse the Colorado River aboard a guided raft for the complete experience.

Closest major league cities (and drive times): Houston—246 miles (4 hours and 15 minutes); Kansas City—512 miles (9 hours and 50 minutes).

IN THE VICINITY

Consider taking a road trip to **Austin, Texas**, the state's capital city, which offers a nice blend of history and nightlife. The atmosphere on **6th Street** is comparable to New Orleans' Bourbon Street, or Crescent and Saint Laurent streets in Montreal. There are dozens of nightclubs and restaurants with just about every kind of music you could hope to find.

One of the city's other claims to fame is that it is home to the live music TV show **Austin City Limits**, which is shown around the country on PBS. The show is taped August–February with 100 seats available to the public for each show. Tickets are free, but go quickly, so call (512) 471-4811 ext. 310 or 475-9077 well in advance.

The **Lyndon B. Johnson Library**, at 2313 Red River Street, is the most visited presidential library in the country. It is open from 9 to 5 daily, and admission is free. For more information, call (512) 482-5137.

The historic **Driskill Hotel** is a great place to stay, right in the heart of the action, at the corner of Brazos and 6th Street. For more information about things to do and see in Austin, call the **Convention and Visitors Bureau** at (800) 888-8287.

◆ CHICAGO ◆

*All ballparks should look like (old) Comiskey Park.
Modern parks are too antiseptic. You come here, and
it feels like baseball.*

TOM SEAVER

*Wrigley Field is a Peter Pan of a ballpark. It has never
grown up and it has never grown old.*

E. M. SWIFT

THE NEW COMISKEY PARK

A lot of fans think there was no need to replace the original Comiskey Park.
Most folks who have been to both will tell you that the new Comiskey does
not have the old park's charm and intimacy. However, new Comiskey was the
first baseball-only stadium built for major-league play since Kansas City's
Royals Stadium opened in 1972, reversing the trend of building massive, multisport stadiums that lacked the feel of a ballpark. More important, the new
park is a pretty good place to see a game.

While it's true that the new Comiskey has symmetrical outfield dimensions,
a uniform 8-foot outfield fence, a lot of foul territory, and far too many advertising billboards, it also has quite a bit going for it. The playing surface is natural grass, there's a nice variety of affordable seating options, some excellent
concessions, all the modern conveniences you could ask for, and the most
entertaining scoreboard in the major leagues. Comiskey was built by HOK
Sports, who also designed two of the big league's best parks, Camden Yards in
Baltimore and Denver's Coors Field. The infield dirt was transported from
the old Comiskey Park, and the new 140-foot-wide by 30-foot-high exploding
scoreboard was modeled after the original stadium's smaller, manually oper-

ated version. I wouldn't put the new Comiskey in my top-ten favorite ball-parks, but it wouldn't miss by much.

Comiskey seats just 44,321 fans, but is a surprisingly spacious stadium. A long concourse of concession and souvenir stands runs behind the outfield bleachers, contributing to the park's wide-open feel. It also allows fans to follow the game while they stand in line. One of the park's more unique menities is a coat and briefcase checkroom, which I suppose is for business people who sneak away from the office for a nine-inning lunch. And Comiskey is the only major-league stadium that offers a place to check your pet (at gate 7, in center field) in case you just can't bear to leave the house without Fido.

There's also a Kids' Corner in right field, with a play area and concession stand with pint-size concessions. On the left field side of the main and upper concourses, you can have your own personal baseball card made for just $5. Souvenir shops are scattered about the park, and there's an ATM on the main concourse behind home plate. Near the ATM you'll find the White Sox Hall of Fame, which has a $1 entry fee and features artifacts from the past, like Shoeless Joe Jackson's original contract.

As I mentioned earlier, Comiskey has one of the big league's best score-boards. Located in straightaway center field, it consists of a twenty-six-foot high, thirty-seven-foot wide Sony JumboTron screen and a state-of-the-art play-by-play board. Every time a White Sox player hits a home run, pinwheels spin and fireworks spew from the top of the scoreboard.

Our seats also added to the fun. I saw the game from a luxury skybox look-ing right down the third base line from behind home plate. It felt as if the game were being played right outside my hotel room, and all I had to do was open the window to let in all the sights, sounds, and smells of the game. The box came with a completely stocked refrigerator and a private bathroom. Attendants came by and took orders for food, and toward the end of the game, they even wheeled in a dessert cart. The box was also equipped with a loudspeaker, through which official scoring decisions were relayed into the suite. All in all, it was a great way to see a game. I wouldn't want to see every ballgame in a skybox—half the fun for me is being outdoors—but it was cer-tainly nice to have the opportunity to do it once.

Aside from complimentary skybox seats, the lower deck boxes at $22 are the best seat bargain in the park, especially those in sections 120–125 and 140–145, as they are closest to the field. Other options include club level seats at $22, upper boxes for $15, lower deck reserved seats—which are mostly in fair territory near the foul poles—at $17, and upper deck reserved seats for $5–10. Reserved bleachers, which unlike a lot of bleachers do have seat backs, are located on either side of the hitters' background and sell for $14. The park doesn't have too many seats at a price that encourage you to bring the

Close up of the league's most entertaining scoreboard at Comiskey Park.
(Photo by Author)

whole family, but when I was there, they did offer a two-for-one deal on Mondays, so be sure to inquire about specials.

HISTORY

New Comiskey opened April 18, 1991, with an afternoon game against the Detroit Tigers. The game was not exactly what the Sox had hoped for as the Tigers won 16–0. In addition to the stadium's first victory, the Tigers got the park's first-ever walk, hit, double, triple, home run, run, RBI, stolen base, double steal, and shutout. Since then the Sox have been equally unsuccessful in playoff games at the new Comiskey, losing all three postseason games they have played there as the Toronto Blue Jays beat them four games to two in the 1993 ALCS.

In the stadium's brief history, a few milestones have been reached. Comiskey saw Carlton Fisk break Bob Boone's record of 2,225 games played as a catcher on June 22, 1993. Later that same season, Frank "The Big Hurt" Thomas broke the White Sox single-season HR record with his thirty-eighth round-tripper on September 1. The stadium's most electrifying moment may have been on opening day of that same year, when Bo Jackson hit a home run on his very first swing of the season after having hip replacement surgery in the off-season.

GETTING TO COMISKEY
333 West 35th Street

The New Comiskey is located just across the street from where the old park stood, on the south side of Chicago. From downtown Chicago you'll want to take the Dan Ryan Expressway south to the 35th Street exit or Lake Shore Drive south to the 31st Street exit. Parking for those without season-tickets is at 35th Street in a secured lot. Do not try to save a few dollars by parking your car in an unsecured area in the neighborhood surrounding Comiskey Park, as you could come back to find your car missing or vandalized. There are 7,000 parking spots at the stadium.

If stadium lots fill up, there is additional parking, served by a free shuttle, at the Illinois Institute of Technology, two blocks east of the ballpark. The shuttle picks up and drops off at the corner of Wentworth and 35th Street. The ballpark is also served by bus and elevated train from the Chicago area. The "El" platform is conveniently located adjacent to the park and much less expensive than parking your car. For more info on mass transit options, call the Travel Information Center at (312) 836-7000.

WRIGLEY FIELD

Wrigley is just the opposite of Comiskey. The "friendly confines" of Wrigley Field offer almost no amenities other than the basics—no flashy scoreboard, no fireworks, pet check rooms, or other such gimmicks. Just a great baseball park in a great neighborhood where you can see the game the way it should be—up close and personal.

Half the fun of attending a Cubs game is getting to Wrigleyville an hour or two before game time and taking part in the pregame activity. There are a host of bars, restaurants, souvenir shops, and street vendors scattered about a middle-class neighborhood on the north side of Chicago. Many of the bars are so crowded before and after games that long waits can be expected if you show up too close to game time.

The other advantage of arriving early is that convenient parking, within a short walk of the park, is much easier to find at least an hour and a half before game time. Prepare to pay at least $10 to park, as Wrigley has some of the most expensive and scarce parking in baseball. Parking passes in the Cubs green lot, a block north of the stadium on Grace Street, can be ordered in advance for $12.50 when purchasing tickets by mail. Like Fenway Park, Wrigley was built in an era when cars were luxuries and people relied almost entirely on mass transit. Fortunately, Wrigley is still easily accessible by a number of mass transit options.

The third oldest park in use, Wrigley has more character than almost all of the middle-aged parks combined. One its quirks is that its power alleys are

A great day for baseball at the National League's oldest and best park, Wrigley Field. (Photo by Author)

actually shorter than in the corners, because the outfield walls jut out toward home plate to accommodate outfield bleacher seats. A giant, manually operated scoreboard and clock sit just to the right of straightaway center field, beyond the hitters' background. Just below the manual scoreboard is an electronic board that shows who is batting and how he is hitting for the day. On the first base side of the park, under the stands, you'll find the **Friendly Confines Cafe** and the **Cubs Hall of Fame**. Other characteristics unique to Wrigley Field are the bleacher-style seats atop buildings across the street and, of course, the infamous ivy-covered outfield walls.

After each Cubs game, a flag is raised on the center field flagpole to let commuters know if the Cubs won or lost. A white flag with a blue "W" signifies a win, a blue flag with a white "L" indicates a loss. Flags are also hung on each foul pole—Ernie Banks' number 14 from the right field pole, and Billy Williams' number 26 from the one in left. Three flagpoles atop the manual scoreboard host the pennants of teams in each National League division, in their respective order at the beginning of the day—the division leader is at the top of each flagpole and the cellar dweller at the bottom.

As almost any baseball fan knows, Wrigley was the last big league park to add lights and did not play its first night game until 1988. On August 8, the first attempt to play a game under the lights at Wrigley Field was rained out after three innings. The following night, they managed to play a complete game. Since then, the Cubs have deliberately limited night games to a handful each season, making these tickets very difficult to get. The ballpark takes on a surreal quality at night, and the atmosphere in Wrigleyville for night games rivals that of Rush and Division streets.

If I can help it, I won't sit anywhere other than the bleachers. Wrigley "bleacher creatures" are as fun a group as there is in baseball. If you do land bleacher seats don't hesitate to join in a game of "moundball" if one breaks out around you. Moundball is a game where fans all contribute a dollar to a kitty. The kitty is passed from fan to fan every half inning. If the ball ends up laying on the mound after the half inning and you are holding the kitty, you keep it. Who knows, you may end up winning back the price of your ticket, or better yet, your beer tab. I've been to hundreds of games, and every stadium in the big leagues, but only in Wrigley's bleachers have I seen so many "side bet games" pop up in the stands. If the bleachers sell out before you get to the park, don't despair. Even the worst seats at Wrigley are worth the price of admission.

For more information, write the Cubs box office at 1060 West Addison, Chicago, Illinois, 60613. Or call (800) 347-CUBS well in advance of the day you hope to see a game. Another option for purchasing tickets to Cubs and Sox games is the **Chicago Cubs Sports Shop**, which sells tickets for the day of the game or future games. All ticket sales at the Sports Shop are cash only. It's located at 445 North Michigan Avenue and open seven days a week.

If you find yourself in Chicago while the Cubs are out of town, tours of the friendly confines are available on nongame Saturdays during the regular season. Tours last about an hour and a half and cost $10. All proceeds go to Cubs Charities. Call (773) 831-2827 for more information.

HISTORY

Wrigley opened on April 23, 1914, as home to the Chicago Whales of the old Federal League. The Chicago Cubs played their first game there April 20, 1916. Some might be surprised to know that Wrigley actually hosted games 4 through 7 of the 1945 World Series as the Cubs faced the Detroit Tigers. The Cubs lost, and the Series hasn't been played at Wrigley since. The Cubs did reach the NLCS in 1984 and 1989, but lost both times.

Wrigley has been the site of many historic occasions, but a few stand out above the rest. On October 1, 1932, Babe Ruth hit his legendary "called shot" where he allegedly pointed to where he was going to hit a home run off Cubs pitcher Charley Root in game 3 of the World Series. A few years later, on September 28, 1938, Cubs catcher Gabby Hartnett hit the infamous "homer in the gloamin,'" a pennant-winning home run off Pirates pitcher Mace Brown just minutes before the game would have been called a tie because of darkness.

More recently, Pirates second baseman, Rennie Stennett, went 7 for 7 at the plate on September 16, 1975, as the Bucs beat the Cubs 22–0. Hall of Famer Mike Schmidt had one of his best days at the plate as the Phillies came back from a 12–1 deficit to win 18–16 in 10 innings. Schmidt hit four home runs in a single game to become just the tenth player to accomplish the feat. Also worth noting is that Schmidt's effort included home runs off a pair of brothers, Rick and Paul Reuschel.

On September 8, 1985, Pete Rose tied Ty Cobb's career record of 4,191 base hits with a single off Cubs pitcher Reggie Patterson. Rose, of course, went on to set the career base hit record of 4,256 hits.

GETTING TO WRIGLEY
1060 West Addison

Several area hotels offer free shuttles to Wrigley, making a stay there an even greater value when you consider the expense and hassle of parking at the park. There are a number of bus lines from downtown (your best options being the No. 152 Addison and the No. 22 Clark lines). But the "El," Chicago's elevated train system, is my favorite way to get to Wrigley Field, as the trains before and after games are packed with baseball fans. The "El" offers a peek at the field from the platform and a unique perspective of Chicago's neighborhoods between downtown and Wrigleyville. The Howard-Englewood/Jackson Park line runs to and from Wrigley via the Addison Street Station. Taking the "El" to a Cubs game is a big part of the Wrigley ballgame experience, so if at all possible, consider making it part of your plans. Call the Chicago Transit Authority for route and schedule information at (312) 836-7000.

WHAT TO DO AND SEE IN CHICAGO

Chicago, like New York and San Francisco, offers more than you can see and do in a short stay. You may want to begin with the **Chicago Cultural Center**, an impressive structure at 78 East Washington Street, if for no other reason than to visit the **Chicago Office of Tourism Visitor Information Center**.

One "don't miss" attraction is **Buckingham Fountain** in **Grant Park**. The fountain is instantly recognizable from a host of TV shows and movies, and features a spectacular light show from 9–11 PM every night. Grant Park is right on the shores of Lake Michigan and offers a great view of the Chicago skyline. It also has miles of walking trails, several playing fields, and hosts many of Chicago's great festivals. Two of these festivals are certainly worth planning your trip around. **Taste of Chicago** is held in late June through the July Fourth Weekend, and the **Chicago Blues Festival** is generally held toward the beginning of June.

The **Sears Tower** is the world's second tallest building and offers a spectacular view of the city from the 103rd floor skydeck observatory. In the building's lobby, you'll come across "Universe," a giant, 8-ton mobile by artist Alexander Calder. Adult admission to the observation deck is $6, with discounts available for children and senior citizens. The **Navy Pier**, which has been completely remodeled, extends more than a half mile out into Lake Michigan and offers a fantastic view of the Chicago skyline. The pier is a great place for a jog, bike ride, or even a picnic.

Chicago has several fine museums. For information on current exhibits, call (312) FINE-ART. The **Art Institute of Chicago** at 111 South Michigan Avenue is one of the country's best, boasting an outstanding permanent collection of European paintings and sculpture. Admission is $6 for adults, $3 for children and senior citizens, except for Tuesdays, when admission is free for everyone. The **Field Museum of Natural History**, located near **Soldier Field** at Roosevelt Road off Lake Shore Drive, is also one of the best of its kind. The museum's centerpiece is the world's largest mounted dinosaur, a brachiosaurus. Admission is $5, except for Thursdays when it's free.

The **Shedd Aquarium**, within walking distance of the Field Museum, at 1200 Lake Shore Drive, is the largest indoor aquarium in the world. More than 6,000 marine animals are kept here. You'll see sharks, dolphins, otters, sea turtles, and even a few beluga whales among the aquarium's more than 700 species of aquatic life. Admission to both the aquarium and oceanarium is $8 for adults; admission to just the aquarium is $4. You can visit the aquarium free on Thursdays. Advance tickets are recommended. The **Adler Planetarium** is also nearby, at 1300 South Lake Shore Drive, and offers three floors of exhibits on the solar system, astronauts, and space exploration, as well as a fascinating hour-long sky show. Admission is just $4 for adults and $2 for children.

The **Museum of Science and Industry** features thousands of hands-on exhibits that demonstrate basic scientific principles. There are science-related exhibits that change regularly, in addition to permanent exhibits, which include the **Henry Crown Space Center** and **Omnimax Theater**. Admission is $5 for adults. There is no admission charge on Thursdays. The museum is located at 57th Street and Lake Shore Drive. Parking is free.

NIGHTLIFE IN CHICAGO

Chicago has a wealth of things to do at night, certainly more than I could list here. Your best resource is Chicago's excellent weekly alternative newspaper, *The Reader*. Turn directly to the third section for the majority of the nightclub ads. Their "critics' choices" are generally worth heeding, but be sure to peruse the ads as well. Most folks know that **Rush and Division** streets are home to many of Chicago's premiere nightclubs, but there's plenty to do all over the city. Here is a partial listing of Chicago's better nightspots.

LIVE MUSIC

Bamboo Bernies   2247 N. Lincoln Avenue (312) 549-3900   In the heart of Lincoln Park. Indoor beach volleyball and a tropical atmosphere. What else could you ask for?

Blue Chicago   937 State Street (312) 642-6261   Regularly hosts major league blues talent. Not far from Rush Street. Get there early for a good seat.

B.L.U.E.S.   2519 N. Halsted Street (312) 528-1012   Hosts the best in Chicago blues and nationally known artists. Great atmosphere, open until 3 AM.

B.L.U.E.S. Etcetera   1124 W. Belmont (312) 525-8989   Same as above, only bigger and better. National acts on the weekends.

Buddy Guy's Legends   754 Wabash Avenue (312) 427-0333   Owned by the legendary Grammy-winning musician, who occasionally shows up to take the stage with the headliner. On most nights you can expect to see top-name acts and even a few celebrities. Live blues seven days a week.

Cubby Bear   1059 West Addison (773) 327-1662 or 477-SHOW   Across the street from Wrigley Field, but this place is not just for before and after the game. They regularly host a wide variety of top musical acts.

Hi-Topps Cafe   3551 North Sheffield Avenue (312) 348-0009   In the heart of Wrigleyville, with a festive atmosphere, good chow, live music, and satellite sports on all five of their big-screen TVs and thirty-three monitors.

Kingston Mines   2548 N. Halsted (312) 477-4646   Live music seven days a week with a second stage on weekends. Open until 4 AM every day except Saturdays when they are open until 5 AM. A favorite spot with celebrities when they are in town.

Mothers   26 West Division Street (312) 642-7251   One of the places that makes Division Street famous. For twenty years this has been one of Chicago's hottest clubs. Featured in the movie *About Last Night*.

The Wild Hare (and Singing Armadillo Frog Sanctuary)   3530 N. Clark (773) 327-HARE   Claims to be the reggae capitol of the United States, which is hard to dispute. The atmosphere is 100 percent fun, and the place is definitely worth stopping by.

Yakos   1330 N. Halsted (312) 642-7706   One of Chicago's premiere jazz spots. Books top rate jazz musicians and bands on a regular basis.

OTHER PLACES WORTH MENTIONING

ESPN Zone   43 East Ohio Street (at Wabash) (312) 644-3776   Check out the model of Wrigley Field constructed entirely of chewing gum wrappers, the "Baseball Tonight Bar" that tracks the home run battle between Sammy and Big Mac with photos of all the stadiums, where the home runs landed, and their distance. For the VIP treatment, reserve the Sammy Sosa or Ernie Banks skybox.

Murphy's Bleachers   3655 North Sheffield Avenue (773) 281-5356   Right across the street from Wrigley Field. It's always packed with Cubs fans, before and after the game.

She-Nannigans Irish Pub and Sports Bar   16 West Division Street (312) 642-2344   Chicago's oldest sports bar is a good place to start a night on Division Street. She-Nannigans boasts a comfortable atmosphere, friendly staff, reasonably priced beers, and fourteen strategically placed TVs.

COMEDY PLACES

Second City   1616 N. Wells Street (312) 337-3992   Chicago's best-known comedy troupe is essentially a farm team for the Saturday Night Live TV show. You're likely to see tomorrow's stars hamming it up on stage at Second City. Call for reservations, as shows tend to get packed, especially on weekends.

Zanies   1548 N. Wells Street (312) 337-4027   The top national acts in Chicago can usually be found here. Most of the better-known stand-up comedians have played here at one point in time.

WHERE TO EAT IN CHICAGO

Chicago is famous for its steaks, ribs, and deep-dish pizza, so it would be a shame if you didn't try at least one of its specialties while you are in town. Here's a list of some of Chicago's more renowned eateries.

Berghoff Restaurant   17 West Adams Street (312) 427-3170   A Chicago institution offering German specialties as well as steaks, poultry, and fresh fish since 1898. Home of Berghoff Dortmunder beers.

Chicago Chop House   60 W. Ontario (312) 787-7100   Rated as one of the country's top-ten steak houses by the Knife and Fork Club. They specialize in huge steaks served in an upscale atmosphere.

Ed Debevic's   640 N. Wells Street (312) 664-1707   Moderately priced, blue collar, '50s style diner that has become one of Chicago's favorites. Eating here is much more than a meal; it's an experience. Expect to wait for a table.

Gino's East   160 E. Superior (312) 943-1124   *People* magazine rated their deep-dish pizza number 1 and it would be hard to disagree. Dark, cozy atmosphere with friendly, attentive service. Expect to wait during lunch and dinner hours.

Harry Caray's   33 W. Kinzie at Dearborn (312) HOLYCOW   A great base-ball atmosphere packed with baseball fans, specializing in prime steaks and classic Italian dishes. As you might expect in a place owned by the Cubs Hall of Fame announcer, Budweiser is the beer of choice.

Morton's of Chicago   1050 North State Street (312) 266-4820   A big favorite with major league ballplayers. Now you can find Morton's all over the country, but it all began right here in "The Windy City." They special-ize in prime, aged steaks, and whole Maine lobsters.

Nick's Fishmarket   One First National Plaza (312) 621-0200   Locals will tell you it's Chicago's best seafood. Classy atmosphere and attentive wait staff. This place is expensive, but you only live once so what the heck—splurge! Reservations are required.

Pizzeria Uno   29 East Ohio Street (312) 321-1000   The originator of Chicago's deep-dish pizza. Recently renovated, perhaps taking away some of the original charm, but the pizza remains the same. Pizzeria Due is just down the block and offers the same menu with a shorter wait.

Ruth's Chris Steak House   431 N. Dearborn (312)321-2725   Another favorite with ballplayers. Ruth's began in New Orleans but are now located in several major league cities and feature huge cuts of steaks, lamb, veal, pork chops, and live lobster.

WHERE TO STAY IN CHICAGO

Be warned: Staying at a hotel in Chicago costs some major bucks. During the week, there is almost no way around it, as the hotels know they are going to be inundated with business travelers. There are some deals to be had on weekends, however, so inquire about weekend rates, ballgame packages, or other such discounts. If you are going to be in town for a few days or more, you'll probably want to stay downtown and commute to the games. Here is a short list of hotels.

HOTELS NEAR WRIGLEY FIELD

Belmont Suites   3170 North Sheridan Road (773) 248-2100   Near Lincoln Park, a short walk from the stadium.

City Suites   933 West Belmont (773) 404-3400   A short walk from Wrigley. Hotel features inexpensive parking, available two-room suites, and a friendly staff.

Comfort Inn   601 Diversey Parkway (800) 221-2222 or (773) 348-2810   Within a fifteen-minute walk of Wrigley Field. Complimentary breakfast and cable TV.

Surf Hotel   555 West Surf (773) 528-8400   Within walking distance of the park. Inexpensive parking available.

DOWNTOWN HOTELS

Clarion Executive Plaza   71 East Wacker Drive (800) 621-4005 or (312) 346-1721   Overlooking the Chicago River.

Midland Hotel   172 West Adams Street (800) 621-2360 or (312) 332-1200   Complimentary breakfast buffet and early evening cocktails, near the Sears Tower.

Ohio House   600 North LaSalle Street (312) 943-6000   An affordable place to stay in the up-and-coming River North area.

The Seneca   200 East Chestnut (800) 800-6261 or (312) 787-8900   Convenient location with reasonable rates, just east of Michigan Avenue.

DELUXE DOWNTOWN HOTELS

Chicago Hilton and Towers   720 South Michigan Avenue (800) HILTONS or (312) 922-4400   Deluxe accommodations in the heart of the shopping district.

Palmer House   17 East Monroe Street (800) HILTONS or (312) 726-7500   Plush accommodations, great location near Grant Park, Sears Tower, and Art Institute.

Renaissance Hotel   1 West Wacker Drive (800) 228-9290 or (312) 372-7200   Prepare to be spoiled by luxury rooms and a convenient location.

TEAM HOTELS

Hyatt Regency   151 East Wacker Drive (800) 233-1234 or (312) 565-1234   Angels, Indians, Braves, Dodgers, Phillies, and Cardinals.

Westin   909 N. Michigan Avenue (800) 228-3000 or (312) 943-7200   All other clubs.

GOOD TO KNOW

- For schedule information or tickets to White Sox games, call (312) 831-1769. The White Sox official Internet address is www.chisox.com.
- For schedule information or tickets to Cubs games, call (773) 831-2827.
- The White Sox can be heard on **WMAQ 670 AM**, the Cubs can be heard on **WGN 720 AM**. **WMVP 1000 AM** is the Chicago area's leading all-sports radio station.
- For more information on Chicago sights, attractions, and hotels, call the **Convention & Visitors Bureau** at (312) 567-8500. Or write them at 2301 South Lake Shore Drive, Chicago, Illinois 60616. The city's official Web site is www.chicago.il.org.
- I would also suggest calling the **Chicago Office of Tourism** at (800) 487-2446 several weeks in advance of your trip and ask them to send you a

map, guide to hotels, restaurants, nightclubs, as well as a calendar of upcoming events, for no charge.

Closest major league cities (and driving times): Milwaukee—90 miles (1 hour and 50 minutes); Detroit—279 miles (4 hours and 45 minutes); Cincinnati—295 miles (5 hours and 10 minutes); St. Louis—299 miles (5 hours and 40 minutes).

IN THE VICINITY

Field of Dreams, the baseball diamond carved out of a cornfield by Universal Studios in Dyersville, Iowa, is visited by nearly 60,000 people each year. There is no charge to visit the field, but donations are accepted. They encourage you to bring your own bats and balls to play on the field. The site is about 200 miles from Chicago. Because there is no direct route, the trip takes about four hours and twenty-five minutes. For more information, write to 28963 Lansing Road, Dyersville, Iowa 52040. Or call them at (888) 875-8404.

◆ CINCINNATI ◆

Cincinnati is nuts with baseball! They ought to call this town Cincinutty!

BUGS BAER

RIVERFRONT STADIUM

The setting for Riverfront couldn't be nicer. On the banks of the Ohio River, beside the picturesque Roebling Suspension Bridge, the stadium is within a short walk of downtown Cincinnati. Unfortunately, like Three Rivers Stadium in Pittsburgh, the view is much more impressive from the exterior than it is from inside. Completed in 1970, Riverfront is a virtual mirror image of Three Rivers and Veterans stadiums. All three are huge, circular, concrete, multi-sport monstrosities with too many bad seats, artificial turf, and no infield diamonds, per se, just dirt patches at each base.

Riverfront seats nearly 53,000 and has the dubious distinction of being the first major-league stadium to install dirt patches around the bases instead of having a full infield diamond. The outfield dimensions are completely symmetrical: 330 feet in the corners, 375 feet in both power alleys, and 404 in dead center. In 1984 the fence was lowered from 12 feet to a standard height of 8 feet all the way around, allowing more home runs and an outfielder the chance to occasionally rob a batter of a home run. While lowering the height of the outfield wall may have been an improvement, the fence still offers no quirky corners or tricky angles to make a carom off the outfield fence anything but routine.

There is, however, quite a bit to like about Riverfront. The Reds pride themselves on making a day at the ballpark an affordable family outing. They are the last team in the majors to still offer $1 hot dogs. Say what you will about Marge Schott, you have to be impressed with her commitment to keeping a ball game affordable. Tickets for all seating levels are reasonably priced, with the best seats, blue boxes, going for just $11.50. Green level box seats are your second-

115

best option, but are only $1 cheaper. Yellow level box seats cost the same as the green level seats, but are a long way from the diamond. There is shade available in the back rows of every level, so if you are sensitive to the sun, you may want to consider these. Another bonus is that of all the multisport stadiums built in the '60s and '70s Riverfront has the smallest foul territory.

Riverfront's greatest attribute is the fans themselves. Cincinnati, home to the country's first professional baseball team, has fans that are as loyal and knowledgeable as any in the country. It helps, of course, that the Reds are usually contenders, having finished first or second in their division seventeen times between 1969, when divisional play began, and 1996. Even in 1993, when they finished in fifth place, thirty-one games out of first place, they managed to draw nearly 2.5 million fans. With that in mind, you may want to order tickets well in advance.

Riverfront was the first ballpark I visited that served mixed drinks. Since then I've encountered a few others, but at the time it was a welcome surprise. Equally surprising was the price, no more than you'd expect to pay at a bar. After a late night rage at **Covington Landing** the night before, we decided to imbibe a Bloody Mary or three in the early innings of the game. They were not particularly special, but they hit the spot at the time.

HISTORY

Riverfront Stadium replaced stoic Crosley Field in midseason on June 30, 1970. Hank Aaron hit the stadium's first home run that day. Fittingly, Pete Rose got the Reds' first hit in their new stadium. The following day he hit Riverfront's first triple. A week earlier "Charlie Hustle" had hit the last triple in Crosley Field.

On April 4, 1974, Cincinnati saw Hank Aaron tie Babe Ruth's career home run mark of 714. On May 5, 1978, Rose got a single off Expos pitcher Steve Rogers. It was the 3,000th base hit of his career. That same year, on June 16, Tom Seaver threw a no-hitter to beat the Cardinals 4–0. Seaver also recorded his 3,000th strikeout at Riverfront Stadium on April 18, 1991. Keith Hernandez was the victim.

On September 11, 1985, Pete Rose broke Ty Cobb's record of 4,191 career base hits with a single off Padres pitcher Eric Show. Tom Browning threw a perfect game to beat the Dodgers on September 16, 1988. On September 7, 1993, Mark Whiten had a career day and tied two big-league records by hitting four home runs and collecting twelve RBIs in a single game.

GETTING TO RIVERFRONT STADIUM
100 Riverfront Stadium

Because Cincinnati is predominantly a baseball city, you may want to come early; buy tickets at the main gate if you don't already have them, and tailgate

The Reds host the Braves at Riverfront Stadium, the first stadium to install dirt patches instead of a full infield. (Photo by Author)

while you wait for the gates to open. The park is easily accessible from highways I-71, 74, and 75 (exit on Pete Rose Way), and there are several parking lots in the vicinity. There's even one directly below the stadium that accommodates more than 3,000 cars. The stadium is just a short walk from downtown via the **SkyWalk**, which crosses over the highway.

Cincinnati has a clean, open, and safe downtown area that is constantly buzzing with activity on game days. Almost everything is within walking distance and accessible via the innovative sixteen-block SkyWalk system that connects downtown hotels with museums, shopping, dining, and the ballpark.

WHAT TO DO AND SEE IN CINCINNATI

Fans have been supporting professional baseball in Cincinnati for more than 120 years. One reason the people of Cincinnati are such tremendous baseball fans is that the city, small by major league standards, has relatively few "high-profile" things to do. There are, however, enough sights in the area to keep a baseball fan busy for a two or three-game stay. Many of the area's best attractions offer free or nominally priced admission.

Fountain Square is a wide-open plaza in the heart of downtown that bustles with activity before and after Reds games. Tables and chairs surround the fountain, and street vendors sell smoky bratwursts, hot dogs, and sodas. It's a great place to sit down to eat and people watch before a game.

The **Museum Center at Union Terminal** offers a half-million square feet of exhibit space in a beautifully remodeled art deco style train station. The terminal is home to the **Cincinnati Museum of Natural History, Omnimax Theater**, the **Historical Society Museum**, and **Library**. The museum's collection is quite extensive, so plan to spend several hours here. A combination ticket to both museums and the Omnimax Theater is a bargain at $11.95 for adults.

The **Cincinnati Museum of Art** recently underwent a major interior remodeling and features a sizable collection of paintings, sculpture, photos, and period pieces, representing 5,000 years of visual arts history. The museum is located northeast of downtown in Eden Park. Admission is $5, but free on Saturdays and Wednesday evenings. Call in advance for exhibit information and hours. Eden Park is also home to the **Krohn Conservatory** and **Playhouse in the Park**.

The **Cincinnati Zoo** is the second oldest zoo in the country and has a substantial collection of rare and exotic animals. Its other claim to fame is the fact that it's home to the world's first and largest insect exhibit. *Newsweek* magazine refers to the Cincinnati Zoo as "the sexiest" in the country, which may or may not have something to do with their outstanding success in breeding wild animals in captivity. Admission is just $6.75 for adults.

Paramount's Kings Island, one of the country's better amusement parks, is about half an hour north of the city. It features more than 100 rides and attractions including "The Beast," one of the fastest and longest wooden rollercoasters in the world. It reaches a top speed of nearly sixty-five miles an hour. Park admission enables you to ride as many rides as you like, as often as you like, and costs $23.95 for adults.

Being just across the river from Kentucky, you might expect that there would be a thoroughbred racetrack in the area. **River Downs**, along the banks of the Ohio River, offers races all spring and summer at 6301 Kellogg Avenue. There's even a climate-controlled clubhouse that's open to the public. Call in advance for starting times and directions.

NIGHTLIFE IN CINCINNATI

Some of the best options are across the river in Covington, Kentucky, with a nice view of the city skyline, so don't limit your search to just the Ohio side of the river. Here's a short list of places on both sides of the river.

The **Wharf at Covington Landing**, at the foot of the scenic Roebling Suspension Bridge and within walking distance of the stadium, is the country's largest floating entertainment complex. For one cover charge you have your choice of three nightclubs, in addition to three restaurants, and a number of specialty shops. There is a great view of the city at night, as well as one of the city's premiere chili joints, **Skyline Chili**. Cincinnati Chili is nothing like Texas Chili, in that it is not nearly as spicy and, believe it or not, uses cinnamon and chocolate as part of the recipe. Don't let that fact keep you from trying it; it's as good as it is different.

Oldenberg Brewery is a tremendous microbrewery and brew pub, five miles south of downtown in Fort Mitchell, Kentucky. Free guided tours of the brewery are offered daily.

WHERE TO STAY IN CINCINNATI

Choices are limited when it comes to downtown hotels in Cincinnati, but there are a few within a mile or so of the ballpark. Several offer shuttles to and from games, as well as weekend packages. Rooms can be hard to come by, so be sure to book a room as soon as you have secured tickets to a game. Following is a partial listing of area hotels.

DOWNTOWN HOTELS

Cincinnatian Hotel 601 Vine Street (800) 942-9000 or (513) 381-3000 Newly renovated historic hotel, deluxe accommodations, minutes from Fountain Square and the stadium.

Crowne Plaza 15 West 6th Street (800) 2CROWNE or (513) 381-4000 Nice accommodations within walking distance of Fountain Square and Riverfront.

Regal Cincinnati Hotel 150 West 5th Street (800) 876-2100 or (513) 352-2100 Reasonably priced accommodations opposite the Convention Center and connected to the SkyWalk system, within walking distance of Riverfront Stadium and Fountain Square.

Holiday Inn Downtown 800 West 8th Street (800) HOLIDAY or (513) 241-8660 Nice hotel with free parking and a rooftop bar with an outstanding view of the city.

Omni Netherland Plaza 35 West 5th Street (800) THE-OMNI or (513) 421-9100 A luxury hotel near the ballpark that offers reasonably priced rooms on the weekends.

TEAM HOTELS

Hyatt Regency 151 West 5th Street (800) 233-1234 or (513) 579-1234 Dodgers, Phillies, Pirates, Cardinals, and Padres. Ask about Reds packages. Official Reds gift shop in lobby.

Westin 21 East Fifth Street (800) 228-3000 or (513) 621-7700 Braves, Cubs, Rockies, Marlins, Astros, Expos, Mets, and Giants. Two blocks from the stadium. Ask about Reds packages.

OTHER AREA HOTELS

Embassy Suites   10 East River Center Boulevard, Covington, Kentucky (800) EMBASSY or (606) 261-8400   Closest hotel to Riverfront Stadium, just across the Roebling Suspension Bridge, next to Covington Landing.

Clarion Hotel   5th Street, Covington, Kentucky (800) 252-7466 or (859) 491-1200   Minutes from stadium and downtown. Reds packages available.

GOOD TO KNOW

- For schedule information or tickets to Reds games, call (513) 421-4510.
- Reds games can be heard on **WLW 700 AM**. **WSAI 1360 AM** is the leading all-sports station in the area.
- For more information on Cincinnati sights, attractions and hotels, call the **Convention & Visitors Bureau** at (513) 621-2142.

Closest major league cities (and drive times): Cleveland—253 miles (4 hours and 30 minutes); Detroit—272 miles (4 hours and 45 minutes); Pittsburgh—298 miles (5 hours); Chicago—295 miles (5 hours and 10 minutes).

IN THE VICINITY

On the first Saturday in May, the **Kentucky Derby** is run at Churchill Downs in Louisville, Kentucky, about ninety miles southwest of Cincinnati. America's premiere horse race recently celebrated its 123rd running and remains one of the classiest and most spectacular sporting events in the world. As such, tickets to the best seats are almost impossible to come by. To request tickets (at least six months in advance) write to Churchill Downs, 700 Central Avenue, Louisville, Kentucky, Attn: Harriet Howard. If tickets are available, you will be notified and billed two months prior to the race.

Crosley Field, the Reds' home from 1912–1970, was the sight of major league baseball's first ever night game, in 1935. The park's original scoreboard, with its giant Longines clock, has been moved to the New Crosley Field in Blue Ash, Ohio, just northeast of Cincinnati. The scoreboard still shows the Giants and Reds line-ups and out-of-town-scores, as if it were still June 24, 1970, when the last pitch was thrown in old Crosley Field.

◆ DENVER ◆

Once again, Colorado proves it's major league.

GOVERNOR ROY ROMER

COORS FIELD

In the heart of downtown Denver, in what used to be a warehouse and industrial section near Union Station, Coors Field has rejuvenated an entire section of town. Within walking distance of a number of hotels, restaurants, cafes, bars, and microbreweries, a game at Coors Field becomes an event. The new park was built by Mortenson/Barton Malow and designed by HOK Sports, the same folks who built and designed Oriole Park at Camden Yards.

The end result is one of the shining new stars among major-league ballparks. Originally designed to have a capacity of just 43,000 fans, the number of seats at the park was increased by more than 7,000 as a result of the Rockies setting attendance records for their first two years in the league.

Coors Field features an old-fashioned, red brick exterior reminiscent of Camden Yards and the Ballpark in Arlington. The main entrance is at the corner of 20th and Blake Streets, under an antique-looking, double-sided analog clock. The playing field is natural grass, and the outfield dimensions are asymmetrical with an 8-foot high fence from foul pole to foul pole, except for an 80-foot section in the right field corner, which is 16 feet high.

The Rockies maintain one of the longest distances from home plate to the deepest corner of the outfield, 424 feet in right-center field. Nevertheless, Coors Field is a hitter's park for three reasons: the ball travels 9 percent farther in the thin mountain air; pitcher's curve balls tend to break less; and foul territory is the third smallest in the National League. With just 56 feet 4 inches between home plate and the front row of seats, some fans are actually closer to the batter than the pitcher is. The distance between the foul line and the stands is especially small past the diamond, turning many would-be foul pop-up outs into souvenirs.

A giant scoreboard and information center, similar to the one at Cleveland's Jacobs Field, sits beyond the left-center field wall, and a small section of 2,300 Wrigley Field style bleacher seats overlook center field. These bleacher seats, known as the "Rockpile," are a long way from home plate, but are very popular. Most are sold in advance for $1–4, but 1,000 seats are held and go on sale two and a half hours before game time. Beyond center field, fountains nestled among rocks and trees simulate a mountain terrain.

Some of the stadium's other novelties include: a single row of purple seats in the upper deck to indicate the "mile high mark" of 5,280 feet above sea level; the **Rounders Brewery**—an on-site microbrewery and restaurant operated by Coors; a manually operated out-of-town scoreboard in the right field corner; and a 350-yard main concourse that makes it possible to watch the game as you stand in line for concessions. Another nice touch is the lack of an upper deck in left field, which allows for a great view of the Rocky Mountains from most upper level seats. The city skyline can be seen behind home plate. Coors Field, like The Ballpark in Arlington, also has a nice variety of baseball-related artwork throughout the park.

The crowds in Denver are among the most enthusiastic in baseball and have continued as such since the Rockies moved into their new baseball-only park. The Rockies' first opening day at Mile High drew an all-time major league baseball record of 80,227 fans. Ever since then, the crowds in Denver have been record-setting, taking only 17 games to draw 1 million fans and selling nearly 4.5 million tickets in their first year of play. Tickets are somewhat easier to come by these days, as the novelty of simply having a major league team appears to have worn off.

If you are in town while the Rockies are on the road, you can take a one-hour tour of the park on non–game days. Call (303) 762-5437 for more information.

HISTORY

Perhaps indicative of things to come, Coors Field opened on April 26, 1995, with a 14-inning barn burner against the Mets that the Rockies won 11–9 on a Dante Bichette 3-run home run. Later that year, on July 3, Andres Galarraga collected 6 hits in a 15–0 victory over the Astros.

On October 1, 1995, the Rockies earned a wild-card berth by beating the Giants 10–9. The Rockies set a modern record by reaching the playoffs in just their third year of play. The previous record had been eight years, set by the Mets, who started playing in 1962 and made the playoffs in 1969. In the first playoff game hosted by Coors Field, the Atlanta Braves beat the Rockies 5–4 by scratching out a run in the ninth inning on October 3, 1995.

Cardinals first baseman John Mabry hit for the cycle in a 9–8 loss to the Rockies on May 18, 1996. Mabry actually completed the cycle in order by

Aerial view of Denver's Coors Field. (Courtesy of the Colorado Rockies)

getting a single, double, triple, and home run in his first four at bats. He was intentionally walked his fifth time up. On September 17, 1996, Dodger pitching phenom Hideo Nomo tamed the league's best offensive lineup in baseball's foremost hitter's ballpark when he threw his first career no-hitter to beat the Rockies at Coors Field.

GETTING TO COORS FIELD
Blake and 20th streets

The area where the new ballpark is located is called Lower Downtown or LoDo. There are few mass transit options other than the MAC RTD Light Rail Line that runs from Broadway and I-25 to the 16th Street Mall, just four blocks from the stadium. There is also a shuttle bus that runs up and down 16th Street from the Civic Center Station near the State Capitol Building to the Market Street Station in Lower Downtown. Call (303) 299-6000 for other RTD routes and schedules. New bus and carpool lanes on I-25 ease traffic for folks taking advantage of Rockies Ride shuttle buses or for those folks who ride to the park in groups of three or more.

Fortunately, Coors Field is easy to get to by car. You'll find the park just south of the intersection of I-70 and I-25. As you travel along I-25, take exit 212C or exit 213. Parking spaces in the immediate vicinity of the ballpark are scarce and can cost $10–15. If you purchase tickets in advance, you can buy a parking pass for $5 at the same time. Call (303) ROCKIES for more information.

WHAT TO DO AND SEE IN DENVER

The easiest place to start a tour of the Denver area is downtown, as many of its premier sights and attractions are within an easy walk of each other. The gold-domed **Capitol Building**, modeled after its namesake in Washington, D.C., offers a 360-degree view of the city at an altitude of 5,500 feet above sea level. The building features wide spiral staircases with big brass railings, impressive portraits, and stained-glass windows. It is also home to both the State Senate and House. In a rare display of humor on the part of politicians, the House chamber features a penalty box, complete with a "no whining" sign. Once you get to the third floor you can climb another ninety-three steps to the top of the Rotunda for a magnificent view of the city, with the Rocky Mountains in the background. The Capitol is open to tour only on weekdays beginning at 9:00 AM, and admission is free.

A short walk away at 13th and Broadway, you'll see the **Colorado History Museum**, which traces the state's history back to the days of the old West. Artifacts and dioramas depicting the days of cowboys and Indians, trappers, gold miners, and the original pioneers are on display. Admission is $3 for adults. Also nearby is the **Leanin' Tree Museum of Western Art**, located in what used to be Denver's classiest bordello and gambling hall. Today it houses the country's third largest collection of Western art. Admission is free. Call ahead for hours and exhibit information.

The **Denver Art Museum**, located at 14th Avenue and Bannock Street, opposite Civic Center Park, is more than 100 years old and has an extensive collection of 40,000 pieces of art. Its collection includes the most comprehensive display of Native American art in the world, as well as European masterpieces. The museum is open Tuesday through Sunday, and admission is just $3 for adults but free to all on Saturdays.

Larimer Square, Denver's oldest street, was recently renovated and now is filled with shops, galleries, streetside cafes, and restaurants. Within walking distance of the new ballpark, it is not the closest place to Coors Field to get a bite to eat or a cold drink before the game, but it is certainly one of the best, offering a variety of options.

There are also a number of interesting attractions outside of Denver's downtown area. One of the more convenient ways to get to some of the attractions both in and away from the downtown area is the **Cultural Connection Trolley**. The Trolley, actually a city bus painted to look like a trolley, runs from 9:30 AM to 5:50 PM daily and allows you to get on and off as often as you like in a given day.

City Park, the largest of Denver's more than 200 city parks, is home to the Denver Zoo, the Denver Museum of Natural History, and the City Park Golf Course. The Zoo is spread out over 70 acres and has more than 1,300 animals, representing nearly 400 species, displayed in natural settings. Admission is just $6 for adults. The Museum of Natural History is the nation's fifth largest natural history museum and features dinosaur fossils, geology, and wildlife exhibits, as well as an IMAX theater and planetarium. Coincidentally, dinosaur bones, estimated to be sixty-six million years old, were discovered during the excavation of the Coors Field site, and in cooperation with the museum, are displayed at the park.

NIGHTLIFE IN DENVER

Denver has a nice variety of brew pubs, sports bars, comedy clubs, and billiard halls within a short walk of the ballpark. Like Fenway, Wrigley, and Camden Yards, you'll want to come early and check out some of these places before and after the game. For a listing of what's happening in Denver nightspots pick up a copy of *Westword*, a free entertainment tab at area restaurants and bars. To get a copy in advance, write to P.O. Box 5970, Denver, CO 80217 or call (303) 296-7744.

Breckenridge Brewery and Pub 2220 Blake Street (303) 297-3644 Located catty-corner to the park it offers five exquisite brews in a brew pub setting. There is a fairly extensive bar menu of sandwiches, burgers, soups, and salads.

Champion Brewing Company 1442 Larimer Square (303) 534-5444 Contemporary home-style grub, great atmosphere, and a number of outstanding local beers.

Comedy Works 1226 15th Street (303) 595-3637 Around the corner from Larimer Square. Denver's premier comedy spot with top-rated national comedians.

Crocs 1630 Market Street (303) 436-1144 Within a short walk of the new ballpark. Mexican food, burgers, sandwiches, and beers in a fun-filled musical atmosphere.

Gate 12 2301 Blake Street (303) 292-2212 Right across from Coors Field. Occasional live music, billiards, and a sports bar atmosphere.

Herman's Hideaway 1578 South Broadway (303) 777-5840 Live blues, bluegrass, and jazz. Free valet parking. Cover charge varies with acts.

Old Chicago 1415 Market Street (303) 893-1806 A great place before and after the game with live music in the beer garden. They offer 110 different beers; try them all and become a member of their "Hall of Foam." I recommend the Wrigley Red. Deep-dish pizza and pasta dishes are their specialty.

Wazoos on Wazee   1819 Wazee Street (303) 297-8500   A short walk from the ballpark. Casual atmosphere; patio, and pool tables. Specializes in gourmet pizza cooked in a woodburning oven.

Wynkoop Brewery   18th and Wynkoop (303) 297-2700   A brew pub and restaurant downstairs, and plush billiard hall upstairs. Just a short walk from Coors Field.

WHERE TO STAY IN DENVER

Denver does not have an abundance of hotels, so you may want to reserve a room well in advance. If at all possible, stay in downtown Denver near the ballpark. Many of the area's best nightclubs and restaurants are within walking distance. There are some bargains to be had on the outskirts of downtown. Many of these hotels offer free shuttles to downtown attractions. Airport area hotels may not be a bad second choice. They are isolated, but the downtown area is only a short drive away by highway.

DOWNTOWN HOTELS

Denver Marriott City Center   1701 California Street (800) 228-9290 or (303) 297-1300   Luxury hotel located in the heart of downtown with weekend packages available.

Embassy Suites   1881 Curtis Street (800) EMBASSY or (303) 297-8888   One- and two- bedroom suites not far from the stadium.

Holiday Inn-North   4849 Bannock Street (800) 465-4329 or (303) 292-9500   Nice accommodations in midtown Denver. Ask about their ball game packages that include a ticket, room, transportation to and from the game, and breakfast.

La Quinta   3500 Park Avenue West (800) 531-5900 or (303) 433-2246   A great bargain and one of the closest hotels to the ballpark.

Oxford Hotel   1600 17th Street (800) 228-5838 or (303) 628-5400   Very nice accommodations. Also happens to be one of the closest hotels to the ballpark.

Radisson   1550 Court Place (800) 333-3333 or (303) 893-3333   Nice accommodations at a bargain price on weekends. Ask about their Rockies package.

Regency Hotel   3900 Elati Street   (303) 458-0808   A little past its prime, but not far from the new ballpark. Reasonably priced with clean rooms and a friendly staff.

TEAM HOTELS

Hyatt Regency Denver   1750 Welton Street (800) 233-1234 or (303) 295-1234   Reds, Dodgers, Phillies, and Padres. Ask about their Rockies package.

TEN BEST-KEPT SECRETS IN BASEBALL

10 If you are sitting close to the infield in a section full of beautiful women, you are probably in the players' wives section. Be careful whom you boo.

9 The best way to "upgrade" your seats is to wait until the third or fourth inning, scope out a few unoccupied seats, fill your hands with concessions, and head toward the seats as if you own the place.

8 If you need to leave your newly "upgraded" seats, to stock up on concessions or use the rest room, be certain that you talk to the usher at the top of your section on the way out. When you return, he'll remember your face and won't ask to see your tickets.

7 At the Ballpark in Arlington they only play one verse of "Take me out to the ballgame" before breaking into a square-dance tune. You might look silly if you start singing the second verse all by yourself.

6 Programs sold outside the stadium are generally half as expensive as those sold inside. They may not be as slick, but they do contain all the information you need to keep score. The same applies for food and souvenirs.

5 Traveling bartenders wander the lower level stands at Olympic Stadium in Montreal. They'll mix you a cocktail right at your seat if you'd rather not go to the concession stands. Tip them well and they'll be back often.

4 Several parks allow you to bring in your own food and drinks as long as your cooler will fit under your seat and you enter through the proper gate. They do not allow bottles, cans, or alcohol.

3 The Kansas City Royals allow fans into the stadium for free after the seventh inning.

2 There are beer vendors in the bleachers of Miller Park. But if you want a beer, you need to get up and head toward the concession stands because the vendors generally sell out their trays before they even get to the stands.

1 Several stadiums reserve a section of bleacher seat sales until an hour or two before game time. Candlestick, Camden Yards, and Coors Field offer some of the best "day of game" seats. There is usually a long line but you'll notice that people in these sections are generally having the most fun once the game is underway.

Westin Tabor Center   1672 Lawrence Street (800) 228-3000 or (303) 572-9100 Braves, Cubs, Marlins, Astros, Expos, Mets, Pirates, Cardinals, and Giants.

GOOD TO KNOW

- For schedule information or tickets to Rockies games call (800) 388-7625.
- Rockies games can be heard on **KOA 850 AM**. **KYBG 1090 AM** is the area's leading all-sports station. Televised games can be seen on KWGN channel 2.
- The **Denver Visitor Information Center** is located at 225 West Colfax and offers over 500 free brochures on area sights and attractions.
- For more information on Denver sights, attractions, and hotels, call the **Convention & Visitors Bureau** at (303) 892-1112. The city's official Web site is www.denver.org.

Closest major league city (and drive time): Kansas City—615 miles (10 hours).

IN THE VICINITY

Boulder, Colorado is a beautiful college town with a wealth of outdoor activities, just 40 minutes northwest of Denver. Bike rentals are very popular and the trail on campus along the river is safe, well marked, and fairly easy. Hikers will want to check out some of the parks nearby. **Chautauqua Park**, just off Baseline Road, has several modest trails with endless wildflowers and terrific views of Boulder as well as the Flatirons. More difficult trails include the Flagstaff Mountain Loops and Green Mountain Loops. Bear in mind that Boulder's elevation and thin air make what would generally be an easy hike considerably more difficult.

Much less challenging, but nearly as much fun, is the **Pearl Street** pedestrian mall in downtown Boulder. Pearl Street is closed to cars and offers a wonderful selection of galleries, cafes, and shops. My favorite places were the Busch Gallery, a fascinating sculpture and painting gallery, and Rocky Mountain Joe's, a comfortable place to read the paper and enjoy breakfast or lunch as shoppers pass by. Joe's is upstairs and easy to miss if you're not paying attention, but it's worth seeking out, especially for a made-to-order breakfast. Boulder also offers a surprisingly diverse restaurant scene and, as you might expect in a college town, a number of microbreweries and nightclubs.

◆ DETROIT ◆

"This place is so big they ought to call it Comerica National Park!"

A VISITING TEXAS RANGER

COMERICA PARK

Words can barely describe the transition from Tiger Stadium to Comerica Park, especially from the outside. The main entry plaza, along the first base side on Witherell Street, is steeped in baseball charm. A pair of 80-foot-tall baseball bats are situated on either side of a menacing 15-foot high, 25-foot long tiger statue. Four more giant tigers are perched above the entrance. Encircling the exterior of the park, tiger-head sculptures hold lighted baseballs in their mouths as families approach the park in wide-eyed amazement.

Unlike other new ballparks geared toward home run hitters, Comerica in its current configuration is a pitcher's park. The power alleys and corners are deeper than those of Tiger Stadium, while center field is shorter, but still a long way from home plate at 420 feet. My first game at Comerica was a 1–0 Tiger victory over the Twins. They scratched out their run in the first, with a single, a double, and a Dean Palmer sacrifice fly. Pitcher Jeff Weaver did the rest, coming within one out of tossing a complete game shutout. What more could a purist ask for? There's even a flagpole near the left-center field wall, reminiscent of Yankee Stadium before the 1974–75 remodeling.

The field is below street level and incorporates the open-air feeling of Wrigley Field and many new ballparks, even offering those without tickets a glimpse of the park from the sidewalks and buildings along Adams Street. Looking beyond center field and the right field stands from inside the park, there's also a view of the downtown skyline. The scoreboard, with a pair of giant tigers along the upper edges, is one of the largest in baseball. The tigers' eyes are said to light up when a Detroit player hits a home run. The scoreboard also has a large analog clock, TV replay board, and matrix message board. It presents the lineup of the team at bat, inning-by-inning scoring, hits, runs and errors, as well as statistics of the player at bat. An electronic out-of-town scoreboard makes up the outfield wall between the center field hitters' background and the terraced bullpens in right field. Auxiliary scoreboards showing balls, strikes, outs and inning, as well as pitch speeds and the number of balls and strikes thrown, are located between the upper and lower decks along the infield.

Below and to the right of the main scoreboard are the retired numbers of Tiger greats (including Ty Cobb, who played before jerseys were numbered) and statues of these same players—Willie Horton, Al Kaline, Hal Newhouser, Hank Greenberg, Charlie Gehringer, and Cobb. In some parks, baseball-related art borders on the ridiculous, but Comerica's stainless steel statues are my favorite works of art in the big leagues. The various poses of players sliding, batting, pitching, and fielding are spectacular, done by the same artists who created the Michael Jordan sculpture at the United Center in Chicago.

Tiger fans may miss the familiar blue interior of old Tiger Stadium, but the playing field at Comerica is every bit as nice, there are no obstructed views, and all seats are angled toward the mound. The outfield wall is eight and a half feet tall from pole to pole, except for a 100-foot section in right-center that goes up to eleven and a half feet high. The park seats only 40,000 fans, more than 12,000 fewer than Tiger Stadium, and available seats range from $8 in the Pepsi family section to $30 for infield box seats. Mezzanine seats offer a great view and are a relative bargain at $15, while pavilion seats, essentially a left field bleacher section with seats, are $14 each.

Kids of all ages will dig the 50-foot high Ferris wheel that can be seen from outside the park, behind the Brush Street entrance. The Ferris wheel is located along the third base line and has twelve baseball-shaped cars that hold up to five adults each. There's also a carousel in the center of the food court near the Witherell entrance. Instead of horses, the illuminated, orange and black carousel features 30 hand-painted tigers and two chariots—one seats four adults, while the other can accommodate two wheelchairs. Just above the hitters' background, in front of flagpoles flying Tiger championship banners, a fountain sets off liquid fireworks during the seventh-inning stretch and when a Tiger hits a home run.

I miss the stadium-style mustard served with hot dogs at Tiger Stadium. These days, aside from the gyros and frozen daquiries, the concessions at Comerica are pretty forgettable, but the prices are no worse than most ballparks. Adults should check out the Brushfire Grill, which features a microbrewery, open-pit barbecue specialties, and seafood entrees. The Brushfire is near the Ferris wheel and has a large outdoor patio. Purists may complain that there are too many non-baseball amenities at Comerica Park, and I cer-

View of infield and scoreboard from first base side. Just to the left of the flagpole are the statues and retired numbers of Tiger greats. (Photo by Author)

tainly feel there is no reason to put a McDonald's behind the right field stands; but, all in all, the park is a tremendous place to bring the family for a baseball game.

HISTORY

Tiger Stadium opened on April 20, 1912, with a 6–5 victory over the Cleveland Indians, but it wasn't until October 1935 that the Tigers won their first championship with a 4–3 victory over the Cubs in game 6 of the World Series. Babe Ruth's 700th home run actually left the stadium on July 13, 1934. The stadium was called Navin Field at the time and did not have a second deck. On September 30, 1945, Hank Greenberg returned from World War II to hit a home run in the last game of the season, clinching the pennant and leading the Tigers to another World Championship. Again, at the Cubs' expense.

On June 15, 1948, the Tigers hosted their first night game. On May 15, 1952, Virgil Trucks fired a no-hitter to beat the Washington Senators. He wasn't assured of the win until Vic Wertz hit a two-out homer in the bottom of the ninth inning. Denny McLain won his thirtieth game of the season on September 14, 1968. On July 15, 1973, Nolan Ryan threw his second no-hitter of the season, striking out seventeen batters on the way to 6–0 victory.

Red Sox rookie Fred Lynn had a career day in Detroit on June 18, 1975, by hitting three home runs and driving in ten runs in a 15–1 victory over the Tigers. On June 14, 1983, Kirk Gibson became one of just 26 players to hit a home run out of Tiger Stadium since the second deck was added in 1938. On October 4, 1994, the Tigers beat the Padres in the World Series, thanks in part to Gibson's two home runs in the deciding fifth game. Boston pitcher Roger Clemens tied his own major league record by striking out twenty batters in a game at Tiger Stadium on September 18, 1996. On April 20, 1997, Mark McGwire became just the fourth player to knock a ball out of Tiger Stadium over the left field stands.

Opening day at Comerica Park was April 11 vs. the Seattle Mariners. Juan Gonzalez hit an inside-the-park home run on September 2 off Kenny Rogers of the Texas Rangers. The Tigers sold out seventeen games for the 2000 season, a team record, and overall attendance was 2,533,752, second only to their 1984 championship season.

GETTING TO COMERICA
2100 Woodward Avenue

Closer to the arts district than Tiger Stadium, the neighborhood surrounding Comerica is fan-friendly and offers a few outstanding places to fuel up before and after a game. The park is near the intersection of I-75 and route 10 and easily accessible by car. Parking is not plentiful, but certainly better than at the old ballpark and lots range from $10 a few blocks away to $20 right beside the stadium.

Detroit's version of mass transit, the People Mover, serves a limited area with stops around downtown. The fare is only fifty cents, with the nearest stops to the ballpark being Broadway and Grand Circus Park, just a few blocks southwest of the stadium. SMART and D-Dot buses also offer routes with stops near the ballpark, but Motor City is not a town I'd recommend visiting without your own transportation.

If you want to eat and drink before the game, **Hockeytown Cafe** is diagonally across from Comerica Park, at 2301 Woodward Avenue, and offers a great view of the stadium's main entry plaza from the upstairs deck. Hockey fans will absolutely love this three-story sports bar. Statues of Steve Yzerman and Bobby Hull are just within the front entrance, ice cold beers are served from inside a Zamboni, and Red Wings memorabilia is scattered about the place. Just up the street, at 100 West Montcalm, **The Town Pump Tavern** is a warm, enthusiastic place that welcomes baseball fans to indulge in their "pub grub" before games and stop by afterward to sample some of their eighteen beers on tap.

WHAT TO DO AND SEE IN DETROIT

A visit to Detroit would not be complete without stopping by **Lindell A.C.**, the nation's original sports bar. Since 1948, fans and players have been going here before and after games at Tiger Stadium. Lindell A.C. is an intimate place with a classic collection of original sports memorabilia, reasonable drink prices, and a limited menu of burgers and steaks. Located at 1310 Cass Avenue (at the corner of Michigan Avenue), it only seats 150 folks, so be sure to get there early on game days.

The **Detroit Institute of the Arts**, the nation's fifth largest art museum, consists of more than 100 galleries and has an outstanding collection of paintings, sculpture, and ethnic art. In addition to work by van Gogh and Rodin, you'll want to see the ancient Egyptian treasures, the William Hearst Collection of Armor, the Tannahill Collection of Impressionist paintings, and a huge Diego Rivera mural commissioned by the Ford family. The museum is located in the **University Cultural Area** at Woodward and East Kirby avenues. It is open Wednesday through Sunday, and admission is just $4 for adults.

The **Henry Ford Museum and Greenfield Village**, minutes away from downtown Detroit in Dearborn, Michigan, is a testament to American ingenuity and inventiveness. The complex is spread out over ninety-three acres, at 20900 Oakwood Boulevard, and offers a fascinating glimpse of Americana. The exterior of the museum is a replica of Philadelphia's Independence Hall, but the articles inside are quite genuine. Among the more interesting items are one of the lunar rovers designed and built to be used on the moon, the chair Abraham Lincoln was sitting in at the time he was assassinated, a collection of presidential cars (including the Lincoln limousine that President Kennedy was riding in that fateful day in Dallas), a number of early model planes and locomotives, and of course, an exhibit of unique antique and contemporary automobiles.

Greenfield Village grounds feature the actual Menlo Park laboratory in which Thomas Edison conceived and invented the phonograph, lightbulb, and telephone. There's also the Wright Brothers' bicycle shop, the homes of Henry Ford and Noah Webster, the Logan County Courthouse, where Lincoln practiced law before becoming president, a 1913 carousel, and a working steamboat and steam engine train. A two-day combination ticket (good for admission to both the museum and village) is $20 for adults, and well worth it as you could easily spend an entire day here and still not see everything the museum and village have on display. Separate admission to either the museum or village is $12.50 for adults.

Detroit is also home to the **Museum of African-American History**, the largest museum of its kind, where you can see African masks and other works of art, photos, and video footage. The museum is located at 315 East Warren Avenue, and is open Wednesday through Sunday, from 9:30 AM to 5 PM. Admission is $3 for adults, with discounts available for children.

The Detroit Zoological Park is just 10 miles north of downtown Detroit, at 8450 West Ten Mile Road in Royal Oak, Michigan. It's one of the largest and best designed zoos in the nation, spread out over 125 acres and featuring cageless exhibits grouped by continent. Admission is $6 for adults.

NIGHTLIFE IN DETROIT

Building on the success of the casino built a few years ago just across the river in Windsor, Canada, Detroit is now home to a few casinos of its own. Motor City Casino, Greektown, and the MGM Grand have all sprouted up near the ballpark. They all offer entertainment at night and a nice selection of restaurants.

In Pontiac, you'll find **Industry**, one of the area's hottest dance club, at 15 South Saginaw. This multilevel dance club occupies what used to be the Eagle Theatre, a classic venue with girded balconies and galvanized cocktail tables. Music ranges from disco to alternative to live jazz.

Second City, located next door to Hockeytown in the theater district at 2301 Woodward Avenue, is only the third of its kind in the nation. The original started in Chicago and brought us Dan Aykroyd, Gilda Radner, and John Candy. The Detroit troupe is not quite that famous, but performs similar skits based on national current events that are sure to make you laugh. Reservations are strongly recommended, especially on weekends. Not far away, in Harmony Park, check out **Center Street Pub**, a good-sized place with pool tables, video games, sit-down dining that packs them in on game days. The surrounding area has become a popular area with a considerable influx of new pubs and restaurants.

Another of downtown Detroit's worthwhile attractions is the **Greektown** entertainment district. Greektown, centered around Monroe Street between St. Antoine and Beaubien, is packed with restaurants, shops, galleries, and nightlife. Not far from the stadium, the **Old Shillelagh** is a genuine Irish Pub that has been a fixture in Greektown, at 349 Monroe Street, for more than twenty-five years. One of Greektown's well-established restaurants, complete with belly dancing, is the **Bouzouki Lounge**, at 432 East Monroe. If that's not your speed, you are sure to find something exactly to your liking as you wander up and down Monroe Street.

Many of the folks I talked to in and around Detroit suggested that if I really wanted to throw down, I needed to cross the border and visit **Windsor, Canada**. Certainly worth checking out are a pair of outstanding Irish pubs. **Kildare House**, in the Walkerville neighborhood of Windsor, has the feel of an Old World pub, live music, and a great menu. **Patrick O'Ryan's** has a more upscale atmosphere, while offering live music and a solid menu. **Casino Windsor** features three stories of gaming, including such popular favorites as blackjack, roulette, baccarat, and slot machines. It's open twenty-four hours a day, 365 days a year, and has become Canada's number one commercial tourist attraction.

WHERE TO STAY IN DETROIT

Downtown Detroit has a number of fine hotels that offer the added convenience of being within a short walk of "The People Mover," an elevated monorail that runs along a three-mile loop with thirteen conveniently located stations around downtown Detroit. If you are not at the mercy of public transportation and taxicabs, you may want to stay at a hotel just outside the city.

Dearborn is just east of Detroit off route 12 and offers an abundance of affordable hotels to choose from. The city of Troy has a number of moderately priced hotels along I-75 that are less than twenty minutes north of downtown Detroit. Pontiac is just a little further north of Troy, and also has quite a few hotels to choose from in every price range. Another consideration is Windsor, Canada which is just south of downtown Detroit, across the Detroit River. Hotels in Canada also offer the advantage of a favorable exchange rate.

DOWNTOWN HOTELS

Crown Plaza Pontchartrain   2 Washington Boulevard (800) 537-8483 or (313) 965-0200   Luxury hotel with weekend packages available.

Detroit Courtyard   333 Jefferson Avenue (800) 321-2211 or (313) 222-7700   Luxury accommodations with weekend packages available.

Hotel Saint Regis   3071 West Grand Boulevard (800) 848-4810 or (313) 873-3000 Affordable, newly renovated hotel in the heart of downtown.

Omni Detroit Riverplace   1000 Riverplace (800) THE-OMNI or (313) 259-9500   Deluxe hotel on the river, just a mile and a half from Comerica Park.

WINDSOR HOTELS

Compri Hotel   333 Riverside Drive West (519) 977-9777   Nice accommodations not far from Casino Windsor, minutes from downtown Detroit.

Quality Suites by Journey's End   250 Dougall Avenue (800) 228-5151 Affordable, clean, two-room suites that are a bargain for families or small groups.

Ramada Inn of Windsor   480 Riverside Drive West (800) 228-2828 or (519) 253-4411   Nice accommodations on the banks of the Detroit River.

Travelodge of Windsor Downtown   33 Riverside Drive East (800) 255-3050 or (519) 258-7774   Affordable, conveniently located hotel with free parking.

Windsor Hilton   277 Riverside Drive West (800) 445-8667 or (313) 962-3834   Luxury hotel with an indoor pool, health club, restaurant, and bar.

TEAM HOTELS

Athenum Hotel   (313) 962-2323   Indians.

Hyatt Regency Dearborn   (800) 233-1234 or (313) 593-1234   Angels and Mariners.

Ritz-Carlton Dearborn   (800) 241-3333 or (313) 441-2000   Orioles, Red Sox, White Sox, Royals, Brewers, Twins, Yankees, A's, and Rangers.

Westin Renaissance   (800) 228-3000 or (313) 568-8358   Blue Jays.

GOOD TO KNOW

- For schedule information or tickets to Tigers games, call (313) 258-4437.
- Tigers games can be heard on **WJR 760 AM**. **WSFN 1600 AM** and **WVFM 730 AM** are the area's leading all-sports stations.
- For more information on Detroit sights, attractions, and hotels call the **Convention and Visitors Bureau** at (800) DETROIT or (313) 259-4333. The city's official Web site is www.visitdetroit.com.
- Windsor's airport is actually closer to downtown Detroit than is Detroit Metropolitan Airport, and sometimes it's less expensive to fly there than directly into Detroit.

Closest major league cities (and driving times): Cleveland—178 miles (3 hours and 15 minutes); Toronto—257 miles (4 hours and 20 minutes); Cincinnati—272 miles (4 hours and 45 minutes); Chicago—279 miles (5 hours and 30 minutes).

IN THE VICINITY

America's "Motor City" is home to the **Detroit Grand Prix**, a formula one race held every year in mid-June on Belle Island. You can catch a glimpse of the race for free, but the very best seats sell quickly. For upcoming dates and ticket information call (313) 393-7749.

Labor Day weekend marks the **Montreaux Detroit Jazz Festival**, an annual jazz festival held at Hart Plaza. The festival kicks off with a benefit show at Music Hall and continues with a series of eighty free shows playing on three stages throughout the festival.

◆ HOUSTON ◆

*"Until the Astrodome came along, baseball was always
played outside. There's a natural appeal to watching
baseball outdoors."*

TAL SMITH

ENRON FIELD

Three million fans can't be wrong! Especially when you consider how poorly
the Astros played their first year at Enron Field. Nevertheless, fans showed up
in droves to check out Houston's new downtown digs. Baseball, played outdoors on a natural grass field, a roof that slides open and closed, a hill and
flagpole 435 feet from home plate in center field, and people watching the
game from atop Union Station—what more could a baseball fan ask for?

Less, perhaps. While Enron is a colossal improvement on the Astrodome,
sometimes less is more. Incorporating the old Union Station rail terminal
building as the park's main entrance is a stroke of urban renewal brilliance,
but do fans really need a locomotive and coal car chugging along the outfield
wall every time an Astros player hits a home run? And how exciting is an over-
sized gas pump that tallies up the home team's home runs? There's a fine line
between quirks and gimmicks. To a traditional baseball fan, Enron Field may
cross that line.

On the upside, Enron's manually operated out-of-town scoreboard in left
field is reminiscent of much older yards. The wide-open concourse areas allow
fans to watch the game as they purchase souvenirs and sodas. Vendors will
come to your seat with everything from cotton candy to cold beer. The scoreboards are so informative and nicely situated that no matter where you sit,
it's easy to follow the action. The home run porch in left center field offers a
neat standing-room-only perspective on the game and hangs over the outfield,
allowing fans to snag what might otherwise be long pop outs.

137

View of Enron from behind home plate. Note the locomotive, hill, and flagpole in center field and retractable roof stored in the open position. (Photo by Author)

Foul territory is much smaller than it was at the Astrodome. The outfield fence varies in height from seven feet in the right field corner, 326 feet from the plate, to nineteen feet along the manual scoreboard in left, a scant 315 feet from home at the foul pole. The fence also offers a number of challenging angles, especially in the power alleys.

Enron has one of the finest retractable roof systems in the game. Despite costing less than half as much as Bank One Ballpark's, the roof at Enron allows for a more open feeling whether the roof is open or closed. Three huge glass panels slide into place as the roof closes, presenting a nice view of the Houston skyline beyond the left field wall. The three-section roof rolls on and off along a rail system similar to the one at Safeco Field, and when it's open, only a few rows of upper-deck seats are still covered.

Enron seats 42,000 fans, 12,370 fewer than the Astrodome accommodated for a baseball game. If seats near the infield are unavailable, check out the $15 bullpen boxes under the giant scoreboard in right field or the $17 Crawford boxes, just above the out-of-town scoreboard. Both spots should be good places to snag home run balls. There are plenty of concession stands and restrooms on all levels. Families may want to check out the Squeeze Play family area in the right field corner, with pint-sized concessions and a variety of interactive games.

Food and drinks are remarkably affordable at Enron, and if you're willing to walk around you can find some unusual items. In addition to hot dogs, peanuts, and pizza, fans on the main-concourse level will find fajitas at **Conductors Wrap Company**, chili from **Sheriff Blaylock's**, strawberries and cream or seedless watermelon slices at **Smalltown Produce Company**, and good-sized burgers at the **Dining Car Grill**. My favorites, though, are the turkey legs and Texas-style barbecue at **Maverick's Smoke House**. Imported and domestic beers are just $5 for a 21-ounce draft at **Whistle Stop Libations**. The **Sports Legacy Art Gallery**, also located on the main-concourse level, offers original sports paintings and drawings.

Ruggles restaurant offers a unique perspective on a game at Enron. It's open for lunch and dinner even when there is no game, but on game days, fans can reserve a table on the terrace overlooking center field. For $100 you'll get $60 of food and drink and a great view of the game. Their desserts are legendary, so be sure to save room.

Nearby, on Crawford Street between Prairie and Preston, you'll find a view of the game even if you don't have tickets. Stone archways that support the roof rails have a number of windows overlooking the field below from deep behind center field.

HISTORY

Enron Field opened with an exhibition game against the Yankees on March 30, 2000. The first regular season game was at 7:05 on April 7 of that season against the Phillies.

Aside from introducing artificial turf to baseball, the Astrodome saw its share of milestones and outstanding performances. Willie Mays clocked his 500th home run there on September 13, 1965. Astros pitcher Don Wilson threw a no-hitter against the Atlanta Braves on June 18, 1967. The 2–0 victory was the first-ever no-hitter thrown at the Astrodome. On April 30, 1969, Reds pitcher Jim Maloney no-hit the Astros. The very next night Don Wilson came back with a no-hit victory over the Reds.

On June 15, 1976, a game was actually "rained out" because of flooding of nearby streets. Nolan Ryan recorded his 4,000th career strikeout on July 11, 1985. Danny Heep was the victim. On September 8, 1993, Houston's Darryl Kile tossed a no-hitter against the Mets.

GETTING TO ENRON FIELD
501 Crawford Street

In the northeast corner of downtown Houston, Enron is just one block west of US 59. Signage directing you to Enron Field along major roads is helpful once you get near downtown. My visit coincided with the Texaco Grand Prix, which was just a few blocks away, and traffic was not unreasonable. There is ample parking, which ranges from $10–20, depending on how far you are willing to walk.

On game days, Home Run Express buses leave Park & Ride lots on the outskirts of town every fifteen minutes and deliver fans to the Metro Transit Center, one block south of the stadium. Shortstop Shuttle buses provide free transportation to downtown stops west and south of the ballpark. They also drop fans off at the Metro Transit Center. For more shuttle and parking information, call (713) 799-9500.

WHAT TO DO AND SEE IN HOUSTON

While Houston may be a little short on "major tourist attractions," it has a surprising nightlife scene and offers a remarkable number of outstanding eateries. Directly across from the Astrodome, you'll find **Six Flags AstroWorld**, a 75-acre amusement park at 9100 Kirby Road. There are more than 100 rides to choose from, including nine roller-coasters. All-day admission is $21.95 for adults and is good for all rides. **Six Flags WaterWorld** is adjacent to AstroWorld, but requires a separate admission. Given Houston's hot, humid climate, it may very well be worth it.

Space Center Houston at 1601 NASA Road One, was designed by Disney at a cost of $70 million. It is next door to the **NASA/Johnson Space Center** about twenty-five miles southeast of Houston. Check out the behind-the-scenes tram tour of Johnson Space Center and exhibits from the past, present, and future of space exploration. You'll see a lunar lander and an Apollo moon capsule, operate simulators, and more. Two highlights include a space shuttle mock-up and the giant-screen film *To Be an Astronaut.*

What many consider to be the area's best museum, the **San Jacinto Monument and Museum of History**, is actually twenty miles east of downtown Houston, in La Porte, Texas. The San Jacinto Monument is a fifty-story stone obelisk with a museum in the base that depicts four centuries of Texas history. An elevator takes you to an observation deck atop the 489-foot tower, where you can enjoy a magnificent view of the surrounding countryside. The museum is open seven days a week and is free to the public. There is a separate charge for the elevator ride and the multimedia slide presentation of *Texas Forever!*

Houston's museum district is located just southwest of downtown, near the intersection of Montrose and Bissonnet Boulevard. The **Museum of Fine Arts** has a permanent collection of more than 27,000 works of art and frequently hosts touring exhibits. The museum's collection of Frederic Remington works is one of the best in the country. The museum is closed Mondays, and admission is just $3 for adults.

Sam Houston Race Park offers Thoroughbred racing five days a week at a state-of-the-art racing facility. The track is located on the northwest side of town, just off Sam Houston Parkway, between 290 and I-45. The Houston area is also home to the world's largest greyhound racing facility, **Gulf Greyhound Park**. The track is just off the Gulf Freeway, in La Marque, Texas, on the way to Galveston.

NIGHTLIFE IN HOUSTON

There are just a handful of worthwhile places near the ballpark. Not far from the stadium's clock tower, you'll find **Irma's Southwest Grill** at the corner of Texas and Austin. Aside from a few baseball-inspired light sconces, nothing about this upscale place is reminiscent of baseball. The food, however, is outstanding and the margaritas are top-notch. A little further away, at **Flying Saucer Draught Emporium** at 705 Main Street, beer fans will think they've died and gone to heaven. China plates hang on the walls and ceilings, giant-screen televisions show your favorite games, a good-looking crowd mills about, and the menu offers a decent selection of sandwiches, salads, and wraps. But the handcrafted beers are what packs the place.

Cabo, at 419 Travis, serves Mexican sandwiches, fajitas, and burritos, as well as reasonably priced drinks. The place is packed on weekends and game days, so expect a wait. **Frank's Pizza** is next door and offers pizza by the slice, sub sandwiches, and happy hour from 3 to 8 PM. A number of thumping techno dance clubs, oddly tucked away in former retail store locations, are just around the corner at Preston and Main.

Because Houston has no zoning laws, there are nightclubs and restaurants scattered all over the city, even in residential areas. But the bulk of Houston nightlife seems to be located along Richmond Avenue, Washington Avenue, or Westheimer Boulevard. Richmond Avenue also offers a nice selection of restaurants and specialty shops. *Houston Press*, the area's leading entertainment weekly, is available for no charge at restaurants and retailers around town.

The **Fabulous Satellite Lounge**, at 3616 Washington Avenue, hosts some of the biggest names in music. **Joe's Crab Shack** has a let-it-all-hang-out attitude and offers some of the best, most unpretentious chow I came across in the city. There's nothing pretty about the place, but Joe's has been so successful that this original location has spawned dozens just like it across the country.

The **Magnolia Bar & Grill**, at 6000 Richmond Avenue, is one of the Richmond Entertainment District's original inhabitants. A great place for a hearty seafood dinner, they also have live jazz and rhythm and blues music Thursday through Sunday.

Dave & Buster's at 6010 Richmond Avenue is a tremendous place with seven bars, billiards, a "play for fun" casino, a million-dollar game room, and much more. Just across the street at 6025 Richmond Avenue, you'll find **Billy**

Blues Barbecue Bar & Grill. Just look for the giant blue saxophone standing out front. This place features the hard-to-beat combination of pecan-smoked barbecue and live blues. Although not together, the restaurant and music room are separated by a pair of garage doors and a hefty cover charge. The acts are often more regional than national, and get kicking around 8:30 every evening. The area's premiere blues venue is **The Big Easy** at 5731 Kirby Drive. The Big Easy is an authentic blues room booking some serious blues talent on the weekends.

SRO, at 6982 West FM 1960, claims to be Texas' biggest sports bar. With 100 TVs, 5 satellites, and a huge game room, that claim may be hard to dispute. A second SRO is reportedly being built not far from the Skybox.

Perhaps the city's most intriguing brew pub is the **Saint Arnold Brewing Company**, named after the patron saint of beer. Be sure to ask one of the three brothers who run the place to tell you the story behind the name, it's a doozy! Saint Arnold is located at 2522 Fairway Park Drive. A newer brew pub is **Rock Bottom Brewery**. Rock Bottom, sprouting up in a number of cities after a successful debut in Denver, has become a major part of the Houston night scene. Good food, outstanding microbrewed beer, and a comfortable setting attracts a handsome young crowd on the weekends and after work.

WHERE TO EAT IN HOUSTON

The first lady of Mexican cuisine in Houston is Ninfa Laurenzo, a minor celebrity among local restaurateurs. Said to be the birthplace of the fajita, Ninfa's, at 2704 Navigation, has been serving them since 1973. Mama Ninfa may or may not have invented fajitas, but she has certainly perfected them. If at all possible, stop by this modest, genuine Tex-Mex eatery and soak up some atmosphere and a margarita or two.

If you want another place with Houston roots, look for Pappas. In 1967 the Pappas family opened **Pappas Bar-B-Q** and have become somewhat of a Houston institution since. All across the city you'll find **Pappadeaux Seafood Kitchens**, cajun and creole seafood houses; **Pappamia's Italian Kitchens**, out of this world Italian cuisine; and **Pappasito's Cantinas**, home of some of the city's best margaritas. There's also the Pappas family's crowning achievement, **Pappas Brothers Steakhouse**, an upscale place, at 5839 Westheimer, with a posh 1920s atmosphere, incredibly attentive service, tremendous food, an extensive wine list, and a nice selection of fine cigars.

As you might suspect, Houston is home to countless Mexican restaurants. For authentic Mexican I suggest you try **Cafe Adobe** at 2111 Westheimer. This quaint, two-level place offers huge servings of traditional south-of-the-border fare and terrific margaritas. If at all possible, grab a table on the patio overlooking the street.

WHERE TO STAY IN HOUSTON

Downtown Houston is not exactly hopping at night or on weekends. Nor are there a wealth of things to do and see in the downtown area, so there is almost no advantage in staying downtown. Another thing to consider is the fact that there is no shortage of hotels in Houston. The most convenient areas to stay may be near the **Richmond Entertainment District** or the **Galleria Mall**. Both are located just southeast of downtown Houston, near the 610 beltway.

There are also a number of hotels in the immediate vicinity of the Astrodome that offer the convenience of a shared toll-free reservation service. The Marriott Residence Inn, Holiday Inn, Sheraton, Days Inn, and Radisson Suite Astrodome all can be reached by calling (800) 627-6461.

OTHER HOTELS

Adam's Mark   2900 Briarpark Drive at Westheimer (800) 444-ADAM or (713) 978-7400   Conveniently located, moderately priced hotel.

Comfort Suites   6200 Richmond Avenue (800) 424-6423 or (713) 783-1400   New hotel located in the heart of the Richmond Entertainment District.

Four Seasons   1300 Lamar (800) 332-3442 or (713) 650-1300   Luxury accommodations in the heart of downtown.

Guest Quarter Suites   5353 Westheimer Road (800) 424-2900 or (713) 961-9000   Luxury hotel one block west of the Galleria Mall.

La Quinta   4015 Southwest Freeway (800) 531-5900 or (713) 623-4750   Affordable accommodations with free continental breakfast, local calls, and cable.

Ramada Inn Galleria   7787 Katy Freeway (800) 822-8373 or (713) 681-5000   Nice hotel convenient to nightlife, the museum district, and the Astrodome.

Residence Inn Galleria   2500 McCue (800) 331-3131 or (713) 840-9757   Spacious all-suite hotel convenient to most attractions and nightlife.

Stouffer Renaissance Houston   6 Greenway Plaza East (800) HOTELS-1 or (713) 629-1200   Luxury accommodations, convenient location, pool, and health club.

TEAM HOTELS

J.W. Marriott   5150 Westheimer Road (800) 228-9290 or (713) 961-1500   Braves, Expos, and Marlins.

Westin Galleria   5060 West Alabama (800) 228-3000 or (713) 960-8100   All other National League clubs.

GOOD TO KNOW

- For schedule information or tickets to Astros games, call (214) 647-5700. The Astros official Internet address is www.astros.com.

- Game starting times are 1:35 PM for day games and 7:05 for night games.
- Astros games can be heard on **KILT 610 AM**.
- Tours of the Astrodome are available by calling (713) 799-9544.
- For more information on Houston sights, attractions, and hotels, call the **Convention & Visitors Bureau** at (800) 231-7799, (800) 4HOUSTON or (713) 227-3100. The city's best Web site for tourist information is www.houston-guide.com.

Closest major league city (and drive time): Arlington/Dallas—246 miles (4 hours and 15 minutes).

IN THE VICINITY

It has been said that the best thing about Houston is that it's only five hours from New Orleans. That may be a little harsh, but there is no city in the world like **New Orleans**. The Jazz and Heritage Festival is held every year during the last week of April and the first week of May. With the possible exceptions of Mardi Gras and New Year's Eve, there is no better time to be in New Orleans. The festival runs for ten days and features the best New Orleans jazz, dixie, cajun, zydeco, and blues musicians. All told, nearly 100 musical acts, many of which are nationally renowned, occupy twelve stages. The concerts are held on the infield of the Fair Grounds Race Course and are remarkably inexpensive for the caliber of talent. The race track is just ten minutes from the French Quarter, and the area around **Bourbon Street** is abuzz all night. Hotel space sells out early, so plan well in advance if you intend to go to New Orleans around this time of year. If you can't make it for Jazz and Heritage, any weekend in late spring or early fall is likely to be about as festive as you can handle.

If five hours seems a bit far, **San Antonio** is just 200 miles west of Houston on Interstate 10 and offers one of the more genteel urban atmospheres I have ever had the pleasure of experiencing. The city's claim to fame is of course **The Alamo**, which is right in the heart of the city and thankfully has managed to avoid becoming touristy or schlocky. The fort is considerably smaller than you might expect, which makes the accomplishment of the 187 American soldiers who died defending it from a Mexican onslaught of 5,000 men that much more impressive. A quick tour, including a ten-minute narrative, takes less than one hour. For information on sights, attractions, and lodging in San Antonio, call (800) 447-3372.

◆ KANSAS CITY ◆

Kansas City has great, enthusiastic fans except those who call you up and threaten to kill you.

BUDDY BELL

KAUFFMAN STADIUM

I never thought I'd like any ballpark that had artificial turf, but I must admit Kauffman Stadium is pretty darn nice. It's very clean, and the fountains and waterfalls beyond the outfield fences are even more impressive in person than on TV. I caught an evening game when the clouds and sky accented the fountains perfectly. A row of pines on the embankment just beyond the park helps create the feeling of being miles from anything, despite the fact that the park is located at the intersection of two major highways and sits beside the Chiefs' Arrowhead Stadium.

I did think it was ironic that the only grass in the stadium, at the time, was on the hitters' background, behind the center field fence, and not on the playing field. Fortunately, Kansas City has since replaced the artificial turf with natural grass, so now I can go back to disliking all parks with artificial turf. In addition to changing the playing surface, the Royals moved the outfield walls in ten feet and lowered the fences from twelve to nine feet high, which should result in Kauffman Stadium becoming a hitter's paradise.

There are only three levels of seating, with a capacity of just 40,000. Most of the seats are along the foul lines, so very few of the seats are that far from the field of play. The outfield has two small bleacher areas just past each foul pole. Both are prime home run spots. As I walked around the stadium, I couldn't find a single seat that had a bad sight line. Royals tickets are some of the most reasonable in the big leagues, ranging from a low of $5 for general admission to a high of just $14 for club boxes. General admission seats go on sale an hour and a half before game time at gates C and D. Another bargain

145

available Mondays and Thursdays is the half-price view level reserved seats. These seats are upstairs and normally sell for $9. One thing about the park that I did find peculiar was that the ushers do not allow you into the outfield seats during batting practice, unless you have a ticket for the general admission area. So if you bought a cheap seat, you could catch a home run during batting practice, but if you bought a better seat, you couldn't.

In addition to the fountains beyond the outfield fences, the park's most impressive feature is the scoreboards. A massive scoreboard in the shape of a crown and shield dominates center field, as does a replay board in left center. The scoreboard is twelve stories tall and lights up each time a Royal hits a home run. One of the more pleasant touches is a scarcity of advertising inside the park. The only exceptions are six rotating signs above and behind the outfield fence.

There's a Royals Hall of Fame behind section 107 on the plaza level that consists of little more than jerseys and equipment used by better-known players. Also on display is the 1985 World Series Trophy. If you are traveling with children, be sure to check out the fan amusement area, just inside gate B, where kids can clock their fastball on a radar gun or have their own baseball card made.

HISTORY

On May 15, 1973, Kansas City was the site of Nolan Ryan's first career no-hitter. It's the first of seven he threw over his distinguished career. Ryan's first no-no was also the stadium's first no-hitter. A few years later, on May 14, 1977, Royals fans witnessed another no-hitter, only this time Royals pitcher Jim Colborn threw the gem, beating the Rangers 6–0.

The Royals first home playoff game victory came at the expense of the New York Yankees on October 10, 1976. The Royals got a taste of what it's like to win a World Series game on October 17, 1980, by beating the Phillies 4–3 in 10 innings. The Phillies, however, recovered to win the series. On October 27, 1985, the Royals brought home their first World Series trophy by beating the Cardinals in seven games after trailing the series three games to one.

Bret Saberhagen presented Kansas City fans with another gem when he threw a no-hitter to beat the White Sox 7–0 on August 26, 1991. Paul Molitor became the 21st player to collect 3,000 hits, on September 16, 1996, in a 6–5 loss to Kansas City. Molitor was the first player in history to reach 3,000 hits by hitting a triple exactly three years after Dave Winfield got his three-thousandth hit. On April 29, 1997, Chili Davis hit his 300th career home run. Davis made his milestone homer count as it gave the Royals a tenth-inning victory over the Blue Jays.

View of Kansas City's famous fountains and scoreboard at dusk. With the addition of a grass playing field, Kauffman Stadium is among the nicest in baseball. (Photo by Author)

GETTING TO KAUFFMAN STADIUM
1 Royal Way

Kauffman Stadium accounts for half of the world's first side-by-side football and baseball stadiums. Together, Kansas City's two stadiums are known as the Truman Sports Complex. The complex is located southeast of downtown Kansas City at the intersection of I-70 and 435. Unfortunately, Kauffman Stadium is not close to the airport or downtown, where most of the hotels are. It is, however, easy to find and traffic is not too bad. Tailgating is encouraged in the stadium lots; areas A1–A3 seem to be popular spots with the tailgaters. However, if you are not tailgating, you might consider parking at a restaurant across the street, having something to eat or drink, and save $5 on parking. If you are staying at a downtown hotel, you can take an express bus to the park. The **Royals Express** begins running one hour and fifty minutes before game time and up until fifty minutes after each game. For more information call (816) 221-0660.

WHAT TO DO AND SEE IN KANSAS CITY

Kansas City is a clean, attractive city that offers plenty to do during the day and a good variety of nightlife. If you want to get a quick sense of what there is to do in town, board the **Kansas City Trolley** at one of the downtown hotels, or call to find the stop nearest you. For the modest fee of $4 per day, you can get on and off as often as you like and see the sights as the driver tells you a little about Kansas City's storied past. The **Nelson-Atkins Museum of Art**, in addition to works by Rembrandt, Seurat, Monet, van Gogh, Gauguin, Renoir, Degas, and Cezanne, has the largest collection of Henry Moore's bronze sculptures in the United States. Of particular interest to baseball fans would be Andy Warhol's *Baseball*, a giant silkscreen of an old newspaper photo of Roger Maris's classic home run swing. Admission to the Atkins museum is a bargain at $4 for adults. The museum is closed on Mondays.

Ask anybody in Kansas City what there is to do and they're likely to mention the **Country Club Plaza**. The plaza is an outdoor area of shops, restaurants, and galleries near downtown Kansas City. The fourteen-block area is modeled after the Spanish city of Seville, one of Kansas City's sister cities, and features Spanish architecture, with a number of handsome statues and fountains. Built in 1922, it is reportedly the world's first shopping center.

Before there was a Kansas City, there was Westport. Originally settled in the 1830s as a last chance for westward travelers to stock up on necessary supplies, it has since become **Westport Square**, an area of trendy boutiques, galleries, and restaurants by day and Kansas City's place to be for nightlife. A number of good cafes, restaurants, and sports bars are within walking distance of each other, making this a good place to consider around dinnertime.

The **Negro League's Baseball Museum** is the only museum of its kind. It offers a glimpse of baseball history before Jackie Robinson broke the major league's color barrier by signing to play with the Brooklyn Dodgers in 1947. It's located in the historic 18th and Vine Street section of town, at 1601 East 18th Street. The collection of Negro League memorabilia is the largest in the nation and includes uniforms, photos, film footage, and autographs of Negro League stars. The museum's powerful centerpiece is the **Field of Legends**, a mock field with life-size bronze statues of ten Hall of Fame ballplayers, including Josh Gibson behind the plate, Cool Papa Bell in left field, Buck Leonard at first, and Leroy "Satchel" Paige on the mound.

The **Liberty Memorial** is a 217-foot memorial tower to soldiers who fought and died in World War I. It was dedicated in 1921 by Calvin Coolidge in the presence of all five allied commanders. The top of the tower offers one of the best panoramic views of the city and can be reached by elevator for just $1. At the base of the tower is a museum featuring weapons, uniforms, and other war memorabilia of the era. There's also a full-scale replica of a World War I battle trench. Across the street is the newly remodeled **Union Station**. The second largest train station in the United States, it was renovated to the tune of $253 million and houses a number of restaurants, bars, and shops. **Fitz's** is a two-story place, specializing in a local brew—Boulevard Beer—with a sports bar upstairs and a root beer brewery below.

Worlds of Fun is an amusement park, not far from the ballpark, at I-435 and Parvin Road, offering more than 140 rides and attractions including the world's largest steel roller coaster and the number 1 rated wooden roller coaster. Next door you'll find **Oceans of Fun**, a sixty-acre water theme park. Combination tickets are available.

South of downtown, just off Interstate 435 in Swope Park, you'll find the **Kansas City Zoo**. It recently underwent a $71 million expansion and renovation and has become one of the largest metropolitan zoos in the country. Admission is just $5 for adults, parking is $2 more. Admission is free on Tuesdays from 9 AM until noon.

NIGHTLIFE IN KANSAS CITY

The number of places near the ballpark to go to before and after a game is extremely limited because the Royals play on the outskirts of town. Across the river, about five minutes from downtown in North Kansas City, you'll find **Chappell's Restaurant & Sports Museum** at 323 Armour Road, said to have the largest collection of sports memorabilia in the midwest. You'll find room after room of historical pieces, including the 1973 Oakland A's World Series trophy, a gold glove from 1963, countless baseballs signed by such Hall-of-Famers as Babe Ruth, Dizzy Dean, and Ty Cobb. Just fifteen minutes from the ballpark, it's worth the drive, and don't be surprised to encounter a national sports celebrity while you are there.

Fortunately, what Kansas City may lack for entertainment near the ballpark, it more than makes up for in the downtown area. Your best bet is to pick up one of Kansas City's free entertainment guides, such as the *New Times* and *Pitch Weekly*.

The premiere nightspot for out-of-towners seems to be **Westport Square**, an ideal place to barhop. A popular spot in Westport Square is **Kelly's**. Housed in Kansas City's oldest building, Kelly's has a genuine pub atmosphere with a friendly staff and an excellent menu of inexpensive entrees. If you are in the mood for live music, **The Lonestar** hosts a wide variety of national-caliber acts from folk to heavy metal. Located at 4117 Mill Street, they are certainly worth a phone call in advance, as they tend to sell out many of their more renowned shows.

The **Grand Emporium** is Kansas City's home of the blues. It has twice been awarded the W. C. Handy Best Blues Club in America and honored eight consecutive years as Kansas City's Best Live Music Spot. The atmosphere is that of a classic blues dive; dark, smoky, and intimate. The sightlines are some of the best I've seen, and the acoustics are fantastic. On Mondays they offer alternative music, attracting more of a college crowd, and Wednesdays are slated for reggae music. Thursday through Saturday you're likely to see some of the great blues legends. As you stroll around the place, checking out the posters of past performances, you'll see that almost all the greats played here at one time.

Kansas City has a great jazz heritage and a number of fine jazz places. The current leader of the pack seems to be the **Phoenix Piano Bar and Grill** at 302 W. 8th Street, a cozy place with a casual to dressy atmosphere and an extensive, yet remarkably inexpensive, menu. The *New Yorker* magazine named it one of the best jazz and blues bars in the country. The Phoenix offers live jazz six nights a week (Monday to Saturday) and is open only for dinner. Get there early if you want a good table; the place gets packed not long after they open.

WHERE TO STAY IN KANSAS CITY

There is no mass transit to speak of in Kansas City, and a cab ride from the airport to downtown is more than $20. Kansas City International Airport shuttle vans run pretty regularly, but cost $19 roundtrip to downtown and $30 to and from the stadium. With that in mind, if you plan to see a few KC attractions and don't plan to have a rental car, it may be worth a few extra dollars to stay downtown near the sights and nightlife, especially since a Royals shuttle is available to the ballpark from most downtown hotels.

However, if you are in town primarily for a ballgame or two, you might consider one of the hotels near the stadium, as they are much less expensive than their downtown counterparts. Several of these stadium area hotels also offer convenient airport shuttles.

DOWNTOWN HOTELS

Best Western Seville Plaza Hotel   4309 Main Street (800) 825-0197 or (816) 561-9600   Nice accommodations located between the Plaza and Westport Square.

Embassy Suites   220 West 43rd Street (800) EMBASSY or (816) 756-1720 Within a short walk of both the Country Club Plaza and Westport Square.

Hyatt Regency   Crown Center (800) 233-1234 or (816) 421-1234 Deluxe downtown accommodations connected to the Crown Center via covered walkway.

Marriott Downtown   200 West 12th Street (800) 228-9290 or (816) 421-6800   Very nice accommodations. Convenient to nightlife and cultural district.

The Raphael   325 Ward Parkway (800) 821-5343 or (816) 756-3800   Small, yet luxurious European style hotel across the street from the Plaza area.

Sheraton Suites   770 West 47th Street (800) 325-3535 or (816) 931-4400
Nice accommodations in the Plaza area. Be sure to ask about weekend
packages.

TEAM HOTELS

Ritz Carlton   (800) 241-3333 or (816) 756-1500   Red Sox, White Sox, and A's.
Westin Crown Center   (800) 228-3000 or (816) 474-4400   Orioles, Angels,
Indians, Tigers, Brewers, Twins, Yankees, Mariners, Rangers, and Blue Jays.

HOTELS NEAR THE STADIUM

Adam's Mark Hotel   I-70 at Truman Sports Complex (800) 444-ADAM or
(816) 737-0200   Located across the street from ballpark, it offers two
restaurants and two bars.
Drury Inn   3830 Blue Ridge Cutoff (800) 325-8300 or (816) 923-3000
Directly across the street from ballpark. Airport shuttle available.
Holiday Inn   4011 Blue Ridge Cutoff (800) HOLIDAY or (816) 353-5300
Nice hotel that allows you to park your car and walk across the street to the
ballpark.

GOOD TO KNOW

- For schedule information or tickets to Royals games call (816) 921-8000.
  The Royals official Internet address is www.kcroyals.com.
- Royals games can be heard on **WIBW 580 AM** and **WDAF 610 AM**.
- For more information on Kansas City sights, attractions, and hotels, call
  the **Convention and Visitors Bureau** at (800) 767-7700. The city's official
  Web site is www.kansascity.com.

Closest major league cities (and drive times): Saint Louis—256 miles (4
hours and 25 minutes); Minneapolis—440 miles (7 hours and 15 minutes).

IN THE VICINITY

The Harry S. Truman Library and Museum is one of the most visited presidential libraries in the country. Truman led the nation during the final months
of World War II, made the decision to drop nuclear weapons on Japan, sent
troops to Korea, and fired General Douglas MacArthur. His terms in office were
far from uneventful. The library/museum is located in Independence, Missouri,
at Highway 24 and Delaware. For more information, call (816) 833-1400.

✦ MILWAUKEE ✦

They know when to cheer, and they know when to boo. And they know when to drink beer. They do it all the time.

GORMAN THOMAS

MILLER PARK

I was never a fan of County Stadium. The fans were terrific, the food among the best in the game, Bernie Brewer and the Klement's Sausage Races hilariously entertaining, and the cozy proximity of the seats to the field allowed fans to be right on top of the action, but the building was—in a word—unimpressive. Think Tiger Stadium with corrugated metal siding and a less scenic field of play. So, it was with eager anticipation that I awaited the arrival of Miller Park.

Unlike many new stadiums with unrelated corporate monikers, I think it's wonderful that Miller Park is named for the big, local beer company. Busch Stadium certainly helped put St. Louis on the map as a great sports town. The Brewers were determined to build a distinctive ballpark and hired HKS of Dallas for construction. HOK Sport of Kansas City and Ellerbe Becket, also of Kansas City, have been the predominant big league stadium builders in recent years, so a fresh, new perspective may be good for baseball. The Brewers took their ideas to local fans, via newspaper surveys, before deciding on the newfangled "fan" roof design. The roof pivots out from behind home plate in seven sections, supported by six arching box chords that give the roof a modern architectural exterior and reach 330 feet above the field. For fans seated around the infield, this virtually removes the roof from sight when opened.

I don't, however, understand the need for a roof in Milwaukee. Wrigley Field is just ninety miles away and is generally regarded as one of the most beloved parks in baseball. I suspect Detroit is every bit as chilly as Milwaukee in the early spring and fall months. The Seligs must be optimists, and expect to play a bunch of home games in late October in the years to come.

This new "fan" design could very well become the future of retractable roof stadiums. Time will tell if the support apparatus, which is seemingly more complicated than the sliding arches of the new ballparks in Seattle, Houston, and Phoenix, will operate without major problems and withstand the heavy snows and harsh winds of Wisconsin.

The stadium has a stark contrast of styles, with the traditional brick and exposed steel stadium, juxtaposed by the ultramodern retractable roof. A local architectural design executive lamented, "It's like putting a spaceship on Yankee Stadium." Love it or hate it, there's certainly no mistaking the building for any other venue as you approach it from the interstate. Like Enron Field in Houston and Seattle, Milwaukee truly had nowhere to go but up. I am certain you won't find too many folks wishing the Brewers still played their home games in antiquated County Stadium.

The outfield fence at Miller Park is close to symmetrical, with a modest bulge enlarging centerfield between the power alleys and no funky corners along the wall. It's deeper down the lines than County Stadium, with the left field foul pole 342 feet from home plate and the left field power alley a respectable 372 feet. Dead center is the deepest part of the park at 400 feet, the right center field wall is marked at 375 feet, and the right field corner is 345 feet from home. The outfield fence is higher in left field, and there is a plexiglass wall in right-center field that allows fans without tickets to see what's going on inside. The main entry plaza, behind home plate, features larger-than-life statues of Hank Aaron and Robin Yount.

Although the average ticket price at Miller Park is $18 as opposed to $12 at County Stadium, baseball in Milwaukee has retained its affordability. The Brewers also created a more intimate atmosphere by eliminating more than 10,000 seats and bringing the seating bowl closer to the playing field.

Milwaukee fans still tailgate in the parking lot before and after games and are likely to pound a few more cold ones once inside Miller Park, as "Roll Out the Barrel" blares over the park's sound system during the seventh-inning stretch. As long as Bernie Brewer occupies his perch in the outfield rafters, the sausage mascots continue to entertain fans, and relief pitchers are delivered to the mound in the sidecar of a Harley-Davidson, fans here will continue to support their beloved Brewers. Who knows? As the commissioner pursues his dream of league-wide parity, the Brewers might even put together a winning team. My apologies to fans of the Cubs and Red Sox, who are at least able to attend home games in two of the finest parks in baseball, but no city deserves it more.

An architectural rendering of Miller Park in Milwaukee. (Courtesy Milwaukee Brewers Baseball Club)

HISTORY

The Brewers opened Miller Park on April 6, 2001, with a game against the Cincinnati Reds, the same team they faced in the final game at County Stadium. Forty-eight years earlier, County Stadium opened on April 6, 1953, as home to the Milwaukee Braves. The Braves left Milwaukee for Atlanta after the 1965 season. Major-league baseball returned to Milwaukee and County Stadium when the Brewers faced the Angels on April 7, 1970. One of the most memorable events at County Stadium happened on May 26, 1959, when Pittsburgh Pirates pitcher Harvey Haddix pitched 12 no-hit innings only to lose 1–0 to the Braves in 13 innings. Despite pitching a flawless game—no hits, walks, or errors—for 12 innings, he is not credited with an official no-hitter.

After becoming home to the Brewers, County Stadium was the scene of several milestone moments. On June 19, 1974, Kansas City Royals ace Steve Busby beat the Brewers with his only career no-hitter. Hammerin' Hank Aaron, finishing up his career in Milwaukee, hit his 755th and final home run off Angels pitcher Dick Drago on July 20th, 1976.

On August 27, 1982, Oakland A's outfielder Rickey Henderson broke Lou Brock's single season stolen base record by swiping his 119th base of the season. The Brewers were the victim as Nolan Ryan earned his 300th career victory on July 31, 1990. Milwaukee's favorite son, Robin Yount, became the third-youngest player in history to get 3,000 hits with a base rap off the Indians on September 9, 1992. On April 7, 1998, the Brewers entered the National League with a 6–4 win over Montreal.

GETTING TO MILLER PARK
201 South 46th Street

The stadium is just a few miles west of downtown Milwaukee, near the intersection of Interstate 94 and U.S. 41. There are no available mass-transit options other than the city bus system. Highways are not particularly well marked, so pay attention as you approach the stadium. Traffic is not a big problem and parking is adequate. Lots adjacent to the park offer the best tailgate opportunities as well as public rest rooms.

WHAT TO DO AND SEE IN MILWAUKEE

It's almost impossible to visit Milwaukee during the summer months and not be there for one of its many ethnic festivals. Several of the larger festivals coincide with the major league baseball season. One of the city's most popular festivals, **River Splash**, is held along the banks of the Milwaukee River in downtown Milwaukee's new **RiverWalk** area. The winding pathway along the river was expanded at a cost of $9.6 million.

Milwaukee's largest and oldest festival, **Summerfest**, is held along the shores of Lake Michigan in Maier Festival Park, on the western edge of downtown. It's hailed as "The World's Greatest Music Festival" and is generally scheduled to run from the last Saturday in June through the second Sunday in July. **Festa Italiana** is slated for the second to last weekend in July, followed by **German Fest**, which runs from noon to midnight, Friday through Sunday of the last weekend in July. **Irish Fest** is held annually on the third weekend in August, followed by **Mexican Fiesta** the next weekend. All four ethnic festivals are held in Maier Festival Park. Milwaukee's festival calendar winds down about the same time the major-league baseball season does, culminating with **Oktoberfest**, also in Maier Festival Park. Despite its name, the festival actually falls on the last three full weekends in September.

The **Milwaukee County Zoo** is considered to be one of the country's finest. The zoo's intricately designed moat system creates the illusion of a natural habitat that is shared by both predator and prey. More than 3,000 animals roam the grounds, which are divided into the 5 continents of the world. The zoo is located ten minutes from downtown, just west of County Stadium, off U.S. 18. Admission is $6 for adults.

The **Milwaukee Public Museum** is located a few blocks west of the Milwaukee River, at 800 West Wells Street. A combination of natural history, science, and fine arts museums, all under one roof, it houses the nation's fourth-largest collection of natural history exhibits, as well as several outstanding environmental exhibits. The museum is open daily from 9 AM to 5 PM and admission is $4.50 for adults.

NIGHTLIFE IN MILWAUKEE

Baseball fans probably won't mind the fact that some of the city's best nightclubs happen to be sports bars. **Fourth Base** is one of the better baseball bars in the country. It's located not far from Miller Park, about ten minutes southwest of downtown, at 5117 West National Avenue. While this is a sports bar through and through, the emphasis is definitely on the nation's pastime. As you enter, you'll cross over home plate embedded in the floor. Once inside you'll be surrounded by baseball memorabilia, and no matter where you sit, you'll have a good view of one of the seven TV screens that encircle a good-size oval bar.

If you prefer to barhop, the **Water Street** area, one block east of the Milwaukee River, in the middle of downtown, offers a good selection of restaurants and a few nightclubs within walking distance of each other. **Luke's of Milwaukee** is at 1225 North Water Street, about three blocks from the Bradley Center. Luke's offers three levels, each with its own sports-oriented bar (baseball, football, and basketball) and forty-two TVs, five of which have large screens.

Lucci's, at 1135 North Water Street, is another three-level sports bar/pizzeria that has become one of the area's hottest night spots, especially before and after events at the Bradley Center. Not too far away, at 1101 North Water Street, you'll find the **Water Street Brewery**, one of the city's many fine brew pubs. What sets it apart from many of the others is the cozy atmosphere and a spectacular view of the city. In addition to brewing their own beer on site, they have a nice selection of appetizers, bratwursts, sandwiches, and dinner entrees.

Another area with a concentration of pubs and clubs is historic **Walker's Point**, along the southern edge of downtown on West National Avenue, between 1st and 2nd streets. All told, the area is home to a dozen European-style pubs and beer gardens, all within walking distance of each other. Or you can take the area trolley from place to place. Speaking of pubs, the **Brown Bottle Pub** has a classic 1930s atmosphere and, despite being located in the historic Schlitz Brewery Park, offers a selection of more than one hundred beers from around the world. The Brown Bottle has an extensive pub menu and is open for lunch and dinner Monday–Friday and after 5 PM on Saturdays. It's located at 221 West Galena, between 2nd and 3rd streets.

Milwaukee has a number of unique restaurants that should not be missed, if at all possible. The **Safe House**, at 779 North Front Street, is one of the most extraordinary restaurants in the country. The place's decor is straight out of a James Bond movie, and you'll have to know the password to gain entrance through the "International Export Office" or be subjected to an entertaining "security check." Monte Carlo "gaming lessons" are held Monday through Thursday.

Mader's German Restaurant, a Milwaukee institution at 1037 North Old World Third Street, is equal parts restaurant, bar, and museum. The dining halls remind you of a medieval castle with their vaulted ceilings and a $2 million collection of knight's armor and old world art. Mader's adjoining bar offers a long list of imported and domestic beers and more than 200 imported wines. It houses hand-carved oak tables and chairs that once furnished Baron Von Richtofen's castle in Germany.

Country music fans will want to check out **Bronco Billy's** at 355 South 27th Street. This is a good-sized place that draws a crowd on the weekends and features line dancing six days a week with occasional live music.

WHERE TO STAY IN MILWAUKEE

Because Milwaukee's sights and attractions are so spread out and there is no mass transit system other than the city bus, it is not critical to stay at a downtown hotel. The biggest concentrations of hotels are in the heart of downtown and near the airport, in Oak Creek, about ten minutes south of downtown Milwaukee.

AREA HOTELS

Astor Hotel   924 East Juneau Avenue (800) 558-0200 or (414) 271-4220   Reasonably priced hotel located in the northeast corner of downtown.

Best Western Woods View Inn   5501 West National Avenue (800) 528-1234 or (414) 671-6400   A nice hotel just eight blocks away from County Stadium.

Holiday Inn Milwaukee City Centre   611 West Wisconsin Avenue (800) HOLIDAY or (414) 273-2950   One of the more conveniently located downtown hotels with regard to the stadium.

Park East Hotel   916 East State Street (800) 328-PARK or (414) 276-8800   Downtown hotel overlooking Lake Michigan.

Ramada Inn Downtown   633 West Michigan Street (800) 228-2828 or (414) 272-8410   Reasonably priced, newly renovated downtown hotel.

Red Roof Inn   6360 S. 13th Street Oak Creek (800) THE ROOF or (414) 764-3500   Inexpensive accommodations located south of downtown, near the airport.

TEAM HOTELS

Hyatt Regency   333 West Kilbourn Avenue (800) 233-1234 or (414) 276-1234   Angels and White Sox.

Pfister Hotel   424 East Wisconsin Avenue (800) 558-8222 or (414) 276-8686 Indians, Blue Jays, and Mariners.

Wyndham Milwaukee Center   139 East Kilbourn Avenue (800) 996-3426 or (414) 273-8222   All other American League clubs.

GOOD TO KNOW

- For schedule information or tickets to Brewers games, call (414) 933-1818 or (414) 933-9000. The Brewers official Internet address is www.milwaukeebrewers.com.
- Brewers games can be heard on **WTMJ 620 AM.**
- For more information on Milwaukee sights, attractions, and hotels, call the **Convention & Visitors Bureau** at (800) 231-0903.
- The **Greater Milwaukee Open** is generally scheduled to start in late August.

Closest major league cities (and drive times): Chicago—90 miles (1 hour and 50 minutes); Cincinnati—385 miles (7 hours and 5 minutes); Minneapolis—398 miles (6 hours and 45 minutes); Detroit—369 miles (7 hours and 15 minutes).

IN THE VICINITY

Green Bay, Wisconsin, is home to the only publicly owned NFL team. The Packers were founded in 1911 and have won an unprecedented 11 league championships, including the first 2 Super Bowls and another in 1997. The Packers play all their home games at ageless Lambeau Field, which holds nearly 60,000 fans. Despite the fact that Green Bay has a population of less than 100,000 people, tickets to Packer's games have been sold out for years and can only be obtained through ticket agencies and from people selling their tickets the day of the game. Even if you don't get to see the Packers play, it's worth a trip to see the **Packers Hall of Fame**, across from the stadium. The Hall of Fame is open daily, and admission is $5.50 for adults. For more information, call (414) 499-4281 or call the Green Bay Convention and Visitors Bureau at (800) 236-3976.

TEN FAVORITE MAJOR-LEAGUE BALLPARK QUIRKS

10 The giant glove and McCovey's Cove at Pacific Bell Ballpark   The old three-finger style glove dominates the area beyond the bleachers and watching the boats slip in and out of the cove in hopes of scoring a home run ball will never get old.

9 Giant "Hefty Bag" wall in Minnesota's Hubert Humphrey Metrodome   The stretched canvas wall is so forgiving in some parts that a fielder can actually reach a ball that is several feet into home run territory.

8 The stainless steel player statues at Comerica Park   No trip to Comerica would be complete without a visit to the concourse beyond the bleachers to see Tiger greats Horton, Newhauser, Kaline, Greenberg, Gehringer, and Cobb.

7 The "Rockpile" bleacher section at Denver's Coors Field   One of the big leagues' best bargains, a section of inexpensive center field seats that go on sale a few hours before game time.

6 Exploding scoreboard at the new Comiskey Park   A bigger, some say better, version of the old park's original fireworks-spewing scoreboard.

5 Bernie Brewers' giant slide into a stein of beer at Miller Park   On those rare occasions that a Brewer hits a home run their daredevil mascot slides into a giant mug of beer from his perch above the center field bleachers.

4 Fountains and waterfalls beyond the outfield fence at Kauffman Stadium   With its new grass playing surface, Kauffman Stadium is one of the most picturesque ballparks in the big leagues.

3 Right field warehouse wall at Camden Yards   Few ballpark quirks define a stadium so completely. It also houses a restaurant, sports bar, and a souvenir shop that are open to the public.

2 Fenway Park's bizarre shape, the "Green Monster," and manual scoreboard in left field   Built to fit in an existing neighborhood, Fenway Park takes on the image of its surroundings.

1 Wrigley Field's ivy-covered outfield wall, rooftop seats across Waveland Avenue, and the giant center field scoreboard   Wrigley is so small that seats across the street on top of neighborhood buildings are closer to the field than upper deck seats at many of the middle-aged, multideck behemoths.

◆ MINNEAPOLIS ◆

It's a travesty. Hit the ball on the ground and it bounces over your head. Hit it in the air and you can't see it.

BOBBY COX

HUBERT H. HUMPHREY METRODOME

The Metrodome is the largest air-supported dome in the world. As you walk in, prepare to be hit with a stiff breeze that seems to be trying to prevent you from coming inside. If you don't like to see baseball played on a carpet under a roof, you may wish the breeze was more successful. I visited the Metrodome right after seeing a game at the Seattle Kingdome. In comparison, the Metrodome is not quite as dark inside, has fewer seats, and, thankfully, the playing field has a few more quirks than the Kingdome. Compared with just about any other stadium, however, it may not fare as well.

It is worth a visit, if for no other reason than to experience a game under such bizarre conditions. The outfield dimensions are about as asymmetrical as they can get. The right field corner is only 326 feet away, the power alley in right is just 327 feet, straightaway center is at 407 feet, the left-center field power alley measures 385 feet, and the left field corner, a relatively deep 343 feet.

The varied fences make things even more interesting. The "Hefty Bag" is a twenty-three-foot high wall in right field that can drive an outfielder crazy when he trys to gauge a ball's carom. The wall's lower seven feet is a regular padded wall, which causes the ball to ricochet back toward the infield, while the upper half is nothing more than stretched canvas with almost no bounce

Exterior view of the Metrodome and Minneapolis skyline. (Courtesy of the Minnesota Twins)

160

to it. Just the opposite is true in left field. The top 6-foot section is made of plexiglass, which the ball takes a big bounce off, while the lower half creates a more subtle carom. The center field wall consists of a seven-foot high stretched canvas, and, like the "Hefty Bag," has almost no rebound at all. When a fielder runs into it, it actually gives, allowing him to catch a ball that would normally be two or three feet past the fence.

Despite its rather deep left field and tall fences, the Metrodome is a hitter-friendly park that has earned its nickname "Homerdome." The Twins must enjoy playing in the Metrodome, as they have won two World Series championships since 1987, without ever winning a series game at the National League opponent's park.

The white ceiling can make for some amusing attempts to field fly balls, and the wall behind home plate kicks wild pitches and passed balls toward first base, turning them into an adventure as well.

Tickets range from $17 for VIP-level seats to $4 for upper deck general admission seats. The foul territory is rather large, especially near the diamond, so seats around home plate are not necessarily the best in the park. Just past first and third base, the stands squeeze in toward the playing field, bringing seats in those sections a little closer to the action with a better chance at snagging a foul ball.

Some of the stadium's highlights include scoreboard replays from cameras directly above home and second base, presenting a great view of stolen base attempts, pitches, swings, and other plays at home. The seats are comfortable, offering a good deal of leg room and a cup holder on the back of each. Concessions are quite good and reasonably priced, although vendors in the stands seemed scarce. There's an out-of-town scoreboard just below the roof in left field, and additional scoreboards do a decent job of keeping you abreast of the action. The replay boards are state of the art, but between innings they feature TV-type commercials that can be annoying—as annoying as the rotating billboards.

A 200-foot-long curtain covering the right and right-center field upper deck was added in 1996 to give the dome a less empty feeling. As a result, nearly 8,000 seats were eliminated for baseball games, bringing the Metrodome's capacity down to just over 48,000. The curtain is fifty-one feet high and features five banners touting the Twins postseason accomplishments and portraits of former Twins stars. Also new since the 1996 season is a Kid's Fun Zone in the upper-deck concourse beyond right field. Kids can test their fastball, have a baseball card made, or try their hand at a video batting cage simulator.

HISTORY

The Metrodome hosted its first regular-season game, a loss to the Seattle Mariners, on April 6, 1982. On October 25, 1987, in seven games against the

Cardinals, the Twins won their first World Series since moving to Minnesota. Four years later, the Twins won a second title, with a hard-fought victory over the Braves on October 27, 1991. This series was even more exciting than their last, and it culminated with a seventh-game 1–0 victory in 10 innings that many consider to be the best World Series game since game 6 of the 1975 series between the Reds and Red Sox.

On September 16, 1993, Dave Winfield collected his 3,000th career hit with an RBI single off Dennis Eckersley in the 9th inning. Only 14,564 fans were on hand to witness the milestone hit as the Twins were on their way to a 5th-place finish. Hometown hero Kirby Puckett earned his 2,000th career hit on April 8, 1994. That same month, on April 27, Twins fans were treated to a no-hitter as Scott Erickson blanked the Brewers 6–0. On June 30, 1995, Eddie Murray, playing with the Cleveland Indians, got his 3,000th career hit with a base rap off Mike Trombley.

GETTING TO THE METRODOME
501 Chicago Avenue, South

Parking is available in a garage right across the street from the stadium for a very reasonable $5 per car. Aside from the local bus, there are no mass-transit options. The express bus from St. Paul is a short twenty-five 167 168 minute ride, only costs $1, and drops you off a few blocks from the park.

If you get to the park early, you may want to check out the **Baseball Museum**, at 910 Third Street South, across from Gate A of the Metrodome. It's worth stopping by, if for no other reason than to see its sizable collection of old uniforms, autographed bats and balls, photos, and record books. Admission is free, and many items are for sale.

WHAT TO DO AND SEE IN MINNEAPOLIS

For a glimpse of baseball as it should be, check out the **St. Paul Saints**, whose schedule runs from June to Labor Day. The Saints, who play in the independent Northern League, have hit the big time recently with players like Darryl Strawberry and Jack Morris spending time with them before returning to the big leagues. The Saints play in Midway Stadium, an ugly outdoor park that you can't help but like. Midway Stadium seats only 6,311 fans, and season tickets are sold out for years to come. Saints ownership goes to great lengths to make a day at the ballpark a good time. Haircuts can be had in a barber chair directly behind home plate, massages are offered in the stands, a potbellied pig delivers balls to the umpire, and Saints promotions are some of the most unusual in the nation. This is not surprising when you consider that the Saints president is Mike Veeck, son of the late great Bill Veeck. Reserved seats cost

$6, and general-admission seats that sell for $4 go on sale two hours before game time.

The area's pride and joy is the **Walker Art Center** and the **Minneapolis Sculpture Garden**, located in the southwest corner of Minneapolis. The Walker Art Center has been called "The most exciting art center in America" by *Vogue* magazine. The museum has a permanent sculpture patio overlooking the sculpture garden that offers a nice view of the city skyline. The garden debuted in 1988 and has been visited by more than two million people since then. It is definitely worth a visit, even if you opt not to go to the Walker Art Center. The Garden is connected to **Loring Park** by a pedestrian bridge which allows you to cross the busy streets safely and wander through the city's biggest downtown park.

The museum itself is located at Hennepin Avenue and Vineland Place. Admission is $4 for adults. The sculpture garden is free. The museum offers free admission to all every Thursday and the first Saturday of every month.

The **Minneapolis Institute of Arts** is well south of downtown, at 2400 Third Avenue (at East 24th Street), but worth going out of your way for. More than 80,000 works of art spanning 4,000 years are on display. There is a particularly impressive collection of French Impressionist paintings and an exhibit of photography from photography's early days to the present. The museum is open every day except Monday, and admission is always free.

The **Minnesota Zoo** is about twenty minutes south of the city, in Apple Valley. It's spread out over 485 acres, making it the second largest zoo in America and has more than 2,000 animals representing 450 species. Admission is $6 for adults.

Also south of downtown, not far from the airport, along the banks of the Mississippi River is **Minnehaha Park and Falls**. The falls are said to have inspired Henry Wadsworth Longfellow's *Song of Hiawatha*. The park also offers miles of cycling and walking trails, as well as statues of Hiawatha and Minnehaha situated above the falls.

Bloomington's **Mall of America** has become one of the area's most-visited attractions. Mall of America is the nation's largest shopping and entertainment complex with more than 400 shops, theaters, restaurants, and bars, occupying 4.2 million square feet of space. The mall's centerpiece is a seven-acre indoor amusement park with twenty-six rides, known as **Camp Snoopy**. It's here you'll find a baseball-related reason to visit. Within Camp Snoopy is the original home plate from Metropolitan Stadium in its original position. Up on a wall, 522 feet away is the seat Harmon Killebrew hit with a home run in June of 1967. It was the longest home run ever hit at the old park. Today you'll find the new mega-mall where the stadium used to be. The mall also has fourteen movie screens and about a dozen nightclubs, including **America's Original Sports Bar**, a huge place with a bunch of TVs and a one-on-one basketball court, **Planet Hollywood**, **Knuckleheads Comedy Club**, and **Fat Tuesday**.

NIGHTLIFE IN MINNEAPOLIS

The place to be is **Hennepin Avenue** near the Target Center. My favorite place is the **Loon Cafe**, actually a block or two off Hennepin at 500 First Avenue North, in what is known as the Warehouse District. The place is a little on the dark side, but very comfortable, with a friendly, outgoing atmosphere. Both *Playboy* and *Esquire* magazines rated it as one of the top 100 bars in America. The **Rock Bottom Brewery**, at 825 South Hennepin, is one of the hotter nightspots in the area and with good reason. The atmosphere is laid-back, but the crowd is dressed to the nines and worthy of some serious scoping.

The Quest is one of the area's better alternative and progressive rock clubs. Located at 110 North 5th Street, this place offers live music or DJs nightly. **Blues Alley**, located in the Warehouse District at 15 Glenwood Avenue, has been around since 1954 and is a good bet for live music. The City's premier comedy club, the **Acme Comedy Company**, generally books regional and nationally known comics. It's located at 708 North First Street.

Another area of town known for its nightlife is **Dinkytown**, located on the east bank of the Mississippi, near the University. Also on the east side of the Mississippi, in St. Paul, is the recently refurbished historic district known as **Lowertown**. While it may not be as happening as Hennepin Avenue, there are a number of nightclubs, restaurants, and cafes to choose from in this area. For a more complete listing of area clubs, pick up a copy of the *City Pages*, Minneapolis's free entertainment weekly.

WHERE TO STAY IN MINNEAPOLIS

Minneapolis sights and attractions are not within an easy walk of each other. Nor is there a convenient form of mass transit that would make it particularly advantageous to stay downtown. With that in mind, you might want to consider staying near the stadium or even in St. Paul, which is just twenty minutes across the Mississippi River. In many cases, hotels in St. Paul or near the airport are less expensive than those in the heart of downtown. Listed below are a few hotels in Minneapolis and St. Paul.

HOTELS NEAR THE STADIUM OR DOWNTOWN

Crown Sterling Suites   425 South 7th Street (800) 433-4600 or (612) 333-3111   Closest hotel to the Metrodome. Connected to area shops and restaurants by Skyway.

Days Inn University　2407 University Avenue (800) 325-2525 or (612) 623-3999　Convenient to the university, Metrodome, downtown Minneapolis, and Saint Paul.

Four Points Hotel　1330 Industrial Blvd. (800) 325-3535 or (612) 331-1900　Within walking distance of the Metrodome. Ask about weekend packages.

Holiday Inn Metrodome　1500 Washington Avenue South (800) HOLIDAY or (612) 333-4646　Nice, well-kept hotel within walking distance of the stadium.

Quality Inn and Suites　41 North 10th Street (800) 423-4100 or (612) 339-9311　Moderately priced in the heart of downtown Minneapolis. Twins packages available.

Sheraton Minneapolis Metrodome　1330 Industrial Boulevard (800) 325-3535 or (612) 331-9100　Within walking distance of the Metrodome. Ask about weekend packages.

HOTELS IN ST. PAUL

Crown Sterling Suites　175 East 10th Street (612) 224-5400　Suite hotel not far from the Lowertown nightlife district.

Days Inn Civic Center　175 West 7th Street (at Kellogg Blvd.) (800) 325-2525 or (612) 292-8929　Affordable, newly remodeled hotel near the Civic Center.

Sheraton Inn Midway　400 Hamline Avenue North (800) 325-3535 or (612) 642-1234　As the name implies, the hotel is midway between the twin cities' downtown areas.

TEAM HOTELS

Marriott City Center　30 South 7th Street (800) 228-9290 or (612) 349-4000　Orioles, Angels, White Sox, Indians, Royals, Brewers, Mariners, Rangers, and Blue Jays.

Minneapolis Hilton and Towers　1001 Marquette Avenue South (800) HILTONS or (612) 376-1000　Tigers and A's.

Radisson Plaza　35 South 7th Street (800) 333-3333 or (612) 339-4900　Red Sox and Yankees.

GOOD TO KNOW

- For schedule information or tickets to Twins games call (612) 375-7444. The Twins official Internet address is www.wcco.com/sports/twins.
- Twins games can be heard on **WCCO 830 AM**. **KFAN 1130 AM** is the area's leading all-sports station.

- For more information on Minneapolis sights, attractions, and hotels, call the **Minneapolis Convention & Visitors Bureau** at (800) 445-7412. The city's official Web site is www.minneapolis.org.

Closest major league cities (and drive times): Milwaukee—398 miles (6 hours and 45 minutes); Kansas City—440 miles (7 hours and 15 minutes); Chicago—465 miles (8 hours and 15 minutes).

IN THE VICINITY

Field of Dreams, the baseball diamond carved out of a cornfield by Universal Studios in Dyersville, Iowa, is visited by nearly 60,000 people each year. There is no charge to visit the field, but donations are accepted. They encourage you to bring your own bats and balls to play on the field. The site is about 240 miles from Minneapolis. Because there is no direct route, the trip takes about five hours and forty-five minutes. For more information, write to 28963 Lansing Road, Dyersville, Iowa 52040. Or call them at (888) 875-8404.

One of the nation's best minor league ballparks is five hours southwest of the Minneapolis area in Sioux City, Iowa. Home to the **Sioux City Explorers** of the Northern League, Lewis and Clark Park seats 3,800 fans and is as intimate a park as you'll find anywhere. Unlike many minor league parks, Lewis and Clark offers comfortable seating, wide-open concession areas, and enjoyable promotions. Despite its handsome design, the stadium cost just $4 million to build, a bargain by today's standards. The Explorers' season runs from June through Labor Day. Tickets range from $3–6, with discounts available for children and seniors. For ticket information, call (712) 277-9467.

◆ ST. LOUIS ◆

*Ozzie Smith just made another play that I've never
seen anyone else make before, and I've seen him make
it more than anyone else has.*

JERRY COLEMAN

BUSCH STADIUM

Busch has a seating capacity of more than 56,000, making it the second biggest
of the four multisport, outdoor stadiums. Despite its massive size, it's also the
nicest. The stadium is among the cleanest and best-kept parks in the majors. It
is also one of the best at disguising the fact that it was both a football and baseball stadium. The reintroduction of a grass playing field in 1997 is a welcome
addition and goes a long way in improving the stadium.

An arched canopy running along the top of the park is crowned by 94
arches 130 feet above the playing field, giving Busch Stadium a distinct look
that helps set it apart from other parks of its genre. If your seats are upstairs
along the first base side you may want to take a peek through the arches for
a view of the Mississippi River and the Gateway Arch. Other unique features
of Busch Stadium are the Cardinal Hall of Fame inside the park on the third
level and a statue of Stan "The Man" Musial outside at the main entrance.
There is also the fantasy play-by-play booth which allows you to make a tape
of yourself calling a portion of the game, a Kids Corner recreation area, ATMs,
and party rooms that can be rented on a game-by-game basis for groups of 25
or more.

The Cardinals have a great baseball history with 15 pennants, 9 World
Series Championships, and 31 players in the Hall of Fame. As a result, St.
Louis has become a great baseball town, and the fans at Busch are some of
the most loyal in the game. The Cardinals regularly draw over two million
fans and, in years that they contend for the division, can be a tough ticket to

come by—especially for games against bitter rivals like the Cubs and Mets. That may change with realignment of the divisions and interleague play, but your best bet is to order Cardinal tickets well in advance.

Tickets are reasonable and range in price from $19 for field and loge boxes to as little as $6 for bleacher seats. Other options include loge reserved, which are located at the back of the first level for $12, terrace boxes for $14, terrace reserved for $11, and upper terrace reserved for $6. The field boxes are well worth the extra few dollars if they're available, as most of the other seats are a long way from the field of play. Bleachers in both left- and right-center fields are a good value; they're close to the field and sell out quickly. Beginning with the 1996 season, the Cardinals offered discount tickets for children with the purchase of adult tickets at regular prices.

The message boards, replay screens, and rotating signs at Busch turn the place into a veritable shrine to Budweiser. Even the hitters background in center field is a huge rotating sign that becomes a Bud billboard when the game is not in progress. They even go so far as to play the Budweiser jingle instead of "Take Me Out to the Ball Game" during the seventh-inning stretch. Anheuser-Busch recently sold the team and stadium to a group of local businessmen, so this may change.

The scoreboards and replay boards are nothing out of the ordinary, but do an adequate job of keeping you up-to-date on the game at hand. A giant mes-

Ninety-four arches encircle Busch Stadium 130 feet above the field and a grass playing surface was added in 1996. Otherwise you might not know whether you are in Pittsburgh, Philadelphia, Cincinnati, or St. Louis. (Photo by Author)

sage board sits beyond left-center field, while a replay board and clock occupy the other power alley. Out-of-town scores are flashed on auxiliary boards along each base path between the first and second levels. The outfield is rather large with symmetrical dimensions of 330 feet down the lines, 378 feet in the alleys, and 402 feet to straightaway center field. The outfield fence is a standard eight-foot high padded wall from foul pole to foul pole.

Concessions at Busch are better than average with a nice selection of traditional and nontraditional ballpark fare including pizza, a variety of Mexican food, steak sandwiches, and as you might expect, lots of Anheuser-Busch beer.

HISTORY

Busch Stadium opened with a 12-inning victory over the Atlanta Braves on May 12, 1966. Since then it has been the scene of many record performances. Bob Gibson struck out a World Series record 17 Tigers en route to a 4–0 win in game 1 of the fall classic on October 2, 1968. Steve Carlton set what was a major-league record at the time by striking out 19 batters against the New York Mets on September 15, 1969. Nineteen strikeouts still remains as a National League record.

Lou Brock broke Maury Wills' single season stolen-base record with his 105th theft of the year on September 10, 1974. On April 16, 1978, Bob Forsch beat the Phillies with a 5–0 no-hit victory. Lou Brock collected his 3,000th hit with a single off Cubs pitcher Dennis Lamp on August 13, 1979. Later that year, on September 23, Lou Brock got the 938th and last stolen base of his career.

On October 20, 1982, St. Louis fans saw the Cardinals win their first World Series title since 1968 with a game seven victory over the Brewers. On October 14, 1985, switch-hitter Ozzie Smith beat the Dodgers with a home run in the bottom of the ninth inning in the fifth game of the NLCS. It was his first career home run from the left side of the plate.

GETTING TO BUSCH STADIUM
250 Stadium Plaza

With the debut of St. Louis' MetroLink light rail system, getting around St. Louis is easier than ever. The MetroLink can bring you right to the ballpark from all over town, including the airport, for just $1. Transfers cost just 10 cents. In the downtown area, there is a "free fare zone" between Union Station, Busch Stadium, and Laclede's Landing, which allows you to travel free between 10 AM and 3 PM, making it easy to leave your car behind. A one-day pass is available for $3, a three-day pass costs just $7, and a weekly pass is just $11. Any of the three allow you unlimited use of the MetroLink, as well as city bus lines. For information about MetroLink schedules and routes, call (314) 231-2345.

The stadium is also convenient to highway 40 from the west, I-55 from the south, and I-70 from the north. It's only a few blocks from the Gateway Arch, so if you head toward the Arch, you won't be far from the stadium. There are three stadium parking lots and a few stadium garages that offer secure, reasonably priced parking. Tailgating is encouraged in the lot at the corner of 7th and Spruce.

WHAT TO DO AND SEE IN ST. LOUIS

No visit to St. Louis would be complete without a visit to the **Gateway Arch.** Even if you don't have time to go up inside the arch, stop by the riverside park known as **Jefferson National Expansion Memorial Gateway Park** to get a close-up view one of the country's tallest and most recognizable monuments. If you decide you want to get to the top, you'll have to wait in line for an egg-shaped pod to take you and three other folks to an observation room at the center of the arch, 630 feet above St. Louis, where a great view of the city awaits. The tram is cramped and hot, but the ride is quick, and the view from the top is well worth the $2.50 fee. Lines for the tram are shortest when the arch first opens at 8:30 in the morning or in the early evening. The **Museum of Westward Expansion** and the **Arch Odyssey Theater**, showing an interesting film about the building of the Arch, are located at the base of the monument. Both are included in the Arch's admission price.

St. Louis is home to one of the nation's best Fourth of July celebrations, the **VP Fair**, which is held underneath the Gateway Arch, along the riverfront. The three-day music, arts, and food festival features a half-dozen free concerts by major acts, and fireworks each night. For more information, call (314) 434-3434.

St. Louis is a great blues city and celebrates its blues background with a series of free outdoor blues concerts at the **Blues Heritage Festival** each year around Labor Day. For the last few years it has been held on the riverfront at Laclede's Landing, near the Gateway Arch. For more information call (314) 241-BLUE.

The **Fox Theatre** is an ornately restored 1929 movie theater located in the Grand Center arts and entertainment district that still hosts plays and concerts. The spectacular decor borders on gaudy and must be seen to be believed. As you listen to the mighty Wurlitzer organ that rises from beneath the stage floor, you can't help but appreciate the building's acoustics. Tours are given at 10:30 AM every Tuesday, Thursday, and Saturday.

Anheuser-Busch offers free tours of their St. Louis brewery Monday through Saturday. The volume of beer produced and the pace at which it's put out is staggering. The original brewery itself is over a hundred years old and has some fascinating buildings, including the stables for the famous Budweiser Clydesdales. If you are fortunate, a team of these magnificent beasts may be on site for your visit. After the tour, complimentary samples of Anheuser-Busch beers are offered in their hospitality room.

Forest Park is a nice escape from the city on the west side of town. The park has seven miles of walking and bicycle paths, as well as two golf courses and a tennis center. The park was the site of the 1904 World's Fair and has since become home to several St. Louis attractions. The **St. Louis Art Museum** is housed in the World's Fair Fine Arts Palace and offers free admission except for occasional special exhibits. The **St. Louis Zoo** is home to more than 3,400 animals and is one of the country's few remaining free city zoos. In the southeast corner of the park is the **Science Center**, which features 500 interactive science and technology exhibits. Kids love the giant roaring dinosaurs and planetarium shows. There is also an Omnimax theater, which has a separate admission fee. The museum is free.

Along Delmar Boulevard, northwest of Forest Park, you'll find the **St. Louis Walk of Fame**, which consists of fifty stars honoring famous St. Louisans, embedded in the sidewalk, as well as plaques listing their accomplishments. Among the stars you'll find baseball players, actors, musicians, and writers who have connections to the city of St. Louis. Some of the ballplayers include Yogi Berra, Bob Gibson, Lou Brock, Cool Papa Bell, Stan Musial, and Joe Garagiola. You'll also find baseball broadcasters Jack Buck and Harry Caray.

Gateway Riverboat Cruises embark from beneath the Gateway Arch. Take a leisurely paddleboat cruise up the Mississippi River. Or if you prefer, visit one of the permanently moored riverboats and eat at one of the onboard restaurants. There are also a number of **Riverboat Casinos** that cruise the Mississippi River.

NIGHTLIFE IN ST. LOUIS

Laclede's Landing is a revitalized nineteenth-century neighborhood, about seven blocks northeast of the stadium, that is generally the place to be before and after Cardinal home games. The area is home to a number of nightclubs, restaurants, and shops. My favorite clubs are **Sundecker's**, which has a pub atmosphere and a good-size deck overlooking the Mississippi River, and **Muddy Waters**, which may sound like a blues club, but actually features a pair of piano-playing comedians singing humorous songs and telling jokes, often at the expense of the clientele. Lacledes Landing is located on the riverfront between the Eads and Martin Luther King Jr. bridges, just north of the St. Louis Arch. It is within walking distance of Busch Stadium and is also served by the MetroLink.

A few blocks north of the stadium, at 100 North 7th Street, you'll find **Mike Shannon's Steak and Seafood**. Shannon played for the baseball Cardinals and went on to become an announcer for Cardinals games on KMOX. Now he owns this upscale sports restaurant that is a popular spot before and after a game.

For live St. Louis blues, the place to go is Soulard, an area on the southern edge of downtown. The **1860 Hard Shell Cafe & Bar**, at 1860 South 9th Street, features live blues on the weekends. The **Great Grizzly Bear**, at 1027 Geyer Avenue, serves a mean lunch and presents local blues acts at night, Tuesday through Saturday. **John D. McGurks Irish Pub**, at 1200 Russell Boulevard, presents traditional Irish folk music, as well as Irish food and beer in an authentic pub atmosphere. **Molly's**, at 816 Geyer Avenue, has a New Orleans-style beer garden, an upstairs game room with billiards, darts, and pinball, as well as occasional live music.

Another downtown nightlife district, albeit in a somewhat trendier, more upscale setting, is at **St. Louis Union Station**, located on Market Street between 18th and 20th streets. Once one of the largest and busiest passenger rail stations in the nation, it's now home to over 100 shops, 25 restaurants, theaters, and a number of nightclubs. Worthwhile restaurants include **Houlihans**, **Landry's**, **Hooters**, **The Casa**, and **Mandarin House**.

For a more complete picture of local nightlife options, pick up a copy of the *Riverfront Times*.

WHERE TO STAY IN ST. LOUIS

St. Louis has a number of nice hotels in the heart of downtown. Most are within walking distance of the stadium, as well as most of the city's major attractions, and several nightlife areas. The addition of the MetroLink light rail system makes it even more advantageous to stay downtown. Listed below are a few of the more convenient hotels in the area. Several area hotels offer Cardinals game packages and shuttles, so be certain to ask before booking a room.

AREA HOTELS

Doubletree Mayfair Suites 806 St. Charles (800) 222-TREE or (314) 421-2500 Within walking distance of the stadium. Single and double rooms available.

Holiday Inn Downtown/Riverfront 200 N. 4th Street (800) 925-1395 or 621-8200 Within walking distance of the stadium. Ask about weekend specials.

Hyatt Regency One Union Station (800) 233-1234 or (314) 231-1234 Deluxe accommodations at the Union Station marketplace.

Regal Riverfront Hotel 200 S. 4th Street (800) 325-7353 or (314) 241-9500 Right next to Busch Stadium and the Gateway Arch.

Sheraton West Port Inn   191 West Port Plaza (800) 822-3535 or (314) 878-1500   Nice accommodations about 30–40 minutes west of Busch Stadium.

TEAM HOTELS

Adam's Mark   Fourth & Chestnut   (800) 444-2326 or (314) 241-7400 Braves, Marlins, Astros, Dodgers, Phillies, Padres, and Giants. Across from the Arch, within walking distance of the park.

Marriott Pavilion   One Broadway   (800) 228-9290 or (314) 421-1776 Cubs, Reds, Rockies, Expos, Mets, and Pirates.

GOOD TO KNOW

- For schedule information or tickets to Cardinals games, call (314) 421-3060. The Cardinals official Internet address is www.stlcardinals.com.
- Cardinals games can be heard on **KMOX 1120 AM. KFNS 590 AM** is the leading all-sports radio station in the area.
- For more information on St. Louis sights, attractions, and hotels, call the **Convention and Visitors Bureau** at (800) 916-0040 for a free visitors guide. Or call (800) 888-FUN1 to talk to a St. Louis travel counselor.

Closest major league cities (and drive times): Kansas City—256 miles (4 hours and 25 minutes); Chicago—299 miles (5 hours and 40 minutes); Cincinnati—356 miles (6 hours and 15 minutes).

IN THE VICINITY

Six Flags over Mid-America is about forty-five minutes southwest of St. Louis, in Eureka, Missouri. The amusement park features more than 100 rides, shows, and attractions and is open daily during the summer. In the spring and fall, it is open only on weekends. An all-inclusive admission is $22.95 for adults. For more information, call (314) 938-4800.

THE WEST

Anaheim Stadium is one of several big league stadiums that allow fans to gather near the dugouts and foul poles to get player autographs and batting practice balls. (Photo by Author)

◆ ANAHEIM ◆

Every player who was playing in the American League when I left ten years ago is either a coach or a manager or a member of the California Angels.

DICK WILLIAMS

ANAHEIM STADIUM

The Angels and their stadium were purchased by Disney in 1996, and, as a result, the city and Disney spent $100 million on a three-year renovation. They turned the stadium into a baseball-only facility with fewer seats, more skyboxes, and upgraded concourse areas. HOK Sport, the builders and architects who built Camden Yards, Coors Field, and Jacobs Field, were in charge of rebuilding the park.

The biggest change was the elimination of nearly 20,000 seats that were added when the NFL Rams began playing home games at Anaheim Stadium in 1979. All remaining seats have been replaced with wider, more comfortable chairs that are angled toward the infield. Other big changes include opening up the area behind the outfield fences and returning the "Big A" scoreboard to its original location, just beyond the outfield fence. There are also a pair of giant Angels helmets that serve as a convenient place to meet friends outside the stadium. While these are all positive steps, the changes don't really create a sense of genuine baseball nostalgia.

Attending a game at the "Big A" is a very "California" experience. The emphasis has been placed on neatness and convenience rather than tradition and intimacy. Like a lot of things in California, Anaheim Stadium is larger than life. Some of the stadium's positive attributes include a beautifully kept natural grass playing field, wide-open ramps and concession areas, and a giant color JumboTron video display board above the left field stands. The JumboTron does a good job of showing replays and up-to-date player stats, while

177

a sufficient number of auxiliary scoreboards and message boards are spread out about the stadium, making it easy to keep up with the status of the game no matter where your seats are. There is no dedicated out-of-town scoreboard, but game scores are shown regularly on the auxiliary boards.

Another nice aspect is the relative lack of imposing advertising billboards. The park is impeccably clean, easy to get to, and has some of the best concessions in major-league baseball. In addition to standard baseball fare, croissants, cinnamon rolls, bagels, pizza, and deli sandwiches are available. Unfortunately, tailgating at the park is limited to certain areas of the parking lot and no charcoal grills are permitted. At the time I visited, you were allowed to bring food into the game, but no bottles, cans, thermoses, or ice chests were permitted inside.

Tickets are almost always available for Angels games and are among the most affordable in baseball. This may change because stadium seating is being reduced greatly, and Disney is not exactly known for the most affordable family entertainment prices. What may very well be the best single-game seats in the park, the MVP section behind home plate, go for just $14.50. The best bargains are the $9 terrace boxes, $8 lower view level seats, and $5 pavilion reserved seats, all of which offer good views of the action. Many of the other seats are a long way from the diamond, especially those in the center field bleachers. Until the Angels begin competing for a division title, you can probably buy your tickets at the stadium on the day of the game. Scalping in California is illegal and at Angels games it's also unnecessary.

Prior to the 1997 remodeling effort, Anaheim Stadium had a remarkable lack of atmosphere and nostalgia. Somehow, despite turning 30 years old in 1996, the park has less of a sense of tradition than most parks built since. The place is simply too big, too new-feeling, and too symmetrical. Nevertheless I found a game at the "Big A" to be an enjoyable, hassle-free experience. Perhaps my favorite aspect of attending a game at Anaheim Stadium was joining the fans along the left field foul line as they razzed A's outfielder Rickey Henderson. Unlike crowds in Boston and New York, Anaheim fans kept it clean, but nevertheless seemed to get to Henderson as he had an off day and shot a look our way as we heckled him in the late innings.

HISTORY

The Angels have not had a lot of success as a franchise, but the "Big A" has seen its share of milestones. As you might expect, Nolan Ryan is responsible for several of those achievements. On September 27, 1973, he set the single-season record of 383 strikeouts as he struck out 16 Twins in his last start of the season. The remarkable story behind this achievement is that he tore a thigh muscle in the 8th inning when he struck out Steve Brye to tie Sandy Koufax's record of 382 Ks in a season. In the 11th inning, he struck out Rich Reese to set the record. Another remarkable aspect of Ryan's single-season strikeout record is that it came in the American League in the very first year of the designated hitter rule, so Ryan never faced a weak-hitting pitcher.

The following year, Ryan set the team record for strikeouts in a game with 19 against the Boston Red Sox on August 12. At the time, 19 Ks in a game was also a major-league record. Later that season, on September 28, he threw his third no-hitter as an Angel, but first one at Anaheim Stadium—a 4–0 victory over the Twins.

Some notable pitching feats by players other than Ryan have taken place here as well. Don Sutton won his 300th game, beating the Rangers 5–1 on June 18, 1986. On April 11, 1990, Angels pitchers Mark Langston and Mike Witt combined on a 1–0 no-hit victory over the Seattle Mariners.

Anaheim Stadium has also been the scene of some memorable base hits. Minnie Minosa became the oldest player to get a hit in the big leagues, on September 12, 1976, when he singled off Angels pitcher Sid Monge at age 53. Other milestone hits include: Reggie Jackson's 500th home run, off Royals' pitcher Bud Black, on September 17, 1984; Rod Carew's 3,000th base hit on August 4, 1985; and George Brett's 3,000th hit on September 30, 1992.

Ironically, only 17,336 people were on hand as Brett became just the eighteenth player in history to collect 3,000 hits. Brett started the day needing four hits, and fans thought even if he got the first three, he wouldn't get the fourth hit until he returned to Kansas City so he could do it in front of the home crowd. In his first three at-bats he got a double and two singles. On his fourth at-bat he slapped a bad hop grounder that got past second baseman Ken Oberkfell and it was ruled a hit. As Brett took his lead off first base, Angels first baseman Gary Gaetti asked Brett if his wife was in the stands. As Brett began to answer him, Angel pitcher Tim Fortugno threw to first and picked him off, spoiling Brett's moment in the spotlight.

GETTING TO ANAHEIM STADIUM
2000 Gene Autry Way

The Angels home field is one of the most conveniently located stadiums in the majors. It's a short distance from the intersection of Interstate 5 (Santa Ana Freeway), State Highway 22 (Garden Grove Freeway) and State Highway 57 (Orange Freeway.) Interstate 5 is the most direct approach from San Diego, to the south, or from Los Angeles, northwest of Anaheim. Parking at the stadium is ample, as Angels games rarely sell out. Coming from Los Angeles you'll want to get off at Katella Avenue and proceed east, make a right on Autry Way (aka State College Boulevard), and you are there.

From San Diego, you exit Interstate 5 directly onto Autry Way and proceed north. The stadium will be on your right, about a block off the interstate. There are no local mass-transit options other than the city bus.

WHAT TO DO AND SEE IN ANAHEIM

Anaheim's biggest attraction is, of course, **Disneyland**. The park itself occupies eighty-two acres, which means you can expect to do a good deal of walking around. The parking lot accounts for another 102 acres, so be certain to remember where you parked, or better yet, take advantage of a hotel shuttle and save the $8 parking charge.

Disneyland is divided into eight different areas, with rides and attractions for both kids and adults. My favorite rides include the **Matterhorn**, a great indoor/outdoor roller-coaster with wild 45-degree turns that will scare the pants off you, and **Space Mountain**, an indoor roller coaster that features planetarium effects and a simulated space launch. Lines for most rides and attractions are ridiculously long and just about everything in the way of souvenirs, concessions, and games is exorbitantly priced, so expect to spend in a big way over and above the price of admission. Admission is $30 for adults.

Knotts Berry Farm is the area's other amusement park, located minutes away at 8039 Beach Boulevard, in Buena Park. The park offers hundreds of rides and attractions in 6 themed areas covering 150 acres. One of the park's newest attractions is the **Boomerang**, a roller-coaster that is more than 110 feet tall and turns you upside-down 6 times. Admission is $25.95 for adults.

About fifteen minutes north of Anaheim, in Yorba Linda, is the **Richard Nixon Library and Birthplace**. This museum and library, dedicated to one of the most controversial U.S. presidents, is visited by hundreds of thousands of people each year. The museum grounds include the humble home Nixon lived in as a child, a rose garden, and a main gallery, which contains the memorabilia of his scandal-shortened presidency. The museum's largest room is centered around the Watergate scandal. Whether or not you are a fan of the man, you are likely to be impressed with the museum's thoroughness and compelling presentation of the events during Nixon's years as a politician and world leader. Expect to spend around two hours. Admission is just $4.95 for adults.

NIGHTLIFE IN ANAHEIM

Most of Anaheim's nightlife is centered around gourmet restaurants, dinner theaters, and hotel bars. There is no one concentration of nightclubs—probably because the city's primary attraction is the family-oriented Disneyland theme park. Your best bet may be to ask your hotel concierge for suggestions or to pick up a copy of the *Anaheim Bulletin*. Another option is to stay in L.A. and do the nightclub scene there.

There are a few places to go before and after a game at Anaheim Stadium. **Charlie Brown's** is one of the most established area sports bars. It's located across the street from the stadium at 1751 South State College Boulevard on the NW corner of the stadium. It features inexpensive food and drinks, a sports memorabilia collection, an enthusiastic crowd on game days, and a dozen TVs to watch the game. **The Catch** is not so much a sports bar as a top-notch seafood restaurant that has been around since 1979. Also located just across from the stadium, at 1929 State College Boulevard, The Catch is a popular place with players after the game.

There are also a few standout nightclubs in the area. The **Improv Comedy Club** features top-flight comedy talent seven nights a week. It's located at 945 East Birch Street, in the Brea Marketplace. The **Disneyland Hotel** also has a few theme nightclubs, and eleven bars and restaurants in all. Until recently, Disneyland's entertaining bars and restaurants were Anaheim's best opportunity for barhopping.

A brand-new **ESPN Zone** is directly across from the hotel and is loaded with sports memorabilia, a 14-foot big screen TV, a pair of virtual-reality Indy race cars, a 30-foot climbing wall, and 163 TVs in all. Baseball fans will want to check out the giant flag consisting of 383 fabric-wrapped baseballs. The flag is a tribute to Nolan Ryan—each ball has the name of one of his strikeout victims and the date from his record-setting 1973 season. You'll also find scads of Anaheim Angel memorabilia and an ironic Norman Rockwell-style painting of a Mets-Dodgers game at Dodger Stadium.

Across the street, there's **House of Blues**, a two-story live music hall that books major blues and rock acts five days a week. The music room accommodates nearly 1,000 fans and original blues-related artwork covers the walls. They also serve lunch and dinner.

WHERE TO STAY IN ANAHEIM

Anaheim has 18,000 hotel rooms, but they can become scarce during the summer months as travelers flock to Disneyland. Most hotels offer Disneyland packages and complimentary shuttles to the amusement park. As you might expect, prices tend to escalate $10–20 per night as it gets into the heart of the tourist season, which according to most area hotels is mid-June through August. In addition, the city of Anaheim, like many travel destinations, adds a hefty 13% tax on your stay.

AREA HOTELS

Anaheim Ramada Inn   1331 East Katella Avenue (800) 228-0586 or (714) 978-8088   Reasonably priced accommodations within a mile of the stadium and Disneyland.

Anaheim Sportstown Travelodge   1700 East Katella Avenue (800) 255-3050 or (714) 634-1920   Well-kept hotel within walking distance of the stadium.

Doubletree Hotel   100 The City Drive (800) 222-8733 or (714) 634-4500   Very nice accommodations just a mile and a half from the stadium.

Holiday Inn Express   435 West Katella Avenue (800) 833-7888 or (714) 772-7755   One block from Disneyland and three miles from Anaheim Stadium.

Sheraton Anaheim Hotel   1015 W. Ball Road (800) 331-7251 or (714) 778-1700   Located at the back entrance of Disneyland within three miles of Anaheim Stadium.

TEAM HOTELS

Anaheim Hilton   777 Convention Way (800) HILTONS or (714) 750-4321 Yankees.

Anaheim Marriott   700 West Convention Way (800) 228-9290 or (714) 750-8000   Red Sox.

Doubletree Hotel   City Drive at Chapman (800) 222-8733 or (714) 634-4500   Indians, Tigers, Royals, Brewers, Twins, A's, Mariners, Rangers, and Blue Jays.

Hyatt Regency   Harbor at Chapman (800) 233-1234 or (714) 750-1234 White Sox.

GOOD TO KNOW

- For schedule information or tickets to Angels games, call (714) 740-2000.
- Angels games can be heard on **KMPC 710 AM**, which is also the area's leading all sports station.
- For more information on Anaheim sights, attractions, and hotels, call the **Convention & Visitors Bureau** at (714) 999-8999. Or write them at 800 West Katella Avenue, P.O. Box 4270, Anaheim, CA 92803.
- The last Saturday and Sunday before the regular season begins marks the annual meeting of the Angels and Dodgers in the **Freeway Baseball Series**. Call Anaheim Stadium at (714) 634-2000 for additional information.

Closest major league cities (and drive times): Los Angeles—25 miles (45 minutes to one hour); San Diego—100 miles (1 hour and 45 minutes); San Francisco/Oakland—400 miles (7 hours and 30 minutes).

IN THE VICINITY

If you are interested in turning your trip into a two-sport adventure, the **Disneyland Pigskin Classic** is played at Anaheim Stadium every August. Two of the previous year's top-ten college football teams are invited to take to the gridiron to kick off the intercollegiate football season. Call (714) 999-4445 or (213) 626-8605 for more information. While it may not be a bowl game, it is two of the country's best teams going head-to-head and tickets are much easier to come by.

◆ LOS ANGELES ◆

The game has a cleanliness. If you do a good job, the numbers say so. You don't have to ask anyone or play politics. You don't have to wait for the reviews.

SANDY KOUFAX

DODGER STADIUM

The Dodgers did it right when they set out to build their own ballpark. After moving out of Brooklyn, they played at the Los Angeles Coliseum from 1958 to 1962 while they scouted a location and built Dodger Stadium. What they ended up with is one of the premier parks in baseball. Located in the Chavez Ravine, just north of Los Angeles, Dodger Stadium is a 300-acre oasis of green grass and tropical foliage nestled in surrounding hills. The view from behind home plate is a treat, with giant palm trees just beyond the outfield fence, and the tree-lined Elysian Hills in the background.

The interior of the stadium is kept remarkably clean. In fact, Dodger stadium is said to be the only park in the majors to receive a fresh coat of paint every off-season. The effort put forth by their full-time maintenance and gardening crew is apparent, as the 35-year-old park looks better than many parks built more recently.

Despite averaging better than 2.6 million fans every year since it opened and being the first park to break the 3 million mark, Dodger Stadium is one of the few parks not to have added seats or undergone major renovations. Apparently the Dodgers are satisfied that they did it right the first time.

Not unlike Yankee Stadium, the park is neither round nor oval, but takes on the shape of the playing field. There are five tiers of seats along the foul lines and two small bleacher sections beyond the outfield fences.

The park was the first to employ a full-color video display screen, which debuted at the 1980 All-Star Game. It has since been replaced with a state-of-the-art DiamondVision, above the left-center field bleachers. The game-in-progress scoreboard sits atop the right field bleachers and does a good job of indicating the batting order, balls and strikes, hits, runs, errors, and lineup changes. There are also scoreboards at field level, along the base paths beside each dugout. There are no support columns to contend with, and every seat has an unobstructed view of the field. Except for the bleacher seats, all seats offer a view of both big scoreboards as well. There are a total of five levels, including the unique dugout level seats. These seats offer a player's level view of the game and are located along the baseline, to the home plate side of each dugout.

Dodger Stadium seats 56,000 people, but keeps the seat options simple. Box seats are $11, reserved seats between the dugouts are $9, all other lower-level reserved seats are $8. Top deck and pavilion seats are $6. Children from 4–12 years old and senior citizens can get tickets in the top deck and pavilion sections for $3. Sales for those seats begin an hour and a half before game time. Children under four years old can attend a game for free. The Dodgers have very few day games, but for the hotter ones you may want to get some shade from the afternoon sun on the third base side. Otherwise, there is some shade at the back of every level of seating.

The outfield fence is 8 feet high, except in the corners between the bullpens and the foul poles, where the fences drop to just 3½ feet tall. While several balls do reach the bleachers during batting practice, the area just above this short fence is the best place to be to grab a ball during batting practice. Behind either foul pole, in fair territory, you can lean over and get ground balls or grab an occasional smash just on the fair side of the pole. The ushers facilitate autograph and ball hunting, and simply ask you to return to your seat once batting practice is over.

Concessions at the park are some of the best in the big leagues. The highlight is the 10-inch Dodger dog. Unlike most ballpark hot dogs, they're grilled instead of steamed or boiled. All of the concession prices are reasonable, especially by southern California standards. As an alternative to standard baseball fare, there is a cafeteria and public bar on the 200 club level.

The park's only downfalls are the symmetrical outfield dimensions, a large foul territory, and the traffic, which can be dreadful when it coincides with rush hour. Unfortunately, the Dodgers do not allow tailgating, so hanging around after the game is not a particularly attractive option.

HISTORY

Perhaps the single most memorable Dodger moment since their move west from Brooklyn is Kirk Gibson's game-winning, pinch-hit home run off Dennis Eckersley in the 1988 World Series. In his only at-bat of the series, Gibson

Aerial view of Dodger Stadium. (Courtesy of the Los Angeles Dodgers, Inc.)

hobbled to the plate to hit a two-run home run in the bottom of the ninth inning to beat the Oakland A's 5–4 in the first game. Gibson's blast set the tone for the series as the Dodgers went on to beat the heavily favored A's 4 games to 1.

Sandy Koufax had a few big games before the Dodger faithfuls. He pitched the deciding game in two World Series at Dodger Stadium. On October 6, 1963, he pitched a 6-hitter as the Dodgers swept the Yankees in 4 games. Two years later, on October 14, he shut out the Twins 2–0 to win Game 7. On September 9, 1965, Dodger fans saw Koufax pitch his fourth career no-hitter, a perfect game 1–0 victory over the Chicago Cubs.

Until 1997 only one man had hit a ball out of Dodger Stadium, Pirates' slugger Willie Stargell. And he did it twice. The first time, on August 5, 1969, he slammed an Alan Foster pitch 506 feet and 6 inches over the pavilion roof. His second shot was four years later, on May 8, 1973, against Andy Messersmith; the ball actually bounced off the roof and out of the stadium. In September of 1997, Mike Piazza became the second player to hit a ball out of Dodger Stadium by bouncing it off the left-center field pavillion roof.

In his rookie year, Ramon Martinez tied Koufax's team record of 18 strikeouts in a game as the Dodgers beat the Atlanta Braves on June 4, 1990.

Martinez wowed the home crowd again with a no-hitter against the Florida
Marlins on July 14, 1995.

GETTING TO DODGER STADIUM
1000 Elysian Park Avenue

As is typical of southern California, there is almost no way to get to the
ballpark other than driving. The Dodgers promote a charter bus to ease the
parking and traffic burden, but that seems directed at local groups rather than
out-of-town visitors.

Dodger Stadium is just a few minutes north of downtown, encircled by the
Pasadena, Hollywood, and Golden State freeways, making it easily accessible
from any direction. All told, the stadium has five entrances, so you shouldn't
miss it.

Parking at Dodger Stadium is ample—16,000 spaces—and fairly priced at
just $5. Each parking section is marked by a giant lighted baseball. It's easy to
get turned around, so make a mental note of what section you park in to facilitate getting out of the lot quickly.

Dodger fans are notorious for leaving games early to beat the traffic, but
not without good reason. Day games often end in the midst of the city's legendary rush hour, and night games generally start before the rush is over. If
enough fans leave a game early, and the game doesn't finish during the
evening commute, the drive home is not unbearable. Weekend afternoon
games generally sell out quickly, but they are also your best bet for avoiding
rush hour altogether.

WHAT TO DO AND SEE IN LOS ANGELES

Los Angeles is made up of five very distinct areas: Downtown, Hollywood,
the Westside, the Coastal area, and the Valleys. Unfortunately, downtown is
the only area to benefit from efficient mass transit. This makes it impossible
to see everything the city has to offer without also spending an awful lot of
time in your car. The city is currently installing a subway system encompass-
ing the majority of the L.A. area, but only three lines are currently up and
running. With that in mind, you may want to plan on seeing all the sights of
a particular area in one day, rather than crisscrossing the area via L.A.'s infamous freeways.

When most people think of Los Angeles, they think of Hollywood and its
trademark attractions, such as the Walk of Fame, Mann's Chinese Theatre,
and of course, the huge white **Hollywood** sign atop Mount Lee. The **Walk of
Fame** runs for about a mile along Hollywood Boulevard, between Gower
Street and La Brea Avenue, and continues along Vine Street just south of
Hollywood Boulevard. Each month a new name, along with a terrazzo and

brass star, is added in a public ceremony. So far, more than 1,850 stars have been embedded in the world's most famous sidewalk. **Mann's Chinese Theatre** is a short walk away, at 6925 Hollywood Boulevard. Here you'll find the handprints and footprints of stars from the past and present in the concrete of the courtyard in front of the theater.

Just a few miles south of Hollywood, the **Rancho La Brea Tar Pits** and the **George C. Page Museum** are located at 5801 Wilshire Boulevard. The museum displays fossils of prehistoric animals that became trapped in the tar pits during the Ice Age. The museum's fascinating guided tour illustrates the process of extracting the animals and reconstructing them before they are put on display in the museum. Admission is $6 for adults, guided tours of the tar pit are free.

Of course, Hollywood is also home to many of the country's movie and television studios. The two biggest studio attractions, Universal Studios and Warner Brothers Studios, actually on the outskirts of Hollywood, just a few miles to the north. **Universal Studios** has become equal parts amusement park and movie studio, attracting five million visitors a year. The studio occupies more than 400 acres, which you'll tour via guided tram and a walking tour. Along the way you'll pass by several familiar backdrops and sets, see the stars' dressing rooms, and come upon a number of catastrophes and calamities, recreating scenes from some of Universal's more memorable movies and TV shows. You may also get the chance to be part of an audience during the taping of a TV show. The amusement park rides are some of the best I've ever been on, especially the *Jurassic Park* and *Back to the Future* rides, but also have some of the longest lines I've ever had to endure. If possible, go to the park during the week when lines are shortest. Admission is $29 for adults.

Warner Brothers Studios takes a much more subtle approach, offering small group tours (12 people or less) of the actual moviemaking process. This allows visitors to get a genuine behind-the-scenes look at the various processes involved in making a movie. It's a lot less glitzy, but offers a far more authentic glimpse into the industry's goings-on. Admission is $24 for adults. Because tours are limited to just two a day, it's suggested that you call at least one week in advance to reserve a space for yourself or your group.

The Westside is where you'll find Beverly Hills, with its ritzy shops, boutiques, and massive celebrity homes, with their lofty protective walls. Ironically, it's also where you'll find the **Museum of Tolerance**, at 9786 West Pico Boulevard. The one-of-a-kind museum's mission is to illustrate the history of racism and prejudice throughout the world. Its "coup de grace" is the exhibit on the Holocaust, which features a full-scale reproduction of a portion of a concentration camp. Suffice it to say, you can't see the place and walk away unchanged. The museum is closed on Saturdays.

The Coastal area is home to several of the area's museums and, of course, L.A's miles and miles of beaches. Along Pacific Avenue, between Santa Monica and Marina Del Ray, is **Venice Beach**, one of L.A.'s trendiest areas. You may have seen Venice Beach depicted in the movie *White Men Can't Jump*. The public basketball courts are pretty much as shown in the movie; lots of incredible athleticism and hotdogging, highlighted by a stream of never-ending trash talking. I could have spent the entire afternoon watching these guys play hoops if it weren't for the equally impressive talent milling about on the beach and boardwalk. The beach itself is not quite as packed, or perhaps as nice as Mission Beach in San Diego, but the boardwalk is absolutely incredible. Jammed with shops and cafes overlooking the ocean, it's a nonstop parade of gorgeous women, muscle-bound men, in-line skaters, and street entertainers. Just taking a seat with your friends at an open-air cafe and watching the crowd stroll by is an entertaining way to spend a few hours. **Figtree's** is my favorite place along Venice's Ocean Front Walk to grab a bite or a cold drink and people watch.

Not far from Venice Beach, up the Pacific Coast Highway, between Santa Monica and downtown Malibu, is the **John Paul Getty Museum**. Without a doubt, this is one of the finest art museums on the West Coast. The museum occupies ten acres and has a massive collection of Greek and Roman sculpture, pre–twentieth-century European paintings including works by Manet, van Gogh, and Renoir, and artifacts ranging from silver settings, to porcelains, tapestries, and furniture. Admission is free, but parking is very limited. Visitors must call seven to ten days in advance to reserve a spot. Walk-in visitors without an appointment are not allowed.

The **Natural History Museum of Los Angeles** has a collection of more than sixteen million artifacts. Its highlights include animal dioramas and dinosaur fossils, including one of the most complete and most well-preserved Tyrannosaurus Rex skulls in the world. The museum is located between downtown and the Westside, in Exposition Park, at 900 Exposition Boulevard. Admission is $5 for adults, but free the first Tuesday of the month.

NIGHTLIFE IN LOS ANGELES

Los Angeles has no end of places to go at night, but they are very spread out. Your best bet for barhopping is in West Hollywood, along **Sunset Boulevard**. Also known as the Sunset Strip, it's home to many of the city's biggest and best known nightclubs. Santa Monica also has a number of outstanding, less trendy nightclubs. To help plan your evening's entertainment, check out *L.A. Weekly*, *Los Angeles View*, and *Los Angeles Reader*.

One of the more recent additions to Sunset Strip is the **House of Blues**, at 8430 Sunset Boulevard. The L.A. version of H.O.B. hosts national acts ranging from blues and jazz to reggae and '70s pop. The restaurant offers generous serv-ings of above-average chow and a terrific view of the city from its patio dining area. If you can't get in at night (the club's $25–30 cover charge may also dis-courage you), check out their Sunday gospel brunch.

The **Whisky a Go Go** is an L.A. institution and is still a great place to catch some of the area's hottest music. On days that they don't have a national act, you can generally see four or five local bands for $10–12. The Whisky is located at 8901 Sunset Boulevard. The Whisky's sister club, the **Roxy The-atre**, is just up the street at 9009 Sunset Boulevard. The Roxy books a solid mix of regional and local acts, usually presenting three or four bands each night. The cover charge varies with the quantity and quality of talent booked.

Dublins Irish Whiskey Pub, a newcomer at 8240 Sunset, is as close to a local watering hole as you'll find in West Hollywood. Dublins has a good selec-tion of beer and cigars; a friendly, helpful staff; pool tables; several TVs; and darts. It didn't hurt when we visited that the place was jammed with a good-looking crowd.

Sunset Strip also offers two of the area's better-known comedy clubs, the **Comedy Store** and the **Laugh Factory**. The Comedy Store, at 8433 Sunset Boulevard, has three different comedy showcases, the Main Room, the Belly Room, and the Original Room, under one roof. The Original Room generally hosts nationally known headliners on the weekends. Cover charge and promi-nence of comedians varies so be sure to call in advance. The Laugh Factory, at 8001 Sunset Boulevard, also offers top-notch stand-up comedy with sev-eral showtimes each night, as well as dinner and valet parking. Both clubs have a two-drink minimum.

Another great choice for nationally known stand-up comedy is the **Impro-visation**, where Robin Williams is said to have gotten his start. The Improv is located at 8162 Melrose Avenue in West Hollywood.

B.B. King's is really two bars in one. The main hall is a restaurant that serves classic Delta cooking, seats over 400 people, and hosts some of the best blues in the area. BB's not-so-conveniently located at **City Walk**, in Uni-versal City, at 1000 Universal Center Drive, but offers a gospel brunch every Sunday at noon that is said to be the best in town. I'm not sure which was better—the buffet or the show. Either way, it's 2 hours and $25 well spent. Make reservations in advance and show up around 11:30 AM for the best seats.

WHERE TO STAY IN LOS ANGELES

Because L.A.'s sights and attractions are so spread out, it is not necessary to stay downtown, particularly during the week when business travelers fill up many of the hotels there. Most of the area attractions are in and around Hol-lywood, but the beaches, museums, and nightlife are so scattered about town that you might lose any advantage of staying in this area—especially when you consider the nightly rates of some of the hotels in Hollywood. You might be just as well off staying in the suburbs and commuting to the area sights. Listed below are a few of the area hotels.

DOWNTOWN HOTELS

Best Western Dragon Gate Inn   818 North Hill Street (800) 282-9999 or (213) 617-3077   Inexpensive hotel in the heart of downtown, two miles from Dodger Stadium.

Holiday Inn Convention Center   1020 South Figueroa (800) HOLIDAY or (213) 748-1291   Reasonably priced accommodations within five miles of Dodger Stadium.

Holiday Inn Downtown   750 Garland Avenue (800) HOLIDAY or (213) 628-9900   Just off highway 110, only a few miles from Dodger Stadium.

Metro Plaza Hotel   711 North Main Street (800) 223-2223 or (213) 680-0200   Nice hotel within walking distance of Chinatown and Olvera Street.

Westin Bonaventure   404 South Figueroa Street (800) 228-3000 or (213) 624-1000   A well-kept, 35-story hotel, just 2 miles from the stadium.

OTHER AREA HOTELS

Beverly Hills Plaza Hotel   10300 Wilshire Boulevard (800) 800-1234 or (310) 275-5575   Luxury hotel a short drive from most of Hollywood's worthwhile sights.

Courtyard by Marriott   10320 West Olympic Boulevard (800) 321-2211 or (310) 556-2777   Very nice, yet reasonably priced, hotel near Beverly Hills in Century City.

Embassy Suites Hotel   9801 Airport Road (800) EMBASSY or (310) 215-1000   Moderately priced two-room suites, southwest of downtown, near LAX Airport.

Radisson Bel Air Summit   11461 Sunset Boulevard (800) 333-3333 or (310) 476-6571   Nice accommodations a short drive from Beverly Hills, Hollywood, and beaches.

TEAM HOTELS

Glendale Red Lion 100 Glenoaks Blvd. (800) 547-8010 or (818) 956-5466 Marlins.

Hilton   930 Wilshire Boulevard at Figueroa (800) HILTONS or (213) 629-4321   Reds.

Hyatt Regency   711 South Hope Street (800) 233-1234 or (213) 683-1234 Giants.

Inter-Continental   251 Olive Street (213) 617-3300   Rockies and Phillies.
Sheraton Grande   333 South Figueroa (800) 325-3535 or (213) 617-1133
   Braves, Cubs, Astros, Mets, Pirates, Cardinals, and Padres.

GOOD TO KNOW

- For schedule information or tickets to Dodger games call (213) 224-1448.
  The Dodgers official Internet address is www.dodgers.com.
- To order by mail, send a check or money order to: **Los Angeles Dodgers**,
  Ticket Office, File #51100, Los Angeles, California 90074-1100. Add $3
  for handling.
- Dodger games can be heard on **KABC 790 AM**. The area's leading all-
  sports radio station is **KMPC 710 AM**.
- For more information on Los Angeles sights, attractions, and hotels, call the
  Convention & Visitors Bureau at (800) 366-6116 or (213) 624-7300. They
  can be reached via the Internet at www.lacvb.com.
- To get the latest scoop on the arts, special events, and festivals, call (213)
  688-ARTS.

Closest major league cities (and drive times): Anaheim—25 miles (45 minutes to an hour); San Diego—124 miles (2 hours and 25 minutes); San Fran-
cisco/Oakland—400 miles (7 hours and 30 minutes).

IN THE VICINITY

If you are driving north toward San Francisco from the L.A. area, you may
want to consider taking **U.S. 1** along the coast, between San Luis Obispo and
Santa Cruz. It adds about three or four hours to your trip, but the view of the
Pacific Ocean meeting the cliffs of the California coast is absolutely incredible,
and well worth going out of your way. If you are planning to stop for a night
between L.A. and San Francisco, and split the drive up over two days, the
additional time goes unnoticed.

One word of caution: The roads are very curvy and the cliffs very steep, so
drive carefully and plan to stop before nightfall, because you don't want to
miss any of the scenery. You'll probably want to fill your tank before you leave
San Luis Obispo because the gas stations along U.S. 1 tend to jack up their
prices considerably.

✦ OAKLAND ✦

Look how drab this place is. All gray cement. Players call it the Oakland Mausoleum.

SAL BANDO

OAKLAND-ALAMEDA COUNTY COLISEUM

The park I saw had its downfalls, such as a huge foul territory, symmetrical outfield dimensions, and a uniform eight-foot outfield fence, but it was a whole lot different than the one Sal Bando describes. The Coliseum is one of those round multisport arenas built in the late '60s with too many seats and a lot of exposed cement, but it has been remodeled since and has become a decent place to see a game. The playing surface has been natural grass since the day it opened; the backstop area was reduced from 90 to 60 feet in 1969, and the seating was recently reduced to just over 47,000.

Prior to the addition of skyboxes for the NFL Raiders, the area behind the outfield bleachers was a wide-open, sloped grassy area with a view of the hills beyond the outfield stands. That view is somewhat obscured now, with luxury suites occupying a good deal of the area beyond the outfield fences. Just above the grassy area in left, is a game-in-progress scoreboard and a message board. A replay board occupies the center field spot and a manual out-of-town scoreboard, installed in 1986, sits beyond the right field fence. No matter where you sit, you'll have an unobstructed view of the field and, unless you are in the bleachers, you'll also have a good view of the scoreboards.

There are three levels of seating, not including the loge and skybox level. Every seat in the stadium is a good way from the infield diamond because the Coliseum has the largest foul territory in the majors. Prices range from a high of $17.50 for MVP seats, $13–14 for field level and plaza level seats around the infield, to $3.50 for upper deck reserved seats. Bleacher seats are only $4.50 and, unlike many ballparks, can be ordered in advance.

192

What used to be a wide open area beyond center field in the Alameda County
Stadium is now a section of skyboxes built to accommodate Raiders fans.
(Photo by Author)

Concessions at the park are exceptional and rival the Angels, Red Sox, Marlins, Orioles, Dodgers, and Brewers for the best in baseball. Options include
your standard ballpark fare of hot dogs, peanuts, and Cracker Jacks, as well as
sub sandwiches, Chinese food, pizza, espresso, and a nice selection of local,
domestic, and imported beer. Most concession items are reasonably priced
and available throughout the ballpark. The **Coliseum Cafe** has two locations,
one behind section 114, the other behind 120. The **Family Entertainment
Center** and **Family Place** are located there as well. The park's only ATM is
located behind section 120.

One of the best-kept secrets in Oakland is **Sam's Hof Brau** at the corner of
Hegeberger Road and Coliseum Way. A small lot behind the restaurant offers
free parking within walking distance of the stadium. The television reception
leaves a lot to be desired, but the cafeteria-style food is exceptional and the
drinks are inexpensive.

HISTORY

The A's franchise had gone through two cities (Philadelphia and Kansas
City) and a postseason drought of more than forty years before moving into

the Coliseum in 1968. That year, on May 9, Jim "Catfish" Hunter thrilled the crowd with a perfect game 3–0 victory over the Minnesota Twins. Hunter also drove in all of his team's runs. Baltimore ace Jim Palmer no-hit the A's at Oakland on August 13, 1969. Oakland was also the site as Vida Blue pitched a no-hitter against the Minnesota Twins on September 21, 1970. Blue also holds the team record for strikeouts in a game as he set down 17 batters in 11 innings of a 20-inning game on July 9, 1971.

On September 28, 1975, four A's pitchers—Vida Blue, Glenn Abbott, Paul Linblad, and Rollie Fingers—contributed to a no-hitter against the California Angels. The Oakland Coliseum has the dubious distinction of being the birthplace of "the wave," one of my least favorite sporting-event activities. It is said to have been started by "Crazy George" Henderson during the seventh-inning stretch of the final game of the 1981 playoff series between the A's and Yankees. The Yankees won the game, but the wave has since managed to rear its ugly head at just about every sports arena in the nation.

Rickey Henderson broke Lou Brock's career record of 938 stolen bases on May 1, 1991, by stealing third base after getting on board via an error in the fourth inning against the Yankees. The A's were the victims of a second Baltimore pitching gem on July 13, 1991, as Bob Milacki, Mike Flanagan, Mark Williams, and Gregg Olson combined to throw a no-hitter.

Getting to Oakland-Alameda County Coliseum
7000 Coliseum Way

The Coliseum is located in south Oakland off Highway 880, between 66th Avenue and Hegenberger Road. Even if you are staying in San Francisco, you can take the Bay Area Rapid Transport (BART) directly to a platform beside the Coliseum. BART is fast, clean, safe, and runs daily until midnight. Unless you need to have your car directly before or after the game, I would recommend giving BART a try—especially when you consider the hassle of stadium traffic, parking costs, and when traveling from San Francisco you'll have to pay a toll for crossing westbound over the San Francisco-Oakland Bay Bridge.

If you do drive to the stadium, bear in mind that the neighborhood immediately surrounding Oakland Alameda County Stadium is not exactly hospitable. In fact, aside from Yankee and Tiger stadiums, no stadium in the majors is situated in a more daunting setting than Oakland's. The fenced parking lot, however, offers 11,500 well-lit, secured spaces and is reasonably priced at $7.

WHAT TO DO AND SEE IN OAKLAND

San Francisco. Just kidding! Oakland's premiere attraction is **Jack London Square**, a charming waterfront area on the Inner Harbor. The area's premiere establishment is **Heinhold's First and Last Chance Saloon**, a favorite watering hole of author Jack London. Heinhold's has been around since 1883 and was built from the timbers of old whaling vessels. The interior consists of little more than a bar with five stools, three tables, a few gas lamps, and a pot bellied stove. The floor is tilted as a result of the 1906 San Francisco earthquake, and the bar's clock remains stopped at the exact moment that the quake hit.

Also in the vicinity are the **Jack London Museum**, which is dedicated to the author and other Bay area writers; **Jack London's Yukon Cabin**, a sod-roofed cabin that can be viewed only from the outside; and the U.S.S. *Potomac*, Franklin D. Roosevelt's huge presidential yacht, also referred to as the "Floating White House." Ferry service from the Square is available to and from San Francisco, until 6 PM daily.

Two restaurants worth checking out in the area are **Kincaid's**, an upscale place specializing in seafood, chops, and steaks at One Franklin Street, and **Il Pescatore**, an Italian place with a warm atmosphere and top-notch entrees. Both places overlook the water, but don't expect to catch a game on TV at either place.

A little over a mile from the Square is the **Oakland Museum**, at 10th and Oak streets. The emphasis of this surprisingly solid museum is on Californian art, natural sciences, and history. There is also a rooftop garden with a nice view of downtown Oakland. Admission is free, except for special exhibits. The **Paramount Theater** is much farther north, at 2025 Broadway. The 1930 Art Deco movie palace is considered an area landmark and still hosts shows, movies, and concerts.

The **Oakland Zoo** is southwest of downtown Oakland, in Knowland Park at 9777 Golf Links Road. The zoo occupies 70 acres and is home to more than 300 animals, representing 90 species. Admission to the zoo is just $5 for adults.

NIGHTLIFE IN OAKLAND

Aside from the bars and restaurants in Jack London Square, Oakland does not seem to have one distinct nightlife district. Telegraph Avenue is home to a tremendous selection of ethnic restaurants, ranging from simple American cafes to Ethiopian, Indian, Thai, and Middle Eastern cuisine. Oakland's best source for nightclub and concert news is the *East Bay Express*, a weekly entertainment tabloid that is available free at many area retailers, hotels, and restaurants.

Cato's Ale House, at 3891 Piedmont Avenue, offers a casual pub atmosphere, a diverse menu of soups, salads, sandwiches, burgers, and pizzas, and a selection of twenty-two beers on tap. They also host live music on Sunday and Monday evenings. **Clem Daniel's End Zone** is a happening sports bar, at 1466 High Street, in East Oakland. The End Zone offers a decent bar menu, large-screen satellite sports, live music, and it occasionally books regional comedy acts. The **Oakland All-Stars Cafe** is a great place to catch a game in Jack London Square, with a diverse menu, lots of TVs, and friendly service at the corner of Embarcadero and Washington.

The **Pacific Coast Brewing Company**, at 906 Washington Street opposite the Convention Center, stands out among the crowd of northern California brewpubs. Pacific Coast offers a handsome traditional pub atmosphere and a wide selection of ales, porters, and stouts brewed on site. **Yoshi's**, at 6030 Claremont Avenue, may be one of the most unique live music venues on the planet. They bill themselves as a "Japanese restaurant and world-class jazz house" offering a fine selection of Japanese cuisine, a genuine sushi bar, and there is no disputing the fact that they book some of the nation's best jazz acts nightly.

WHERE TO STAY IN OAKLAND

Oakland does have a number of outstanding hotels that are generally less expensive than similar places across the Bay. Listed below is a partial list of area hotels.

AREA HOTELS

Best Western Jack London Square   233 Broadway (800) 633-5973 or (510) 452-4565   Affordable hotel located beside Jack London Square, just six blocks from downtown.

Dockside Bed & Boat   77 Jack London Square (510) 444-5858   As unique a lodging experience as you'll find anywhere. All the comforts of a bed and breakfast aboard a dockside yacht.

Executive Inn Oakland   1755 Embarcadero Drive (800) 346-6331 or (510) 536-6633   Waterfront location, courtesy shuttle to airport and BART station.

Holiday Inn Airport   500 Hegenberger Road (800) HOLIDAY or (510) 562-5311   One of the closest hotels to the stadium. Free parking and shuttle available.

Marriott City Center   1001 Broadway (800) 228-9290 or (510) 451-4000   The largest hotel in the city, located right next to the BART line.

Washington Inn   495 10th Street at Washington (800) 477-1775 or (510) 452-1776   A historic hotel one block from BART station.

TEAM HOTELS

Airport Hilton   One Hegenberger Road (800) HILTONS or (510) 635-5000   All American League clubs except the Red Sox, Mariners, Blue Jays, Tigers, and Yankees.

Parc 55   55 Cyril Magnin Street (800) 338-1338 or (415) 392-8000   Red Sox, Mariners, and Blue Jays.

Waterfront Plaza   10 Washington Street (800) 729-3638 or (510) 836-3800   Tigers and Yankees.

GOOD TO KNOW

- For schedule information or tickets to A's games, call (510) 762-2277. The A's official Internet address is www.oaklandathletics.com.
- A's games can be heard on **KFRC 610 AM**.
- For more information on Oakland sights, attractions, and hotels, call the **Convention and Visitors Bureau** at (800) 262-5526.

Closest major league cities (and drive times): San Francisco—8 miles (30 minutes); Los Angeles/Anaheim—400 miles (7 hours and 30 minutes).

IN THE VICINITY

The **Winchester Mystery House** in San Jose was owned by Sarah Winchester, the heiress to the Winchester fortune. A fortune-teller told her that the spirits of all the people killed by Winchester rifles would haunt her unless she continued to build at her San Jose estate. She did just that for thirty-eight years, spending millions on construction crews to build around the clock. What resulted was a 160-room mansion with 2,000 doors, some of which open into walls, 10,000 windows, 47 fireplaces, and stairs that lead nowhere. Guided tours that last just over an hour are available, beginning at 9 AM daily. Admission is $9.50 for adults. Call (408) 247-2101 for more information.

Just north of Oakland, in Vallejo, **Marine World Africa USA** is the only combination wildlife park and oceanarium in the United States. The oceanarium features killer whales, dolphins, and sea lions, but the highlight is an eerie trek through an underwater tunnel while sharks swim by above, below, and beside you. The wildlife park is home to tigers, chimpanzees, orangutans, and birds of prey. Admission is $22.95 for adults. For hours or more information call (707) 643-6722.

If you'd like to check out the Napa Valley wine region, consider doing it in style aboard the **Napa Valley Wine Train**. This upscale passenger train offers year-round gourmet dining excursions for brunch, lunch, or dinner. Call (800) 427-4124 or (707) 253-2111 for more information. If you are outside California, call (800) 522-4142.

◆ PHOENIX ◆

BANK ONE BALLPARK

Phoenix may be responsible for the ugly trend of corporate-named baseball parks, which in my mind puts it in the same company as the Astrodome for introducing artificial turf to the game of baseball. Phoenix is, nevertheless, home to an impressive baseball stadium. Bank One Ballpark has a retractable roof similar to the SkyDome in Toronto. Unlike its Canadian cousin, "BOB" is a baseball-only facility with a natural grass playing field and 85 percent of its 48,569 seats located along the foul lines. Because there are so few seats between the foul poles beyond the outfield fence, and no obstructed views, almost any seat is a good one.

The movable portion of the roof covers more than five acres and takes just five minutes to slide into place. A dozen wall panels beyond the outfield fence also swing open to help give the ballpark a more open feel. These panels are 60 feet tall, 30 feet wide, and weigh 32 tons each. They swing open in ninety seconds and make up a giant baseball mural along Jefferson Street. The stadium cost $350 million to build. Judging by the 33,000 season tickets already sold, the citizens of Phoenix think it was money well spent.

Located in the city's warehouse district, across from the America West Arena, BOB's brick exterior and airplane hangar roof fit in nicely with the surrounding neighborhood. The stadium was designed by Ellerbe Becket, who also designed Atlanta's Turner Field. The designer's obvious attention to detail is evidenced by wide, comfortable seats and aisles, drink holders at every seat, and steep-banked upper decks that allow the cheap seats to remain close to the field of play.

Outfield dimensions are slightly asymmetrical with 380-foot power alleys, 402 feet to straightaway center, 328 feet down the left field line, and 335 feet to the right field corner. Outfield fences that meet at drastic angles should make for some interesting caroms as outfielders try to gather in potential doubles and triples. The grass playing field will be different than those of most major league parks because it will feature a zoysia hybrid turf instead of the blend of rye and Bermuda grasses found at most ballparks.

Another unique aspect of Bank One Ballpark is the **Pool Party Pavilion** located 430 feet from home plate beyond the outfield wall. This outdoor swimming pool will be available to private parties of twenty-five to thirty-five people. The retractable roof, 8,000 tons of air conditioning equipment, and countless strategically placed ceiling fans help keep the stadium cool despite the 100-plus temperatures that are common in Arizona summers.

The Diamondbacks have done a nice job offering a variety of seating choices. Ticket prices range from $1 for two sections of upper deck seats in the corners, similar to Turner Fields' skydeck sections, to $50 for lower level seats between the dugouts. The least expensive lower level seats are just $9 for outfield bleachers, while the most expensive upper deck seats are $13.50 for those directly behind home plate.

GETTING TO BANK ONE BALLPARK
Jefferson Street (between 4th and 7th Streets)

The stadium is located on Jefferson Street between 4th and 7th streets in downtown Phoenix. Public transportation is limited to local bus lines that stop at the main bus terminal just one block away. Call (602) 253-5000 for schedules and fare information.

Getting around Phoenix by car is not difficult, and stadium routes are clearly marked. Bank One Ballpark is conveniently located between I-10 (Papago Freeway) and I-17 (Black Canyon Highway) in southwest Phoenix. More than

A hard-to-achieve view of Bank One Ballpark. (Photo courtesy of Arizona Diamondbacks)

18,500 parking spaces are available within a 15-minute walk of the stadium, and a 1,500-car garage is being built next to the stadium.

WHAT TO DO AND SEE IN PHOENIX

Phoenix is not a big city like New York, Los Angeles, or Chicago, but it does have a few things to keep you occupied on those days you decide not to see a ballgame. A lot of what Phoenix has to offer is outdoors: desert Jeep tours, hot-air balloon rides, tubing down the Salt River, even horse-and-carriage rides. There are also a number of worthwhile indoor activities to get you out of the sun.

The **Arizona State Capitol Museum** is in the heart of downtown at the corner of West Washington Street and 17th Avenue. Built in 1900, this tuff stone and granite building served as the state capitol until 1974, when the adjacent capitol building was opened. The legislative chambers are open to the public from 8 AM–5 PM Monday through Friday. Admission to the museum and legislative hall is free. Guided tours are available at 10 AM and 2 PM Monday through Saturday.

Encanto Park is a beautiful city park, at 2705 North 15th Avenue, with an abundance of walking trails, paddle boats, tennis, basketball and volleyball courts, and an affordable public golf course. Serious golfers may want to check out the **TPC at Scottsdale**. This Tom Weiskopf-designed course, at 17020 North Hayden Road in Scottsdale, hosts the PGA Phoenix Open every year and is open to the public.

Papago Peaks Park, at Galvin Parkway and Van Buren Street, offers simple bouldering and hiking trails with a number of caves and terrific views of the surrounding valleys. The **Desert Botanical Garden** and **Phoenix Zoo** are also located within the park. The zoo occupies 125 acres and is home to more than 1,300 animals. Admission is $7 for adults. The botanical gardens showcase more than 150 acres of desert foliage. Admission is just $6 for adults.

The **Heard Museum**, at 22 East Monte Vista Road, is the area's premiere cultural attraction. The emphasis here is on Southwestern Native American history and art with an impressive collection of baskets, pottery, jewelry, and kachina dolls. Admission is just $5 for adults with discounts available for kids and seniors. Entry is free for everybody on Wednesdays. The museum is open every day at 9:30 AM except Sunday, when it opens at noon.

The **Phoenix Art Museum** is two blocks south of the Heard at 1625 North Central Avenue. The museum boasts an extensive collection of nineteenth- and twentieth-century art including work by artists such as Frederick Remington and Georgia O'Keeffe. Admission is $4 for adults and $3 for children. Like the Heard, admission is also free on Wednesdays.

For something completely different try **Waterworld Safari** at 4243 West Pinnacle Peak Road. This water park offers twenty acres of water slides and wave pools and can be a refreshing break from Arizona's torrid summers. If you'd rather try the real thing, head to nearby Mesa. **Salt River Recreation**

Inc. is among a handful of outfits that offer shuttle service and rental tubes for a long, lazy ride down the Salt River.

NIGHTLIFE IN PHOENIX

The best source for nightclub and restaurant information is the *New Times* entertainment weekly, which lists nightclubs by the type of music they generally offer and which has a separate listing for sports bars and comedy clubs. They also list restaurants by location and offer mini-reviews and a pricing guide.

The area's premiere blues club is **The Rhythm Room** at 1019 East Indian School Road. The Rhythm Room offers live blues seven days a week and books better-known national acts every weekend, so be sure to call for upcoming acts and cover charge information. Two of the city's better music venues are located on Indian School Road near 23rd Street. **Warsaw Wally's** is a blues-oriented club, at 2547 East Indian School Road, that generally hosts top-notch regional blues musicians and offers a separate pool room. Just up the street you'll find **The Mason Jar**, a dark yet popular alternative and rock music club at 2303 East Indian School Road.

One of Phoenix's best sports bars is owned by former Suns player Dan Majerle. **Majerle's Sports Grille** is not far from the new ballpark at 24 North Second Street. If you're staying downtown, **America's Original Sports Bar**, located in the Arizona Center at 455 North Third Street, is another place to be before and after a big game. Check out the highlights on fifty-three TVs and seven giant screens, or join in the action on their outdoor volleyball court. **Sports Fever** is another giant sports bar at 2031 Peoria Avenue. Sports Fever offers satellite sports on thirty-eight TVs and four large screens. They also have a sports memorabilia room, pool tables, darts, basketball, a DJ, and a dance floor.

The **Pink Pony**, at 3831 North Scottsdale Road in Scottsdale, is a terrific baseball fan hangout. Not far from the Giants spring training complex, the Pink Pony's walls are plastered with baseball memorabilia, and their steaks are some of the biggest and best in the area. Another popular spot in Scottsdale is **Don & Charlie's**, at 7501 East Camelback Road. Famous for their ribs, Don & Charlie's is frequented by ballplayers throughout spring training, and it's likely to be the same throughout the summer, once Phoenix and the Diamondbacks host regular season ball. Cubs fans will want to stop by **Steve Stone's Chicago Grille** in nearby Mesa, Arizona. This baseball theme bar/restaurant, owned by Cubs broadcaster Steve Stone, is at 161 Centennial Way just a short drive from the Cubs new HoHoKam Park.

For stand-up comedy, check out **The Improv**, at 930 East University Drive in Tempe, which hosts nationally known comedians seven days a week. **Knuckleheads**, at the Arizona Center, offers nationally renowned comedy talent Tuesday through Sunday with two shows on Friday and Saturday nights. Cover charge varies, but they do not have a drink minimum.

For killer Mexican food, I enthusiastically recommend **Macayo**. This local chain offers several locations throughout the area, so no matter where you are staying, you're bound to be near one. We hit the one at 4001 North Central Avenue and enjoyed it so much, we returned a second time before leaving town.

The city's original microbrewery is the **Coyote Springs Brewery** at the corner of 20th Street and Camelback Road in the Town & Country Shopping Center. Coyote Springs offers a full menu of appetizers, salads, sandwiches, burgers, pizzas, and other specialties, as well as a fine selection of handcrafted ales and lagers. In the same shopping center you'll find **Ed Debevic's**, a Chicago institution with great diner food and intentionally surly service.

Speaking of Chicago institutions, **Gino's East** has a location in Tempe at 1470 East Southern Avenue. If you have never tried their deep-dish pizza, you owe it to yourself to stop by for a slab. The Tempe location does not offer the same charm and character as their original Chicago location, but the pizza is some of the best you'll ever have.

WHERE TO STAY IN PHOENIX

Places in the immediate downtown area near the Arizona Center come at a premium but offer the advantage of being within walking distance of the ball-park and a number of the city's more popular, albeit trendy, nightspots and restaurants. More reasonably priced hotels in the northeastern part of the city offer proximity to many of the city's better nightclubs along Camelback and Indian School roads.

AREA HOTELS

Courtyard By Marriott   2101 East Camelback Road (800) 443-6000 or (602) 955-5200   Moderately priced accommodations in the Biltmore nightlife district.

Crowne Plaza Phoenix   100 North First Street (602) 257-1525   Luxury accommodations with bargain summer rates, one block from the stadium.

Embassy Suites Biltmore   2630 East Camelback (800) 362-2779 or (602) 955-3992   Luxury accommodations in the Biltmore area, not far from nightlife district.

Hilton Suites at Phoenix Plaza   10 East Thomas Road (800) HILTONS or (602) 222-1111   Luxury accommodations just two miles from the stadium.

Hyatt Regency   122 North Second Street (800) 233-1234 or (602) 252-1234   Luxury accommodations one block from the stadium.

The Phoenix Inn   2310 East Highland Avenue (800) 956-5221 or (602) 956-5221   Very nice, moderately priced accommodations in the Biltmore area.

Ritz Carlton   2401 East Camelback Road (800) 241-3333 or (602) 468-0700   Luxury 11-story hotel within a short walk of nightlife district.

GOOD TO KNOW

- The Phoenix and Valley of the Sun Convention and Visitors Bureau can be reached at (602) 254-6500. The city's official Web site is www.arizona-guide.com.
- Diamondback games can be heard on **KTAR 620 AM**. The leading all-sports talk radio station is **KMVP 860 AM**.
- For additional information on Arizona sights and attractions, call the Arizona Office of Tourism at (800) 842-8257.

Closest major league cities (and drive times): San Diego—350 miles (6 hours and 20 minutes); Los Angeles/Anaheim—369 miles (6 hours and 35 minutes).

IN THE VICINITY

Take a forty-five-minute drive north of Phoenix and you'll find the make-believe Wild West town of Cave Creek. In the heart of town is the **Black Mountain Brewery** and **Crazy Ed's Satisfied Frog Saloon**. Black Mountain Brewery produces several outstanding brews including Frog Light, Black Mountain Gold, and a chili beer. All three can be sampled next door at the Satisfied Frog, where they are served ice-cold in mason jars. The saloon also offers terrific barbecue, steaks, ribs, and Mexican entrees. The town itself is a little cheesy, but the food and beer at the Satisfied Frog make it well worth the trip.

The **Grand Canyon** is three and a half hours north of Phoenix. The canyon is by far the most impressive natural wonder in the United States, perhaps in the world. Be sure to get up early to see the sunrise, as the canyon is at its colorful best when the sun rises and sets. You can spend your days hiking or riding a mule to the basin, aboard a helicopter riding through the interior, or taking a guided raft down the mighty Colorado River, the best white water ride in the nation. Accommodations within the National Park range from rustic cabins along the southern ridge to luxury rooms with fine dining in the main lodge. Make your reservations well in advance as cabins, mule rides, and rafting trips sell out quickly.

Sedona, a popular spot between Phoenix and the Grand Canyon, offers a wealth of incredible desert scenery that approaches the natural beauty of the Grand Canyon. Sedona was originally an artist community that has since become something of a retirement mecca with an abundance of shops, galleries, restaurants, and some terrific bed and breakfast lodges. Sedona also has several outstanding outdoor areas worth checking out. **Red Rock State Park** is just west of Sedona and offers five hiking trails of varying degrees of difficulty through some of the nation's prettiest countryside. **Slide Rock State Park** has a plunge pool at the bottom of a natural rock slide that is a lot of fun for the whole family. The park gets crowded on the weekends and traffic can be brutal in the summer.

◆ SAN DIEGO ◆

Tradition in St. Louis is Stan Musial coming into the clubhouse and making the rounds. Tradition in San Diego is Nate Colbert coming into the clubhouse and trying to sell a used car.

BOB SHIRLEY

JACK MURPHY STADIUM

Years ago, an area sports editor led the campaign to bring major-league baseball to San Diego. That campaign resulted in the Padres joining the National League in 1969, along with the Montreal Expos. It also resulted in San Diego's stadium being named after that editor. Since then, despite having rosters stocked with such players as Fred McGriff, Tony Gwynn, Joe Carter, Dave Winfield, Ozzie Smith, Gary Sheffield, Tony Fernandez, Benito Santiago, Garry Templeton, Craig Nettles, Andy Benes, Randy Jones, and Rollie Fingers, the Padres have accomplished little else.

Fortunately, the ballpark is better than the ball team has been. Unfortunately, it's not much better. Jack Murphy Stadium is another multipurpose arena that went up in the late '60s with little regard for the game of baseball. While they did have the sense to install natural grass and not put a roof on the place, the park has almost no character and even less nostalgia. The outfield dimensions are symmetrical, and the fence is a standard height except for a small section in right center that is a few inches higher. Foul territory is huge, and the stadium, with a capacity of 59,700, has far too many bad seats.

Needless to say, Padres' tickets are pretty easy to obtain. With the Padres being more competitive lately, tickets to good seats are harder to come by, but games rarely sell out. When I was there last, I was able to park two rows from the main gate and buy tickets for that day's game in the lower level near the diamond. In hindsight, I wish I had bought tickets in the right field bleachers, which were filled with folks much more concerned with getting a good tan and checking out the opposite sex. Given the general lack of talent on the playing field at the time, that was probably not such a bad idea. The stadium does have one unique feature. In each outfield corner there is an area in foul territory that can't be seen by anybody in the infield. An outfielder could feasibly catch a ball in the corner and a runner trying to tag up would have no idea when and if the fielder caught the ball. For that matter, the umpires might not know.

I do have one fond memory of my first visit to Jack Murphy Stadium. The Padres are one of those clubs that let you sit in the outfield during batting practice and vie for the occasional home run ball, even if your seats are located elsewhere. In the summer of 1993, Jack Murphy became the first major league park in which I snagged a batting practice home run ball. I'd like to say I snared a hot smash, but the truth is that I managed to out-scramble a few other folks for a ball that bounced around the left field seats. Nevertheless, despite seeing hundreds of regular season and spring training games, it's the only time I have ever managed to come home from a ballpark with a ball.

The stadium's other bright spot is its concessions. Everything I tried was better than average, and the selection was nothing short of remarkable. I did not have the courage to sample the sushi or fish tacos, but other, more tempting options included a make-your-own tostada and fajita bar, deli sandwiches,

Two new sections of seats and a brand-new scoreboard dominate right field in San Diego's Jack Murphy Stadium. (Photo by Author)

and gourmet sausages. There's also a Sports Club, open to the public, in section 21 of the plaza level.

HISTORY

For a franchise short on history and even shorter on memorable victories, Jack Murphy Stadium has hosted a number of extraordinary moments. In 1969, the stadium's debut season, Willie Mays collected his 600th home run on September 22 with a dinger off Padres pitcher Mike Cockins. The following year, Dock Ellis threw a no-hitter against the Padres on June 12, while allegedly tripping on LSD. The Padres were also victim to Chicago Cubs pitcher Ferguson Jenkins' 3,000th strikeout on May 25, 1982.

On a more positive note, aided by an error on Cubs first baseman Leon "Bull" Durham, the Padres wiped out a 3–0 deficit versus the Cubs in game 5 of the NLCS to win 8–3 on October 7, 1984. The Padres had trailed the series two games to none. Three days later, the Padres won their only World Series game, a 5–3 victory over the Detroit Tigers.

Between 1984 and 1996, about the only thing Padre fans have had to cheer were the scantily clad sunbathers in the right field bleachers and the play of Tony Gwynn. Gwynn got six hits in one game against the Giants on August 4, 1993. Two days later he singled off Rockies pitcher Bruce Ruffin for his 2,000th career hit.

GETTING TO JACK MURPHY STADIUM
9449 Friars Road

"The Murph" is right off the highway and easily accessible by car. There are not a lot of places in the immediate vicinity to eat or drink before the game, so tailgating seems to be the way to go. Traffic on the way out of the game was the easiest I've ever encountered at a major league stadium. There are no mass-transit options, which is just as well, because in Southern California it's imperative to have a car if you hope to see even a small percentage of the sights and attractions.

WHAT TO DO AND SEE IN SAN DIEGO

San Diego more than makes up for the Padres with its wealth of things to do and see. In fact, one of the reasons the Padres draw as poorly as they do is because there are so many other things to do, especially during the summer months. The **San Diego Zoo** is well known as one of the biggest and best in the world. Plan to start early and spend an entire day if you want to see it all. **Skyfari**, the zoo's aerial tram, offers a neat perspective of the zoo itself and a bird's-eye view of some of Balboa Park's Spanish architecture. Another option for getting around is to take the forty-minute guided tour aboard a double-decker bus. The zoo has nearly 4,000 animals representing 900 species, including many rare and near-extinct species, in some of the most natural settings a zoo can offer. During the long summer season the zoo is open at 9 AM daily. Admission is $12 for adults.

San Diego's other major attraction is **Sea World**, which is home to Shamu the killer whale. It has developed into much more than a dolphin-and-whale show. Today there is also a nautical theme park, aquariums, amusement park rides, a penguin exhibit, and the park's most visited attraction, **Shark Encounter**. This display features the effect of being surrounded by swimming sharks as you pass through a clear tunnel that runs through a shark-infested tank. The park opens at 10 AM every day. Admission is $27.95 for adults.

About thirty miles north of downtown in Escondido, you'll find the **San Diego Wild Animal Park**. The park encompasses 2,150 acres and is home to more than 3,000 animals from Asia and Africa who roam free and raise their young much as they would in the wild. The public can observe safely from a monorail encircling the park. The 1.75-mile Kilimanjaro Hiking Trail wanders through dense foliage and past elephants, gorillas, and big cats. Admission is $17.50 for adults.

San Diego's greatest attraction, however, is its seventy miles of beaches. Whether you want to swim, surf, snorkel, scuba dive, or just walk along the Pacific Ocean, the San Diego area offers thirty-three beaches to choose from. **Pacific Beach**, as well as **North** and **South Mission Beaches** are located on Mission Boulevard. All three offer busy boardwalks full of in-line skaters, cyclists, joggers, and entertainers, with shops, restaurants, and cafes along the way.

You'll find surfers at just about every San Diego beach, but **Ocean Beach**, near the pier off Interstate 8 and Sunset Cliffs Boulevard, is a surfer's paradise. You may also find a number of highly competitive volleyball games up and down the beach.

There are so many beaches to choose from, that each one seems to have its own specific function. If you'd rather get away from it all and just take in the sights, **La Jolla shoreline** has beautiful windswept cliffs and caves, fascinating plant life, and is a favorite among snorkelers and scuba divers. **Dog Beach**, as its name implies, is a beach where our canine friends can run untethered, while **Border Field State Park's** beach does not allow swimming, but rents horses for rides along the beach. There's even an unofficial nude beach known as **Black Beach**, located below some steep cliffs, just north of La Jolla. The easiest way to get there is to take the fifteen-minute hike from **Torrey Pines State Beach**.

The **Gaslamp Quarter** is a sixteen and a half block National Historic District that has been around since just after the Civil War. In the early 1900s, it turned into San Diego's red light district but has since been renovated and become home to some of the area's best dining, nightlife, art galleries, hotels, and shopping. The area is served by both the San Diego and Old Town Trolleys, making it easily accessible from all over downtown. Some of the area's better-known outdoor cafes, restaurants, and taverns can be found along 4th, 5th, and 6th avenues, starting around Broadway and extending down toward the waterfront.

San Diego is also home to **Torrey Pines Golf Course**, one of California's most picturesque golf courses. For scenic, oceanside holes, the course is probably second only to the world-famous Pebble Beach Golf Course in Monterey. The 18-hole municipal course plays host to the Buick Invitational every February. Greens fees run between $39.50–$46 and advance tee times are recommended.

NIGHTLIFE IN SAN DIEGO

San Diego's nightlife options are pretty diverse. Mission Boulevard has a number of clubs and cafes not far from the beaches. As I mentioned earlier, the Gaslamp Quarter has several nightclubs, restaurants, and one of the area's better comedy clubs. **Horton Plaza** offers several blocks of cafes, bars, restaurants, and shops.

Your best bet for a current, more complete listing of area nightlife is to pick up a copy of the *San Diego Reader*. It's available free all around town at area restaurants and bars. Once you are in town, you may also want to solicit the advice of the concierge at your hotel. Below is a partial list of area clubs.

One of San Diego's newest and best sports bars is owned by Junior Seau, the Chargers All-Pro linebacker. **Seau's** is a huge, two-story restaurant with a casual atmosphere, wall-to-wall sports memorabilia, an outdoor patio, and a separate cigar lounge. It's located in the Mission Valley Center at 1640 Camino Del Rio North.

The Gaslamp Quarter has a few sports bars to choose from. **Johnny Love's**, at the corner of 5th and G streets, is a good-size place with better-than-average food, dancing, plenty of TVs, and a basement aviation sports bar with pool tables and darts. **Buffalo Joe's American Restaurant and Bar**, at 600 Fifth Avenue, has a dozen TVs, eighteen beers on tap, and a serious menu of ribs, burgers, even ostrich, buffalo, and alligator entrees and appetizers. They also feature live music seven nights a week.

Jazz fans will want to check out **Croce's**, at the corner of Fifth Avenue and F Street. Croce's is owned by Jim Croce's widow, Ingrid. This multilevel bar/restaurant has a warm, cozy atmosphere and features some of the area's best jazz, and rhythm and blues acts nightly.

Two of the better-known comedy clubs in the San Diego area are **The**

Improv and **The Comedy Store.** The Improv is in the Mission Bay area at 832 Garnett Avenue and features top names in comedy seven days a week. The Comedy Store, at 916 Pearl Street in La Jolla, is open all week long and has nationally known comedians Wednesday through Saturday.

Quite possibly the area's best club for cutting-edge, alternative music, **SOMA Live** at 5305 Metro Street in Bay Park hosts nationally known bands every Thursday, Friday, and Saturday. Another outstanding live-music venue is **4th & B**, at 345 B Street. This downtown music theater showcases top-name musical acts ranging from blues to pop, folk, and country. Tickets are available at the theater box office, open from 10 to 5 every day, or by calling Ticket-Master.

One of the few places to grab a drink or bite to eat near Jack Murphy Stadium is the **San Diego Brewing Company**. About one mile east of the stadium, at 10450 Friars Road, this microbrewery has fifty beers on tap and serves lunch and dinner seven days a week and breakfast on weekends. Another microbrewery worth looking into is **Sports City Cafe & Brewery** at 8657 Villa La Jolla Drive in La Jolla. With more than sixty TVs and eight satellites, they can show eleven different games at a time.

WHERE TO STAY IN SAN DIEGO

Tourism is the area's third largest industry, so there is an abundance of hotel space in and around San Diego. That does not mean you are likely to find a bargain if you don't do some calling around in advance. Not surprisingly, none of the hotels I came across seem to cater to baseball fans or offer any sort of Padres packages. There are, however some deals to be had.

AREA HOTELS

Best Western Shelter Island Marina Inn   2501 Shelter Island Drive (800) 528-1234 or (619) 222-0561   Nice, yet reasonably priced with a great view of the marina.

Comfort Inn Downtown   719 Ash Street (800) 424-6423 or (619) 232-2525 Convenient downtown location. Complimentary continental breakfast, free parking.

Doubletree Inn   910 Broadway Circle (800) 222-TREE or (619) 239-2200   Adjoining the Horton Plaza shopping and entertainment center.

Embassy Suites   601 Pacific Highway (800) EMBASSY or (619) 239-2400 Two-room suites with complimentary cooked-to-order breakfast and happy hour.

Gaslamp Plaza Suites   520 E Street (800) 443-8012 or (619) 232-9500 Remodeled historic hotel in the heart of the Gaslamp district. One block from Horton Plaza.

Radisson Hotel Harbor View 1646 Front Street (800) 333-3333 or (619) 239-6800   Nice hotel convenient to downtown and airport.

Team Hotels

Hyatt Regency   One Market Place (800) 233-1234 or (619) 232-1234   Astros.

Marriott Hotel & Marina   333 West Harbor Drive (800) 228-9290 or (619) 234-1500   Braves, Marlins, Expos, Mets, and Giants.

Marriott Mission Valley   8757 Rio San Diego Drive (800) 228-9290 or (619) 692-3800   Reds, Dodgers, Phillies, and Pirates.

Sheraton Harbor Island   1380 Harbor Island Drive (800) 325-3535 or (619) 291-2900   Cubs and Rockies.

GOOD TO KNOW

- For schedule information or tickets to Padres games, call (619) 452-7328. The Padres official Internet address is www.padres.org.
- Padres games can be heard on **KFMB 760 AM**. The leading all-sports radio station is **X-TRA 690 AM**.
- For more information on San Diego sights, attractions, and hotels, call the **Convention & Visitors Bureau** at (800) 701-WAVE or (619) 236-1212 or (619) 232-3101. Or you can write them at 401 B Street, San Diego, CA 92101. The city's official Web site is www.sandiego.org.

Closest major league cities (and drive times): Los Angeles/Anaheim—124 miles (2 hours and 25 minutes); Phoenix—350 miles (6 hours and 20 minutes); San Francisco/Oakland—533 miles (10 hours and 10 minutes).

IN THE VICINITY

The **U.S. Summer Olympic Training Center** is just southeast of San Diego in Chula Vista on the shores of the Otay Lakes Reservoir. Olympic hopefuls train for track and field, cycling, soccer, field hockey, and rowing teams at the nation's only warm-weather Olympic training center. A short film is shown in the facility's theater followed by a narrated tour along a scenic 1.5-mile Olympic Path overlooking 150 acres of athlete training areas. The guided tour is free, and all proceeds from purchases at the U.S. Olympic Spirit Store support the U.S. Olympic Movement. Call (619) 482-6120 for directions or additional information.

Tijuana, Mexico is just across the border from San Diego. As the San Diego Convention & Visitors Bureau likes to say, the city's proximity to Mexico makes it "a two-nation vacation destination." Because of insurance restrictions, you may not drive a U.S. rental car across the border without additional insurance, which you can purchase on either side of the border. You can park your car at the border in San Ysidro (parking is $5–7) and take a Mexicoach bus to Tijuana for $1 per person each way. Another way to get there, without having to worry about your car or dealing with long waits at customs, is to take the seventeen-mile trip on the San Diego Trolley. Its southern terminus is right at the border and it runs until late at night. Be sure to ask the driver when the last trolley runs. Once you walk through customs and get on the Mexican side, you'll find cabbies who will take you to Tijuana for about $2 per person.

Because of the favorable exchange rate and the fact that Tijuana is a duty-free zone, you can come across some great deals on silver jewelry, serapes, pottery, and a host of other genuine Mexican products, so you may want to bring some extra spending money. Pharmaceuticals and liquor are also available at significant discounts. You are allowed to bring back only one liter of liquor per person.

Nightlife in Tijuana goes on until late at night and is like nothing you've ever seen. My favorite place was an upstairs bar called **The Iguana**, but most of the larger places are pretty hopping and will offer you two-for-one margaritas and in some cases even three-for-one margaritas. Stick with the beer if possible. Believe it or not, Corona, Dos Equis, and Pacifico beers are actually cheaper than Coca-Cola in Tijuana. I would recommend traveling with at least one other person and staying on the main strip, avoiding side-street establishments unless you are with somebody who knows their way around. **You'll need a driver's license or passport to get back into the United States**, so don't forget to bring one or the other.

TOP TEN BASEBALL-RELATED ATTRACTIONS

10 **Original Baseball Hall of Fame**   Minneapolis, Minnesota

9 **The Sports Museum of New England**   Cambridge, Massachusetts

8 **Saint Louis Cardinals Hall of Fame Museum**   St. Louis, Missouri

7 **Legends of the Game Baseball Museum**   Arlington, Texas

6 **Ted Williams's Hitters Hall of Fame**   Hernando, Florida

5 **Negro League Baseball Museum**   Kansas City, Missouri

4 **Yankee Stadium Monument Park**   Bronx, New York

3 **Babe Ruth Birthplace and Museum**   Baltimore, Maryland

2 **Field of Dreams**   Dyersville, Iowa

1 **National Baseball Hall of Fame**   Cooperstown, New York

♦ SAN FRANCISCO ♦

"When you see 41,000 people in the stadium, and you see it all year, it's great. This is a great stadium. The fans here are very good, very loud."

LIVAN HERNANDEZ

PACIFIC BELL PARK

The Giants' new home is everything Candlestick was not—friendly, convenient, enthusiastic, and bordering on intimate. Pacific Bell Park, the first privately financed big league baseball stadium built since 1962, is an absolute jewel of a ballpark. The main-entrance plaza, at the base of Third Street, is a welcome sight with a stunning nine-foot-tall bronze statue of Willie Mays, fronted by a group of palm trees. The park's red brick exterior may be reminiscent of Coors Field, Camden Yards, the Ballpark at Arlington and a few classic yards, but the interior is one of a kind.

The park seats 40,800 fans, with standing-room-only for another 130 people in right field, but has an openness you might not expect in a big league park. There are virtually no seats beyond the right field fence. An open concourse area that stretches behind the bleacher seats from the left field foul pole, underneath the massive center field scoreboard, to the right field corner adds to the park's open feel. The view of San Francisco Bay, the Bay Bridge, and the Alameda hills beyond the outfield fence is absolutely awe inspiring. Seeing the collection of kayaks, sailboats, and yachts cruise into McCovey Cove beyond the right field stands is unforgettable.

A giant scoreboard, replay board, clock, and light tower dominate the center field view, while a giant baseball glove and Coca-Cola bottle are situated above the left field bleacher seats. The vintage three-finger-style glove is an impressive piece, built and designed by a group of female Berkeley artists, while the 80-foot bottle is home to four giant, twisting playground slides. The huge center field scoreboard is among the best in baseball, providing a wealth of stats and game information about individual hitters and the lineup of the team at bat. A pair of scoreboards along the base paths show the speed of each pitch, how many balls and strikes the pitcher has thrown, and his total pitches. Another pair of auxiliary boards along the baselines track the inning, score, balls, strikes, and outs.

Pacific Bell's natural grass playing surface, asymmetric dimensions, and varying outfield fence height add to the nostalgic feel. The outfield wall, just eight feet high from the left field corner to right-center field, tops out at 25 feet tall in the right field corner, a mere 305 feet from home plate. The manual out-of-town scoreboard, with scores from both the National and American league games, sits in the arched insets of the right field wall. The area beyond this wall, between McCovey Cove and right field, allows folks without tickets a glimpse of the game from the bay-side walkway.

The deepest part of the park is 421 feet in right-center field near the all-time home run leader board. This board lists the top 18 home run hitters of all time including four Giants—Mays, McCovey, Ott, and Bonds. Beyond the home run board, a flagpole flies the pennants of western division teams in order of their standings from top to bottom. The left field corner is 339 feet from home plate, and just left of the foul pole is where you'll find retired jersey numbers of former New York and San Francisco Giant greats, as well as Jackie Robinson's omnipresent number 42.

My favorite fan amenity at Pacific Bell is one I couldn't make use of. A miniature ballpark in the left field corner allows kids to participate in a pick-up game of wiffle ball as a Giants staffer pitches to them. Kids who take part in a game here are liable to become fans for life. Bigger kids can check out a variety of interactive baseball games.

In addition to great seats, Pac Bell has good eats. There's been plenty written about the sushi, clam chowder bread bowls, grilled salmon, and other specialty foods at Pacific Bell Park, but my favorites were the Gilroy Garlic Fries and Orlando's Jamaican BBQ sandwich. Orlando's BBQ is behind the left field bleachers and serves a mean steak sandwich and plenty of Red Stripe beer. The garlic fries are potently plentiful and can be found at two locations, one each on the Promenade and View levels, with shorter lines at the center field stand. Other concession stands throughout the park include Say Hey Sausages, Portwalk Pizza, Doggie Diner, Carl's Jr., and John McGraw's Derby Grill.

The stadium has few flaws. There's an abundance of advertising signage. The TD Waterhouse display board in the left corner scrolls stock market activity, and the Chevron billboard, shaped like a car with headlights at field level in the same corner, is obtrusive to the point of jutting above the outfield wall—in play, and in the way of seats in the very bottom rows of that section. Scorekeepers may be interested to know that the sign's letter H

View of Pacific Bell Park from upper level behind home plate. Note the giant glove behind left center field fence. (Photo by Author)

lights up for hits, while the E illuminates when a play is scored as an error.

The bullpens consist of side-by-side mounds along either foul line, just beyond the dugouts. These may provide the home team a slight edge, by adding to the degree of difficulty as fielders go after shallow, foul pop-ups behind first and third, but I prefer the traditional, separate bullpens near the bleacher seats.

Another significant difference between Pac Bell and Candlestick is the tremendous number of places near the park to eat and drink before and after the game. **Momo's** is a martini bar and restaurant directly opposite the Second Street Gate that packs them in on game days. Just up the street you'll find **Paragon**, another happening upscale place to hang out or grab a meal before the game. **21st Amendment Brewery and Cafe** offers a more relaxed atmosphere, an attentive staff, and a modest menu. Even farther from the park, **Eddie Rickenbacker's** is worth the walk. Surrounded by vintage domestic motorcycles, genuine Tiffany lamps, and model trains, you'll be greeted with a smile, offered outstanding seafood, steaks, and burgers from a dinner menu that changes daily. More important, just about all your favorite beverages are offered on tap for a fraction of ballpark prices.

Before attending afternoon games, consider beating the traffic and heading to **Choppers** or **Primo Patio Cafe** on Townsend Street, just a block or two from the park off Third Street. Choppers makes outstanding specialty sandwiches, while both places serve fine omelettes, breakfast burritos, and coffee with comfortable back patio seating. Reasonably priced beer and wine are served at both, but don't overlook the mango mimosas at Primo. At the corner of Third Street and Brannan, you'll find **Zeke's**, a well-worn, indigenous sports bar with a helpful staff, moderately priced burgers, chili, sandwiches and fries. **Bay City Bar & Grill**, also near the stadium on Third Street, offers California-style cuisine in a casual dark, urban setting for lunch and dinner.

There are also a few places to splurge near the park. **Town's End Restaurant & Bakery**, at 2 Townsend Street in the South Beach area, has been a local favorite for years, with friendly service, excellent food, and a stellar brunch on weekends. **Palomino** is farther away, near Embarcadero, but this Seattle-based chain can be counted on for outstanding entrees, an eclectic appetizer menu, exceptional beverages, and attentive service.

HISTORY

In their first year at Pacific Bell Park, the Giants won more games than any other team in the National League. Sadly, Pacific Bell Park hosted just two playoff games that year, albeit memorable ones, as the Giants lost to the Mets in four games after taking the first game 5–1, behind Ellis Burks' 3-run homer. In game two, J.T. Snow tied up in the bottom of the ninth with a clutch home run, just inside the right field foul pole, but the Mets came back to win the game in the 10th.

The Giants have not won the World Series since moving to Candlestick Park in 1958, but the stadium has been the site of many significant achievements and events. Candlestick hosted the All-Star Game in 1961. The wind was so fierce that Giants pitcher Stu Miller is said to have been blown off the mound during his windup. While that may be somewhat of an exaggeration, he was charged with a balk on the play. On September 22, 1963, Giants slugger Willie McCovey belted three consecutive home runs against the Mets.

In one of the ugliest moments in sports, Juan Marichal attacked Dodgers' catcher Johnny Roseboro with his bat on August 22, 1965. Marichal took offense with Roseboro's throwing the ball back to the pitcher so close to Marichal's ear. Words were exchanged, then Marichal proceeded to whack Roseboro with his bat figuring there was no other way to hurt a fully equipped catcher.

The very next year, another pitcher made headlines for his bat handling. On July 3, Atlanta's Tony Cloninger became the first and only National League player to hit two grand slams in the same game. Cloninger nearly had a chance for a third grand slam as he was on deck when Denis Menke struck out on a 3–2 count to end an inning with two men on. On Cloninger's ensuing at-bat, Giants outfielder Len Gabrielson, Jr., scaled the wall to rob the Atlanta pitcher of a potential third round-tripper. For the day, Cloninger settled for two grand slams, nine RBIs, and a complete game 17–3 victory. No small accomplishment for a pitcher!

On July 14, 1967, Eddie Matthews hit his 500th career home run off Juan Marichal. The following season, Candlestick witnessed back-to-back no-hitters as Gaylord Perry blanked the Cardinals 1–0 on September 17 and Cards' hurler, Ray Washburn, no-hit the Giants the following day for a 2–0 victory. Nearly seven years later, on August 24, 1975, Ed Halicki pitched a no-hitter for a 6–0 win over the Mets.

Perhaps Candlestick's most memorable moment came on October 17, 1989, when an earthquake rocked the stadium just before game three of the World Series between the Giants and A's. Remarkably, nobody was hurt in the sold-out stadium, but the 7.1 quake caused the World Series to be postponed for ten days.

GETTING TO PACIFIC BELL PARK
24 Willie Mays Plaza

Situated in northeast San Francisco, along the China Basin Channel between Second and Third streets, Pac Bell is easy to get to on foot, by automobile, Muni Metro, ferry, and Cal Train. BART stations at Montgomery Street and Embarcadero are closest to the park, albeit a long walk from the stadium. Transferring from BART to the Muni Metro is probably a better bet. By car, the park is easy to find, especially via I-80 and 280, as signs directing you to the stadium are virtually everywhere, but traffic can be slow as you leave the highway and approach the park.

Official ballpark parking lots are expensive ($15–20) and limited to just 4,800 cars, encouraging the use of mass transit. A lot on Second Street, near Brannan, has $10 game parking, but fills quickly. The Muni Metro rail line stops directly in front of the park and the CalTrain depot is just over a block away. A ferry from Oakland's Jack London Square drops you off at the park's Marina Gate behind center field. This gate opens two hours before game time and leads to the left and center field bleachers, a great place to field batting practice home run balls. The ferry costs just $4.75 each way for adults. Pay your fare once on board, or call (415) 705-5555 in advance to reserve a spot.

WHAT TO DO AND SEE IN SAN FRANCISCO

San Francisco is my favorite big city in the United States. Every time you turn the corner, it seems that you stumble upon a scene even more beautiful than the last. Despite the fact that the city occupies only 46 square miles, there is no way to see all that San Francisco has to offer in just a few days. With that in mind, the San Francisco Visitor Information Center offers a twenty-four-hour visitor hot line you can reach at (415) 391-2001, to help narrow down the choices. If you prefer to talk to someone directly, stop by their office, at the corner of Market and Powell streets. It's generally worth stopping by, as maps and discount passes to area attractions are available. The visitors center is conveniently located next to a Cable Car turnaround and BART station.

When people think of San Francisco, their first image is generally the **Golden Gate Bridge** and the San Francisco Bay. The bridge is more than 8,900 feet long and its twin towers are the highest in the nation at 746 feet. A walk across the bridge offers a great view of the city skyline, Alcatraz Island, and the surrounding countryside. While the Golden Gate Bridge is San Francisco's most recognizable landmark, it is certainly not the city's only one. Every year nearly one million people take the mile and a half boat ride to **Alcatraz,** America's most famous maximum security prison. You can catch the Red & White Fleet Ferry (for $5.50 round-trip) at Pier 41 for the short trip across San Francisco Bay. Tickets should be ordered well in advance during the summer by calling (415) 546-2700. Once you're on the island, be sure to take a self-guided audio tour (an additional $3), narrated by ex-inmates and guards. You can also wait for a free ranger-led tour to get a good feel for the prison's short but colorful history.

No visit to San Francisco would be complete without a ride on a **cable car**. What used to be the main form of mass transit in San Francisco is now little more than a tourist attraction, as there are only three lines and seventeen miles of track left these days. Nevertheless, more than ten million folks ride the cable cars each year. Despite having a top speed of just nine and a half miles an hour, they are an excellent way to negotiate the city's steep hills. All three lines are fun, but the Powell-Hyde Line, which takes you down Russian Hill, is my favorite.

If you are without a car or are in town for more than two days, you might want to consider buying a **Muni Passport**, which allows you unlimited rides on any regularly scheduled Muni vehicle, including cable cars. A one-day pass is just $6, a three-day pass costs $10, and a seven-day pass is $15. The pass also entitles you to discounts at some area attractions and a reduced fare on the bus to Candlestick Park. For more information call (415) 673-6864.

Lombard Street is touted as "the world's crookedest street." The one-block street makes eight switchbacks and offers a tremendous view of the San Francisco Bay, Telegraph Hill, and Coit Tower from the top. Once you've seen it, you'll be surprised to know that it's neither the steepest nor the narrowest street in the city. Bear in mind, that it's a one-way street, and if you want to drive on it, you have to start at the top, off Hyde Street.

Coit Memorial Tower was a gift to the city from Lillie Hitchcock Coit. The tower stands atop Telegraph Hill and offers a panoramic view of the city, which is especially impressive in the late afternoon. For $3, an elevator takes you to the 210-foot-high observation deck, which is actually over 540 feet above the bay. The tower is open daily.

San Francisco's Chinatown is the best and most authentic in the United States. The main entrance is at the corner of Grant and Bush streets, where you'll find a stone lion and dragon gateway. The 24-block area, also in the northeast corner of the city, is home to some of the best Chinese restaurants you'll ever encounter, as well as open-air markets, shops, and a number of small museums highlighting the contributions made by the Chinese to California's history.

Another of San Francisco's great neighborhoods is Haight-Ashbury, which used to be the hippie capitol of the West Coast, but has become sort of a punk/yuppie hangout with a number of shops, restaurants, and bars. If you are looking for something indigenous to the area (but not too kitschy) to bring home from your trip, this is a great place to look, as there are a number of galleries, record stores, and poster shops along Haight Street.

Golden Gate State Park is the crown jewel of the San Francisco Recreation and Parks Department and home to several of San Francisco's premiere sights and attractions. Within the 1,017-acre park, you'll find the M.H. deYoung Memorial Museum, which has a formidable collection of American art, the Asian Art Museum, home to the Avery Brundage Collection of nearly 10,000 Oriental works of art, the California Academy of Sciences, a fine natural history museum and planetarium, the glass-domed Conservatory of Flowers, as well as the five-acre Japanese Tea Garden. A Culture Pass to all five of the attractions listed above can be purchased for $10 at the McLaren Lodge in GGS Park, the downtown Visitors Center, or at any of the individual attractions.

Also at the park, but not included in the Culture Pass, is the Steinhart Aquarium, which features a 100,000-gallon tank and more than 14,000 aquatic animals. The public golf course within the park is quite challenging and offers some great views of the Pacific Ocean. If not for one of the attractions listed above, you should still consider heading to Golden Gate State Park to make use of the miles of walking and cycling trails, enjoy one of the many lakes, see the two authentic Dutch windmills and the herd of bison. For more information or a free guided tour, call (415) 221-1311. After exploring all there is to see at Golden Gate State Park, you may want to stop by the Cliff House, at 1066 Point Lobos Avenue, for a drink and a bite to eat. The Cliff House offers great food and overlooks Seal Rock and the Pacific Ocean.

Along the northwestern edge of San Francisco itself and across the Golden Gate Bridge, in Marin County, is the Golden Gate National Recreation Area.

The area north of San Francisco offers a great view of the bridge from the rocky cliffs below the bridge, a perspective few tourists ever see. The park stretches from just above **Fort Funston**, in San Francisco, to well into the Marin Peninsula, north of the city. Among other things, there are more than one hundred miles of hiking trails, several beaches, picnic facilities, and a limited number of campsites. Swimming is allowed at Stinson Beach.

The **California Palace of the Legion of Honor** is considered to be one of the West Coast's finest art museums. It is home to nearly 90,000 works of art, including one of the nation's largest collections of sculpture by Auguste Rodin.

Two of the lesser-known attractions in San Francisco are the **Museum of Cartoon Art** and the **Ansel Adams Center**. The cartoon art museum, located at 665 Third Street, features a permanent collection of early animation art as well as occasional traveling exhibits. The museum is open Wednesday through Sunday and admission is just $3 for adults. The Ansel Adams Center can be found at 240 Fourth Street. The museum consists of five galleries of the photographer's work, as well as an ever-changing exhibit of the history of photography. The museum is open Tuesday through Sunday. Admission is $4 for adults.

Baseball fans may want to keep an eye out for **Lefty O'Doul's** on Powell Street near Union Square. Named after the ex-big-league player and minor-league manager, it's an inexpensive place to grab a cold beer and a bite to eat. Be sure to walk around the place and check out the baseball memorabilia on the walls.

NIGHTLIFE IN SAN FRANCISCO

San Francisco is like most big cities in that there's a small pub or tavern on just about every corner, but the closest thing to a nightlife district would be **Union Street**, where there are quite a few singles bars to choose from. For live music, check out the **South of Market Area** along 11th Street, also known as SOMA. Another option is the **Haight-Ashbury** area, where the spirit of the '60s is alive and well, in the form of coffeehouses, street front cafes, and small clubs with poetry readings and acoustic music. Your best bet is to check out one of San Francisco's free entertainment magazines for upcoming shows and events. The *SF Bay Guardian* and the *Bay Area Music Magazine* seem to be the most helpful. Here is a partial list of clubs that stand out from the crowd.

Bottom of the Hill   1233 17th Street (415) 621-4455   An intimate room with live original music nightly, featuring up-and-coming local, regional, and national acts. The kitchen is open 11 AM to 11 PM.

Club Boomerang   1840 Haight Street (415) 387-2996   A Haight-Ashbury mainstay with live local progressive music seven nights a week. Even on weekends, when they present three bands, the cover charge is rarely more than $5.

Club DV8   540 Howard Street (415) 957-1730   One of the bigger, more trendy dance clubs in the SOMA area.

Cobb's Comedy Club   2801 Leavenworth (in the Cannery) (415) 928-4320 Top-rate comics as seen on the Tonight Show, Letterman, and Comedy Channel.

The Fillmore   1805 Geary at Fillmore (415) 346-6000   A San Francisco institution, with the best in live rock and roll nightly. Top-name talent almost every day of the week. Tables and seating are very limited, so get there early. Most shows have a two-drink minimum.

The Great American Music Hall   859 O'Farrell(415) 885-0750   Nationally known folk, jazz, blues, and rock acts nightly. Tickets can be picked up in advance at GAMH box office Monday to Saturday without a service charge.

Lou's Pier 47   300 Jefferson Street (415) 771-0377   A live rock and pop music venue located at Fisherman's Wharf.

Paradise Lounge   1501 Folsom at 11th Street (415) 861-6906   The Paradise is a favorite with the locals and features live music almost every night.

Perry's   1944 Union Street (415) 922-9022   The king daddy of Union Street singles clubs. A good place to start your night, or end up after checking out other Union Street area clubs.

The Punch Line 444-A Battery Street (between Washington and Clay) (415) 397-PLSF   Nationally known comedians appear regularly. Both Jay Leno and Whoopi Goldberg got their start here. Two-for-ones are available in the *Bay Guardian*.

San Francisco Brewing Company   155 Columbus (415) 434-3344   An outstanding brew pub on the edge of the North Beach neighborhood that is home to a number of fine restaurants and cafes.

Slim's 333   333 Eleventh Street (between Folsom and Harrison) (415) 621-3330   Live music most nights. From rock to reggae, generally top-rate, nationally known acts. Cover varies between $8 and $16.

The Warfield   982 Market Street (415) 775-7672   A classic nightclub, restaurant, and bar that presents big-time rock and roll acts that often sell out in advance of show date.

WHERE TO STAY IN SAN FRANCISCO

San Francisco has no shortage of hotel rooms. The trick is to find one that is clean and comfortable, while at the same time affordable and conveniently located near the downtown sights. Candlestick Park is located south of the city near the airport, but it's not an ideal place to stay if you are going to spend any time seeing the sights of the city.

DOWNTOWN HOTELS

Best Western Americana 121 7th Street (800) 444-5816 or (415) 626-0200 A block and a half south of Market Street. Free parking and shuttle to area sights.

Chancellor Hotel 433 Powell Street (800) 428-4748 or (415) 362-2004 Located on the cable car route, within walking distance of Union Square and Chinatown.

The Handlery Union Square Hotel 351 Geary Street (800) 843-4343 or (415) 781-7800 A short walk to cable car route and Chinatown. Heated pool and sauna on site.

Holiday Inn Union Square 480 Sutter Street (800) HOLIDAY or (415) 398-8900 Nice hotel between Union Square and Chinatown, on the cable car route.

Hotel Britton 112 7th Street (800) 444-5819 or (415) 621-7001 Affordable, small hotel within walking distance of SOMA restaurants and nightclubs.

Royal Pacific Motor Inn 661 Broadway (800) 545-5574 or (415) 781-6661 Across from Chinatown, just a short walk from Fisherman's Wharf and Union Square.

Warwick Regis Hotel 490 Geary Street (415) 928-7900 Two blocks west of Union Square. Within walking distance of cable car route, Union Square, and Chinatown.

TEAM HOTELS

Grand Hyatt 345 Stockton Street (800) 233-1234 or (415) 398-1234 Phillies.

Hilton 333 O'Farrell Street (800) HILTONS or (415) 771-1400 Cubs, Rockies, and Dodgers.

Parc 55 55 Cyril Magnin Street (800) 338-1338 or (415) 392-8000 Braves, Reds, Marlins, Astros, Expos, and Pirates.

Westin St. Francis 335 Powell Street (800) 228-3000 or (415) 397-7000 Cardinals and Padres.

GOOD TO KNOW

- For schedule information or tickets to Giants games, call (510) 762-2277. The Giants official Internet address is www.sfgiants.com.
- Giants games can be heard on **KNBR 680 AM.**
- San Francisco Visitor Information Center offers a 24-hour visitor hot line

you can reach at (415) 391-2001. The city's best Web site for tourist information is www.sfchamber.com.

- Football fans may be interested in seeing the annual **Bay Classic** preseason game between the 49ers and Raiders. Call the 49ers' office at (408) 562-4949.
- For more information on San Francisco call the **Convention & Visitors Bureau** at (415) 227-2603 or write them at 201 Third Street, San Francisco, CA 94103.

Closest major league cities (and drive times): Oakland—8 miles (30 minutes); Los Angeles/Anaheim—394 miles (7 hours and 5 minutes); San Diego—518 miles (9 hours and 30 minutes).

IN THE VICINITY

Sausalito sits across the Golden Gate Bridge less than twenty minutes from downtown San Francisco by car. Restaurants and taverns on the waterfront offer a nice view of the San Francisco skyline as you enjoy a cold drink or bite to eat. There are shops and galleries in the immediate area.

Napa Valley and **Sonoma County** are home to more than 200 wineries, many of which offer tours and tastings. The countryside makes for an enjoyable drive except on weekends when the stop-and-go pace can be enough to make you wish you stayed in San Francisco. For a list of wineries, call the Napa Valley Conference and Visitors Bureau at (707) 226-7459 or the Sonoma County Convention and Visitor's Bureau at (800) 326-7666.

Monterey is two and a half hours south of San Francisco, but the drive along the coast is incredible. If there's a more breathtaking stretch of road in the forty-eight contiguous states, I haven't seen it. Once you get to Monterey, you may want to drive along **Pebble Beach Golf Links**. Pebble Beach is one of the world's finest golf courses—the back nine is particularly impressive—featuring a number of oceanside holes and an abundance of wildlife.

Monterey's **Fisherman's Wharf** consists of an active marina, a number of fine restaurants, and it is not nearly as touristy as San Francisco. The city's premier attraction is **Cannery Row**, which was at one time a working fish cannery and the setting for several John Steinbeck novels, but has since been transformed into an area of shops, restaurants, and galleries. It's also where you'll find some of the town's better nightlife and the **Monterey Bay Aquarium**. The aquarium is one of the biggest and best in the nation. Admission is $11.25 for adults. For more information call (408) 648-4888 or (800) 756-3737 for advance tickets.

A little more than twenty miles south of Monterey is **Big Sur**, perhaps the most dramatic and picturesque meeting of the California coast and the Pacific Ocean. For more information on sites in and around Monterey, call (800) 695-0123 or the Chamber of Commerce at (408) 649-1770.

◆ SEATTLE ◆

"They're all starting to look the same. There are only so many quirks you can install to make a stadium look different. It won't be long before we start thinking of Comiskey Park and Kauffman Stadium as unique. "

JAY AHUJA

SAFECO FIELD

Fans whose only big league baseball experience was from the seats of the Kingdome are in for a treat. Safeco follows the lead of Camden Yards, Jacobs Field, Bank One Ballpark, Coors Field, Ballpark in Arlington, and Turner Field with a "nostalgic" brick and exposed steel design. Safeco's view of the skyline beyond the left field foul pole is impressive, but the ingenious manner in which the retractable roof allows the park to open and close is what sets this park apart. Seats in the very top section of right field are under cover when the roof is open, so Safeco more resembles an outdoor park than most other indoor/outdoor stadiums. Designed by a local engineering firm, this could be the wave of the future for retractable-roof ballparks.

Contributing to Safeco's spacious feel is the way the roof rolls into place on its own support columns, so supports are not in view when the roof is open. The 13,000-ton roof slides into place in just twenty minutes and stores in three overlapping sections above the Portland-Seattle railroad line just beyond right field. Trains pass regularly and contribute to the park's ambience as they rumble by.

Safeco Field is also not without it's own unique charm. Fans who enter from behind home plate will appreciate the chandelier of 1,000 luminescent bats hanging in the atrium. At the top of the stairs, on the main concourse level, you'll find another artistic accoutrement underfoot. A terrazzo floor incorporates the Mariner compass logo and the signatures of roster players from the day the park opened. There's also a sweeping view of the entire park from this vantage point. Outside the park, near the left field entrance, you'll find a massive bronze sculpture of a glove with a hole in it, oddly reminiscent of the old Milwaukeee Brewers logo.

The field is within view of concession areas and readily accessed from a number of exceptional common areas, so fans can stand and watch the game from a position that might be better than their actual seats. Perhaps the best such spot is a nearly ground-level standing-room-only plot of real estate beyond the center field fence that must have been built with Ken Griffey, Jr. fans in mind. The center field gates open three hours before game time, so this spot is perfect for snagging batting practice homers.

Other common areas that may offer an interesting perspective include the **Hit It Here Cafe/Terrace**, a casual eatery overlooking right field with a great view of the game, and the picnic/patio area behind home plate—reminiscent of Wrigley Field—where you can't watch the game, but are treated to a remarkable view of Puget Sound and the surrounding mountains. A long way from home plate, in the left field corner of the upper concourse, you'll find **Lookout Landing**, with a sweeping view of the field, downtown Seattle, and Elliot Bay. You'll also find one of the park's concession highlights, **Holy Smoke BBQ**.

The park's scoreboards are top-notch. A dozen boards, strategically placed so that fans everywhere can keep track of the action, provide out-of-town scores, play-by-play information, at-bat stats, pitch speed, official scoring decisions and more. The main scoreboard offers a massive video screen equipped for HDTV and a giant matrix animation board surrounded by billboards above the center field bleachers. A giant Safeco Field sign sits below the left field light stanchion and above the out-of-town electronic scoreboard. A hand-operated scoreboard sits in the left field corner, while four auxiliary statistics boards and two play-by-play boards are situated along the baselines.

On the down side, Safeco is only moderately impressive from the exterior. The home plate entrance has a grand facade and stairway atrium, but outside along the first and third baselines, there is little evidence that a ballgame might be played on the other side of what looks like a department store or hotel exterior. Beyond right field lie the railroad tracks and roof apparatus. The handful of artistic touches scattered about the park fall a little short of creating a genuine nostalgic baseball atmosphere.

The interior concourses offer a tremendous view of the game, but look a lot like the interior of a shopping mall, especially on the suite levels. One also can't help but wonder if the immaculate skybox and club seat sections were a little less opulent would the rest of the park have a more finished and nostalgic atmosphere? The grass playing field is not among the best in the big leagues, and groundskeepers will have their work cut out for them as they maintain the turf under Seattle's challenging weather conditions.

The retractable roof of the new Safeco Field shades a part of right field stands.
(Photo courtesy of Ben Van Houten/MLB Photos)

The asymmetrical outfield wall, suddenly a standard feature in today's new ballparks, doesn't present any particularly challenging caroms. The bullpens occupy some prime long ball territory, denying fans much sought after souvenirs. There's also a somewhat unsightly turf-growing area past right-center field. Safeco is a fine park, however, with every conceivable fan amenity—a tremendous improvement on the old Kingdome.

HISTORY

The Mariners have been playing outdoors since July 15, 1999, and fans may find it to be a very different game. The Kingdome's "arena baseball" provided for some bizarre plays. On August 4, 1979, Seattle's Rupert Jones hit a foul ball that lodged in a speaker suspended above the first base dugout. Four seasons later, on May 20, Ricky Nelson of the Brewers duplicated the feat. Several other balls hit support wires and speakers, some falling in play for base hits, others being caught for outs, and in some cases would-be home runs actually bounced foul.

Seattle has been host to several milestone events. On May 6, 1982, Hall of Fame spitballer Gaylord Perry beat the Yankees 7–3 to earn his 300th win. On June 2, 1990, Randy "The Big Unit" Johnson threw the team's first ever no-hitter in a 2–0 victory over the Tigers. Chris Bosio no-hit the Red Sox for a 7–0 victory on April 22, 1993.

Ken Griffey, Jr., on July 28, 1993, set a record by hitting a home run in eight straight games. Unfortunately, the Mariners lost the game to the Twins, and Griffey's streak was snapped the following game. Edgar Martinez was a one-man wrecking crew October 7, 1995, as he accumulated 7 RBIs to lead the Mariners to an 11–8 victory over the Yankees in game four of the playoffs. The following night, he hit a 2-run double to win game five in the 10th inning.

GETTING TO SAFECO FIELD
83 South King Street

Parking and traffic at the ballpark is not unreasonable, but I recommend considering mass transit. Seattle has one of the nation's best mass-transit systems, including an excellent system of tram/buses that run on electricity in the city and diesel on the highways. An area of more than 120 square blocks in the downtown area makes up the free-fare zone. The free-fare zone ends just two blocks away from Safeco Field. The express bus, which has a stop just outside the airport's baggage claim area, is the most affordable way to get downtown, at $1.10 each way. Other options include a Shuttle Express van that will cost you in the neighborhood of $15. Call 1-800-487-RIDE for reservations.

One way to get to Safeco from the waterfront area is via streetcar. Several 1920s era Australian streetcars run from Pier 70 to the corner of South Main and 5th Avenue. The Occidental Park stop is closest to the stadium. One-way trips take about 20 minutes and cost either 75 cents or $1, depending on the time of day. For just $3, you can purchase a Metro Visitors Pass that allows you one day's unlimited use of the streetcars and Metro Buses, plus one round-trip on the Seattle Center Monorail. For more information, call (206) 624-PASS.

If you opt to drive, there are several reasonably priced fenced parking lots a short walk from the stadium. You may want to get there early and sample the surrounding neighborhood. **F.X. McCrory's**, at 419 Occidental, is a steak, chop, and oyster house, offering a nice atmosphere and thirty-six local, domestic, and foreign beers on tap.

WHAT TO DO AND SEE IN SEATTLE

Seattle is one of my favorite small-market, major-league cities. I say small market because I don't think it's fair to compare it to San Francisco, New York, Chicago, and Boston. Among small-market cities, only Montreal impressed me more. But Seattle has a charm all its own. The people are friendly and down-to-earth, the sights are never-ending, and the night life is staggering. The cultural attractions are also remarkably diverse.

The city's trademark attraction is, of course, the **Space Needle**. Located in the 74-acre **Seattle Center**, the needle offers a terrific 360-degree view of the city and Puget Sound. If you luck upon a clear day, you can see as far as Mount Rainier from the top observation deck, 605 feet above the city. The Space Needle is open from 7 AM to midnight, Monday through Saturday, and 8 AM to midnight on Sunday. When I was in town, the Seattle Center Pavilion was hosting an M.C. Escher exhibit of 250 of his best drawings, paintings, and etchings, that I would have regretted missing. A **Jimi Hendrix Experience Museum** was recently added to the pavilion.

From the Space Needle, you can take the Monorail, for 80 cents each way, to the West Lake Mall. The mall is a short walk from **Pike Place Market**, an indoor/outdoor market with a great selection of seafood, produce, and crafts. The vendors put on quite a show as they hawk their wares. There are a number of good places to eat and a few street musicians scattered about.

There's a long stairway from the Market down to the waterfront. On the banks of Puget Sound, along Alaskan Way at Pier 59, is where you'll find the **Seattle Aquarium** and **Omnidome Film Experience**. A portion of the aquarium is actually under Puget Sound, offering a glimpse of marine life in as natural a setting as you'll find in any aquarium in the nation. You'll also see fur seals, harbor seals, otters, and the world's only aquarium-based salmon ladder. All told, more than 360 species of marine life are on display. The Omnidome is a domed OmniMax theater that features the Academy-Award-nominated film *The Eruption of Mount St. Helens*. The film gives you the feeling of being on board a helicopter as it flies into the volcano. Admission is $5.95 for adults.

There are a number of excellent seafood establishments along the pier, and, of course, it's where you'll find Seattle's ferries and harbor tours. **Spirit of Puget Sound** launches from Pier 70 and offers lunch and dinner buffet cruises with a narrated tour and live entertainment. **Seattle Harbor Tours** departs from Pier 55 and takes you on a two-and-a-half-hour cruise of Elliot Bay, Lake Washington Ship Canal, and through Ballard Locks for a tour of the Seattle area by water. **Bainbridge Island** is also worth checking out.

The **Seattle Art Museum** is just a short walk from either the waterfront or Pike Place Market, down First Avenue at 100 University Street. You're not likely to miss it, as there is a five-story mechanical statue out front. I was most impressed with the collection of 20th-century paintings and sculpture by the likes of Warhol, Homer, and Martin Puryear, as well as some more classical works on the fourth floor. Admission is $6 for adults. The museum is open every day except Monday.

Seattle's **Woodland Park Zoo** is considered one of the country's ten best zoos and is spread out over ninety-two acres. The zoo features more than 300 animal species in natural settings. Particularly impressive is the five-acre African Savanna with elephants, lions, giraffes, and zebras. It's located at 5500

Phinney Avenue, about fifteen minutes north of downtown. Admission is $6 for adults. On your way back, you may want to stop by for a tour of the **Redhook Ale Brewery** at 3400 Phinney Avenue and N. 35th Street. Redhook is one of the area's leading local brews and offers a free tour of the brewery at 3 PM on weekdays and several times a day on weekends. Tours are free and end with a tasting of Redhook Ales. The Trolleyman Pub is on site and open daily.

For something completely different check out **Underground Seattle**, a tour of the original town that has since been built over and exists only as a maze of underground streets below Pioneer Square. The hour-long expedition divulges how the original town had to be forfeited and used as a foundation for the current city as it had become impractical for citizens to traverse the veritable swamp caused by flooding. Be sure to wear comfortable shoes and prepare to be astounded. Guided tours are every two hours starting at 11 AM.

If that's not enough to keep you occupied, consider wandering around Green Way Park, watch the boats as they pass through Chittendon Locks, party with the locals in Freemont, Ballard, and the university area or search for the Troll under the bridge near Aurora and 36th.

NIGHTLIFE IN SEATTLE

As I mentioned earlier, there is no shortage of things to do after dark in Seattle. The area around Safeco Field has a number of outstanding sports bars and restaurants. Pioneer Square offers a nice cluster of clubs and cafes. However, if you don't venture off the beaten path in Seattle, you'll never know what you missed. *Where Seattle* offers a decent map and loads of practical dining and tourist information. *Seattle Weekly*, an alternative tabloid, is another good source for entertainment news.

The Backstage   2208 NW Market   (206) 781-2805   Live music nightly, featuring nationally known acts and local talent. Call for upcoming shows. Cover charge varies.

The Central Cafe   207 1st Avenue   (206) 622-0209   Big-name and local blues, as well as good eats in the heart of Pioneer Square.

Crocodile Cafe   Second at Blanchard   (206) 448-2114   Live music, ranging from alternative to mainstream rock. Also has a happy hour Tues-Thurs 4-8 PM.

Fenix Underground   323 2nd Avenue South   (206) 343-7740   A Pioneer Square "joint-cover charge" participant that generally hosts acoustic music acts.

The Improv   1426 First Avenue   (206) 628-5000   Books top-notch, nationally known comedians, especially on weekends. Call ahead for upcoming acts.

MOE Mo'roc'n Cafe   925 East Pike   (206) 324-2406   A big place in the Capitol Hill district with live progressive bands Wednesday through Saturday.

Under the Rail   2335 5th Avenue   (206) 448-1900   A relatively small venue, but their upcoming show schedule reads like a who's who in rock, blues, and reggae.

WHERE TO STAY IN SEATTLE

Seattle has plenty of nice hotels. Many of those that are located downtown offer the added convenience of free parking and easy access to the city's mass transportation. Most of the city's premiere attractions are within a short walk of each other and those that aren't can be reached by the monorail, trolley, or city bus. With that in mind, you may find that it is worth the extra couple of dollars to stay at a downtown hotel and do without a rental car.

Days Inn Towercenter   2205 Seventh Avenue (800) 648-6440 (206) 448-3434   Inexpensive accommodations within walking distance of the Space Needle.

Moore Hotel   1926 Second Avenue (800) 421-5508   Historic hotel near Pike Place Market and the Waterfront.

Pacific Plaza Hotel   400 Spring Street (800) 426-1165 or (206) 623-3900   Quaint, reasonably priced hotel in the heart of downtown.

Park Inn   225 Aurora Avenue North (800) 255-7932   Indoor pool, Jacuzzi, and exercise room on site. Complimentary parking and breakfast.

Residence Inn by Marriott   800 Fairview Avenue North (800) 331-3131 or (206) 624-6000   All-suite hotel located near the Space Needle.

TEAM HOTELS

Crowne Plaza Holiday Inn   1113 Sixth Avenue (800) HOLIDAY or (206) 464-1980   All American League clubs, except the Yankees.

Seattle Westin   1900 Fifth Avenue (800) 228-3000 or (206) 728-1000   Yankees.

WHERE TO EAT

I've never had a bad meal in Seattle. Listed below are a few eateries I highly recommend.

Anthony's Home Port   A mile or two past the Chittendon Locks and Salmon Ladders on Seaview Avenue, you'll find this warm, inviting seafood restaurant overlooking Puget Sound.

The Brooklyn   Seattle eateries are known for their seafood, steak, and oysters. The Brooklyn does all three well and offers a remarkable wine and microbrew selection.

Lowell's   Watch the ferries pass by as you enjoy breakfast served on three levels overlooking the sound at Pike Place Market. Near the market's main entrance.

McCormick & Schmicks This classic seafood establishment is among the best in the city. Open for lunch and dinner, it's not just a seafood place. The steaks, pasta, and salads are also legendary.

Metropolitan Grill Ask locals what their favorite place for steaks is and you're likely to hear at least a few hearty recommendations for this Second Avenue mainstay. The Met offers polished service, mouth-watering, mesquite grilled steaks, and the opportunity to run into local sports celebrities.

Poor Italian Cafe Perhaps the westernmost authentic Italian restaurant in the U.S., this cafe has an intimate atmosphere and a stellar menu. Located in Belltown at the corner of Second Avenue and Virginia Street.

Ray's Boathouse Next door to Anthony's, Ray's Boathouse has been a Seattle favorite for a quarter century. The formal dining rooms offer a cozy, wood-paneled atmosphere with an outstanding seafood menu, and a sweeping view of the sound.

GOOD TO KNOW

- For schedule information or tickets to Mariners games, call (206) 628-0888. The Mariners official Internet address is www.mariners.org.
- Mariner games can be heard on **KIRO 710 AM**. **KJR 950 AM** is the area's leading all-sports station.
- For more information on Seattle sights, attractions, and hotels, call the **Convention & Visitors Bureau** at (206) 461-5840 or (206) 461-5800. The city's official Web site is www.seeseattle.org.

Closest major league city (and drive time): San Francisco—875 miles (14 hours)

IN THE VICINITY

Perhaps Seattle's greatest attribute is that it offers several scenic wonders within a short drive of the city.

Mount Rainier The drive is long, but worth it once you get there. The mountain itself is 14,410 feet tall and its 34-square-mile glacier system is absolutely breathtaking. For information on camping and hiking in the area call (410) 569-2211.

Mount Saint Helens Farther south than Mt. Rainier, you can hike to the site of the May 18, 1980 volcanic eruption that darkened the skies of the Northwest. Call (504) 274-4038 for more information.

Snoqualmie Falls 26 miles east of Seattle the Snoqualmie River plunges 268 feet into a rocky gorge. About a forty-minute ride east on I-90, it makes for an easy day trip or you can spend the night at the Salish Lodge which is beside the falls. Call (800) 826-6124 for more information.

TEN FAVORITE MAJOR-LEAGUE BALLPARK MENU ITEMS

10 **Orlando's Barbecue Sandwich at Pacific Bell Park**   Not inexpensive, but big and good. Wash it down with a Red Stripe, served at the same stand, and save some room for garlic fries.

9 **Bagel Sandwiches at Anaheim Stadium**   A surprisingly decent deli sandwich found at the concession stands on the third base side.

8 **Dessert Tray in the Comiskey Skybox**   I'm not much of a dessert fan, but when you have a veritable smorgasbord delivered to your seat at a ballgame it's tough to say no.

7 **Primanti Brothers Sandwiches at PNC Park**   Thin-sliced beef and cheese on hearty white bread with the fries inside the sandwich.

6 **Carla's Pizza at Wrigley Field**   Chicago-style pizza in the bleachers at Wrigley Field.

5 **Clam Chowder at Fenway Park**   Fenway used to have some of the worst food in baseball until a new concessionaire brought in a few Legal Seafood specialties.

4 **Bloody Marys at Riverfront Stadium in Cincinnati**   Just what the doctor ordered for a day game after a long night of drinking.

3 **Dodger Dogs at Dodger Stadium**   Grilled instead of boiled or steamed, these ten-inch beef dogs are by far the best in baseball.

2 **Bratwursts at Miller Park**   Only the beer outsells the brats in Milwaukee. Three styles to choose from. I had to try them all and prefer the traditional bratwurst over the spicy or cheese brats.

1 **Crabcake Sandwiches at Camden Yards**   They sell out early so get one as soon as you can. The ones at Memorial were legendary, but Camden Yards comes in a close second.

ON YOUR OWN VERSUS TAKING A TOUR

Anybody who thinks it doesn't make a difference whether a game is played in the Astrodome or Fenway Park probably doesn't think it makes any difference that Alex Trebeck is the host of Jeopardy instead of Art Fleming.

BOB COSTAS

There are countless baseball tour outfits that conduct trips to major-league games across the country. They generally schedule tours from one to six games and cities at a time, and they take care of every detail. All you have to do is pay a tidy sum, get to the city they depart from, and get on the bus or plane. Tours vary from the more economical family-oriented trips to high-dollar packages that put you up in the same hotels as the visiting team, and schedule behind-the-scenes talks with baseball insiders. A good tour operator plans an interesting trip, picking out hotels and arranging for decent seats at the game. They do such a good job that you may want to duplicate one of their trips if you find that their fee is out of reach.

Most tour outfits have been taking people out to ballgames for years and can show you things you might never see otherwise. They also transport you to and from the ballpark, so you don't have to worry about driving, car trouble, or even parking. Tour outfits offer the convenience of one-stop shopping. Just call or write for a brochure, pick out one of their trips that interests you, and hit the road.

If you are contemplating a solo baseball trip, an organized tour can make a lot of sense. You'll travel with a group of avid baseball fans and may very well meet some nice folks. However, tour prices are generally based on double occupancy of a hotel room. If you are traveling alone, allowing a tour operator to assign you a roommate can be a crapshoot. Single occupancy is generally available, but the price is always a good deal more. Some outfitters offer a small discount if you recruit three or four friends to go along.

Organized tours generally have these three things in common: they travel by bus; they charge a pretty hefty fee for providing their services; and their fee represents only a fraction of your total expenses. Their fee includes game tickets, hotel accommodations, perhaps a souvenir of some sort, and bus fare. Their fee doesn't include most meals, "fun money," or airfare to and from the city they meet in. While it may be nice to have somebody else do the driving, if you've ever traveled by bus—or luxury motor coach as tour operators often call it—you know it's few people's idea of living large.

There are a few other downsides to an organized group. You never know who is going to end up on the bus with you. With a group of baseball fans, you'd like to think it would be a fun group, but you never know. Just like any other travel experience, depending on the tour you choose, you could end up with a pile of screaming kids, a group of belligerent drunks, or a bunch of blue hairs who aren't much fun. There's also less flexibility in choosing what nonbaseball activities to take part in while you are in a particular city. You generally see what the tour outfit has set up and not much else.

I've found that organizing a trip of your own is not only more affordable, but also more rewarding, more customized to your own interests, and in many ways, more convenient. One of the biggest advantages is that you can pick your own group. I suggest a small one, perhaps two to four close friends, as it is easier to come up with a consensus on what to see and do that way. A small group is also ideal when it comes to sharing driving time and the costs of a rental vehicle and hotel room(s).

Doing it on your own also allows for more flexibility in choosing a route, where to go, what teams to see, and how many days you want to spend in each city. Most of the longer organized tours center around the New York and Chicago areas. If the teams you want to see aren't there, you're out of luck. If you are doing your own tour and decide en route that you'd like to spend some more time in a particular city, you can make adjustments and do just that. Another advantage of doing it on your own is that you can pick out your own hotels, places to eat, and means of travel.

As far as transportation goes, I'm a big fan of mass transit once I arrive in a major city. If there's an efficient subway or other such transit option, I prefer to use that and park the car. But many of America's major-league cities don't have adequate mass transit, and you'll often find that some of a city's major attractions are not on or near the mass-transit route. With that in mind, I like to know I have the option of taking a car to see a city's sights.

On my very first baseball trip, two friends and I drove a Ford Escort station wagon more than 2,300 miles to 6 games in 9 days, simply because we were concerned more with economy than comfort. We nicknamed our Escort "the Babe Magnet" because nothing could be further from the truth. Despite the basic transportation, we had a great time and absolutely no problems with the car. In cities like New York and Boston we were able to park it and utilize mass transit most of the time we were in town. In other cities, we relied on the Escort to get us everywhere.

We've taken a rental van on almost every trip since then. It costs a little more and doesn't get the same gas mileage, but the roominess and comfort more than make up for the additional expense. One of these days, maybe for spring training, we'll get a recreational vehicle and do it up right. Until then, a van for small groups has been more than adequate. We've also packed as many as eight or nine into a van for weekend trips to Baltimore or Atlanta and had a great time.

Listed below are a number of baseball tour outfits. Call or write some of those nearest you before you plan your own trip—if for no other reason than to get a few good ideas.

Some tours are less expensive than others and claim to provide discount hotel rates and game tickets. It's been my experience that when it comes to travel packages, you tend to get what you pay for. Always be sure to ask where your seats are and what hotels you are going to be staying in. It may also be helpful to know what the rainout policy is. Many sports travel outfits offer a free trip for every twenty trips you book, so if you have a large group, be sure to inquire about group discounts.

Broach Baseball Tours
(704) 365-6500
4425 Randolph Road #315
Charlotte, NC 28211

Jay Buckley Baseball Tours
(888) 666-3510 or (608) 788-9600
P.O. Box 213
LaCrosse, WI 54602

Champs Tours
(800) 382-8087
8301 Torresdale Avenue
Philadelphia, PA 19136

Fields of Dreams Baseball Tours
(405) 840-7080
208 West Silver Meadow Drive
Oklahoma City, OK 73110

Games Away Tours
(800) 422-8972
177 Milk Street
Boston, MA 02109

Roadtrips
(800) 465-1765
177 Lombard Avenue, 7th Floor
Winnipeg, MB Canada R3B 0W5

Sports Fantasy Tours
(800) 379-7767
6917 Wildglen
Dallas, TX 75230

Sports Tours
(800) 722-7701
P.O. Box 84
Hatfield, MA 01038
www.4sportstravel.com

I've also included the address for the **Field of Dreams**, the site of the hit movie, which is reportedly visited by nearly 60,000 people a year.

And if you have deep pockets and would rather play the game with ex-pros than watch the current crop of big leaguers, you may want to call **Dream Week**. They do several weeklong baseball training camps each year, where you are coached by, and play against, ex-major league players and coaches.

Field of Dreams
(888) 875-8404 or (319) 875-8404
28963 Lansing Road
Dyersville, IA 52040
www.fieldofdreamsmoviesite.com

Dream Week Baseball Camps
(800) 888-4376
P.O. Box 115
Huntingdon Valley, PA 19006

APPENDIX B

SPRING TRAINING

That's the true harbinger of spring, not the crocuses or swallows returning to Capistrano, but the sound of a bat on a ball.

BILL VEECK

If you are a baseball fan and you've never been to spring training in Florida or Arizona, you owe it to yourself to do it at least once. Be careful though, it can become habit forming. While there's nothing quite like seeing a major-league game played in a big-league ballpark in the heart of baseball season, Florida and Arizona can be equally inviting in February and March. Just about the time you get sick and tired of winter, big-league players begin tossing the old horsehide around in the Grapefruit and Cactus leagues.

Spring training offers a few advantages over regular-season baseball. The ballparks and training facilities are far more intimate and accessible. Tickets, concessions, and parking are less expensive and easier to come by. Established players are more laid back because they are not competing in a regular-season situation and are often more inclined to sign autographs and chat with fans.

Baseball fans know that spring training games don't offer the same intense competition as regular-season or post-season games. In fact, it's quite possible that a team's star players and pitchers may play only a few innings as clubs tend to take a longer look at their minor-league talent—especially in the early weeks of spring training. But that's a big part of the fun of spring training—seeing who is fighting for what positions. Which rookies are likely to make the trip north with the parent club? What veterans still have it, and who's going to lose his spot to a prized prospect?

I've been fortunate enough to take trips to both Florida and Arizona for spring-training games. Both are great, but offer very different settings. Arizona has the advantage of several teams training within a very short drive of Phoenix, allowing you to check into a downtown hotel and easily see six of the eight ballparks and teams in the Cactus League. Only the Rockies, White Sox, and Diamondbacks, who play in Tucson, are not within a half-hour drive of Phoenix.

Now that the Cubs' HoHoKam Park has been refurbished, all of Arizona's ballparks are very open, scenic, and modern. But best of all, Cactus League stadiums are intimate, single-tier parks with the best seats just a few feet from the baselines. My favorites are the Giants' Scottsdale Stadium; Compadre Stadium, home of the Milwaukee Brewers; and Peoria Stadium, a sports complex shared by the Mariners and Padres. I'm told that the Colorado Rockies' Hi Corbett Field, in Tucson, and the Anaheim Angels' Diablo Stadium in Tempe are two of the nicer parks that I have not yet visited.

Cactus League ballparks also seem to have better concessions than their Florida counterparts. My particular favorite is the Jose Cuervo margaritas served at Scottsdale Stadium. As a bonus, Phoenix offers a surprisingly diverse nightlife scene, as well as relative proximity to Sedona and the Grand Canyon just a few hours to the north. Both are worth the trip. In 1998, the Cactus League added two teams, as the Chicago White Sox moved west to share a training site in Tucson with the expansion franchise Arizona Diamondbacks.

Florida, on the other hand, has the major advantage of being within driving distance of many East Coast cities. Many of the spring training sites are in southern Florida, and it's a manageable drive if you can split your time behind the wheel with a few friends. This, of course, will also save you hundreds of dollars in airfare. Unfortunately, the baseball facilities in Florida are spread out along both coasts, from Fort Lauderdale to St. Petersburg and many smaller cities in between, making it difficult to stay in one city and take day trips to the individual ballparks. It is not impossible, however, if you stick with only one coast. The Tampa/St. Petersburg area is a good central location, with the Tigers, Reds, Blue Jays, Phillies, Yankees, Indians, Royals, and Pirates training sites within a short drive.

The Astros are also not too far away in Kissimmee, and the Braves moved to an impressive new Disney ballpark in Orlando for the 1998 Grapefruit League season, so you can add them to the list of teams playing home games within a short drive of the Tampa area. Braves tickets are said to be the most expensive in either spring training league.

Most of the ballparks in Florida are well established and have been hosting big league teams for years. The parks may not be as new as those in Arizona, but they are home to most of the major leagues' marquee teams and players. In addition to those teams mentioned above, the Expos, Cardinals, Dodgers, Red Sox, Mets, Twins, Rangers, Marlins, and Orioles train in the sunshine state. Florida is also home to many tourist attractions such as DisneyWorld, the Epcot Center, Busch Gardens, and of course, numerous beaches—all of which may make your trip easier to justify if you are bringing along your significant other.

My favorite parks in Florida include the Devil Rays' Al Lang Field, overlooking the bay in St. Petersburg; Chain of Lakes Stadium, an intimate park in Winter Haven that is home to the Cleveland Indians; and the Yankees' new digs, Legends Field in Tampa. The Pirates' McKechnie Field is an older park that has been refurbished to become one of the nicer stadiums in the Grapefruit League. Folks who drive down to Florida may want to consider scheduling a stop on their way back at Turner Field in Atlanta.

Getting a few buddies together and planning a trip can be half the fun of going on a spring training tour. Every winter *USA Today, Baseball Weekly*, and *Baseball America* print preseason schedules. Internet users will want to check out major league baseball's official Web site www.majorleaguebase ball.com for schedule information. You can also call or write the individual teams for schedules and tickets. Phone numbers to order tickets are also listed. Armed with team schedules, a map, and a calendar, it's relatively easy to put together a short road trip.

But if that sounds like a lot of work, call a baseball tour operator and inquire about the spring training trips they offer. The big advantage of taking a tour is that you can leave the driving and planning to them. Just hop on the bus and see a few ballgames. They generally arrange for hotels, tickets, and transportation. Another plus is that you are likely to meet some fellow baseball fans and may very well make some lifelong friends. Tour operators offer some very well-thought-out trips involving five or six games and travel to Florida by bus or plane.

No matter how you do it—on your own or with a tour operator—a spring training trip can't help but be a good time. I always come home with a tan, a little better idea of what's going on with my favorite players, and renewed energy and drive. Of course, it doesn't hurt that I return knowing opening day is just around the corner.

A list of current spring training sites is available from the National League or American League offices at 350 Park Avenue, New York, NY 10022. For more information call (212) 931-7500.

BIBLIOGRAPHY

This book would not have been possible without referring to and being inspired by the following magazines, newspapers, books, and media guides.

Baseball America. *Baseball America's 1996 Almanac.* Durham, N.C.: American Sports Publishing Inc., 1996.

Baseball Weekly. Arlington, Virginia: USA Today 1993–1997.

Blake, Mike. *Baseball Chronicles.* Cincinnati: Betterway Books, 1994.

The Charlotte Observer. Charlotte, North Carolina, 1993–1997.

Dickson, Paul. *Volvo Guide to Halls of Fame.* Washington, D.C.: Living Planet Press, 1995.

Hollander, Zander. *The Complete Handbook of Baseball.* New York: Penguin Books, 1997.

Koppett, Leonard. *The New Thinking Fan's Guide to Baseball.* New York: Simon & Schuster/Fireside, 1993.

Lowry, Phillip J. *Green Cathedrals* (second edition). Reading, Mass.: Addison Wesley, 1992.

Martinez, David H. *The Book of Baseball Literacy.* New York: Penguin Books, 1996.

Nathan, David H. *Baseball Quotations,* New York: Ballantine Books, 1991.

Plaut, David. *Baseball Wit and Wisdom.* Philadelphia: Running Press, 1992.

Richmond, Peter. *Ballpark.* New York: Simon & Schuster, 1993.

Schlossburg, Don. *Baseball Almanac.* Lincolnwood, Ill.: Publications International, 1994.

Seaver, Tom. *Great Moments in Baseball.* New York: Birch Lane Press, 1992.

Will, George. *Men at Work.* New York: Macmillan, 1990.

Wolff, Rick, editorial director. *The Baseball Encyclopedia* (ninth edition). New York: Macmillan, 1993.

Wood, Bob. *Dodger Dogs to Fenway Franks.* New York: McGraw-Hill Publishing Co., 1988.

I also acknowledge city directories, stadium programs, and media guides from the following convention and visitors bureaus, stadiums, and ballclubs:

Anaheim, Anaheim Stadium, and the Anaheim Angels.
Arlington, Dallas, and Fort Worth, Texas, The Ballpark, and the Texas Rangers.
Atlanta, Ted Turner Field, and the Atlanta Braves.
Baltimore, Camden Yards, and the Baltimore Orioles.
Boston, Fenway Park, and the Boston Red Sox.
Chicago, Wrigley Field, Comiskey Park, the Chicago Cubs, and the White Sox.
Cleveland, Jacobs Field, and the Cleveland Indians.
Cincinnati, Riverfront Stadium, and the Cincinnati Reds.
Denver, Coors Field, and the Colorado Rockies.
Detroit, Comerica Park, and the Detroit Tigers.
Houston, Enron Field, and the Houston Astros.
Kansas City, Kauffman Stadium, and the Kansas City Royals.
Los Angeles, Dodger Stadium, and the Los Angeles Dodgers.
Miami, Fort Lauderdale, Pro Player Stadium, and the Florida Marlins.
Milwaukee, Miller Park, and the Milwaukee Brewers.
Minneapolis, Hubert Humphrey Metrodome, and the Minnesota Twins.
Montreal, Olympic Stadium, and the Montreal Expos.
New York, Shea Stadium, Yankee Stadium, the New York Mets, and the Yankees.
Oakland, Alameda County Stadium, and the Oakland A's.
Phoenix, Bank One Ballpark, and the Arizona Diamondbacks.
Philadelphia, Veterans Stadium, and the Philadelphia Phillies.
Pittsburgh, PNC Park, and the Pittsburgh Pirates.
Saint Louis, Busch Stadium, and the Saint Louis Cardinals.
San Diego, Jack Murphy Stadium, and the San Diego Padres.
San Francisco, Pacific Bell Park, and the San Francisco Giants.
Seattle, Safeco Field, and the Seattle Mariners.
Tampa, Tropicana Field, and the Tampa Bay Devil Rays.
Toronto, SkyDome, and the Toronto Blue Jays.